INDICTING AMERICA

Sal DePasquale

Indicting America

Copyright © 2024 by Sal DePasquale

All rights reserved. No part of this book may be reproduced or transmitted in any form or by any means without written permission of the author.

ISBNs:
979-8-218-48970-0 (paperback)
979-8-218-49688-3 (hardcover)

Library of Congress Control Number: 2024918137

Published by: Sal DePasquale
Artlanta, Georgia USA

Dedication

My son and social scientists dedicated
to finding and exposing truth

Contents

Preface 1

Part 1: Foundation for the Charges 7
Opening Statement. 8
Emergence of Wealth and Power and Monotheism 14
Siberian Migration Era 32

Part 2: The Charges. 39
European Invasion Era 40
Barbados 50
New World and White Slaves 68
French-Indian War (1754-1763) and Proclamation Line 81
Settler Colonialism. 97
James Somerset. 105
Revolution or Secession? 120
Indian Removal/Genocide 149
Cotton Seeds of Worldwide War 168
Who Won the Civil War? 181
Post-Civil War 193

Imperialism 211

World Wars 230

Race, Fear and Hate 251

Vietnam 262

2008 Crash 273

American Democracy on the Edge; Civil War; and New
    Constitution 291

Part 3: Closing 303

Closing Argument 304

Notes 305

Bibliography and Video References 321

Appendix 340

Preface

From the beginning of adolescent school years, Americans learn love of country. Reinforced by family, community, religion, and friends; patriotism and reverence for the flag are deeply etched into the American psyche. Love of country, even in the hearts of those left behind by America, is an integral part of Americans and the phenomenon of "God bless America."

This narrative, providing a foundation for love of country, is predicated upon concepts of American History designed for promoting patriotism and love of country. The United States of America, cast as a country valuing freedom and justice, is presented as a land where noble Europeans, inspired by ideas of freedom, risked everything they had, ventured off into the unknown, and created a new government, making their dreams a reality. Pioneers were people seeking religious freedom; opportunities for enjoying the fruits of their labor free from oppressive elites; and creating a place where a person could better himself, or herself, based on initiative. As the story is told, America is a product of the human spirit, demanding equality for all and denouncing societies based on class, such as those led by the Kings and Queens of Europe.

As America approaches its 250th birthday, however, the landscape reflects a stark contrast to this narrative. To be sure, the traditional narrative is deceptive, annunciating ideas that Americans wish to be true, but are anything but true.

America is a country of haves and have-nots; segregated by class, skin color and ethnic origin; deeply divided and certainly not a land of freedom and equality. As a result, Americans remain baffled at how a system allegedly designed in service of the Common Good caters to the needs of the wealthiest, while millions are left behind.

As a member of the baby boom generation, I was raised in post-World War II America. Americans were proud of their country and their government. World War II was a defining moment. Americans joined together in the war against the Nazis. Young men and women went off to war, Rosie the riveter rose up operating America's manufacturing; business, industry, government and academia joined forces for the war effort. I was a less than average student, but I did very well in history, because it told the story about my beloved country, America. It was a story validated by family, friends, church and community.

When the Vietnam War called for recruits, I patriotically stepped forward and joined the Marine Corps in 1969. Slowly but inexorably, my framework for viewing America shifted. The Vietnam War simply didn't make sense. We were there under the pretense of helping the "peaceful villagers of South Vietnam," but we were the greatest threat to them. My disillusionment propelled me to dig deep into the war, long after my service in Vietnam. As the story unfolded, it was painful to accept. I then studied much more about American history, not as told in high school textbooks that were conduits for propaganda, but by reading the works of academic historians whose works were based on verified facts. This tale was infinitely more difficult to take. I had

PREFACE

to conclude that America, as an institution constituted in 1789, is a criminal enterprise, an on-going criminal enterprise that began long before the country was constituted and continues today.

My sources of information are the historians who emerged along with the baby boomers. The massive number of children born from the close of World War II strained the systems that absorbed young adults. Colleges became a sort of relief valve, some say an extended babysitting service, in which high school graduates could continue their education years as the American society made way for integrating them into adulthood. College enrollments before the baby boom remained constant, but come the 1960s, they skyrocketed. Colleges expanded dramatically and jobs for history professors expanded, too. This meant new ideas were given a chance.

The Dunning School, a historiographical school of thought, named in honor of William Archibald Dunning of Columbia who died in 1922, represented a contrived tale of America. The narrative it established set the parameters for history professors. But that narrative seemed to wither away as young vibrant professors emerged in filling the posts created by college expansions. Over the past 50 years, academic works on history produced an avalanche of evidence exposing the Dunning School as a sham. My sources of information are rooted in the academic works of contemporary historians. If their work is faulty or if I fail in faithfully representing their work, then my thesis is simply wrong. I introduce the collected works of scholars into evidence, however, as I argue the charge of America as an on-going criminal enterprise.

Historian Eric Foner has said many times that history must be read forward not backwards. It took me a long time to understand his point, but each time I felt I understood some period in history, something would compel me to explore previous events. Invariably this exercise added more context to what I thought I understood.

My objective in this representation is to connect the dots from our emergence as a separate species within our Ape Family ancestry, maybe 200,000 years ago, on up to the modern day. Understanding the vicious assault upon indigenous peoples, once defined as mere savages, requires recognition that these savages lived in the Americas about 20,000 years before Columbus. The deep and enduring animus aimed at black people only makes sense when placed within the wealth and power derived from enslavement. It has zero to do with some peculiarity of black people.

Chapter One represents an opening statement to a grand jury. Although the book is premised upon the idea of an indictment, it is not constrained by actual legal proceedings. It does fit, however, within the context of this being the first presentation of an opening charge. If the grand jury finds sufficient evidence to indict, the case then goes on to a petit jury for determination of guilt. Moreover, the charges are not based on a statutory crime, but crimes based upon a sense of morality, right and wrong.

Chapter Two provides a foundation for the accusation suggesting that the crime charged is part of changes in the Human Experience making possible predatory human behavior.

Chapters Three and Four stipulate two distinctive eras of America, the Siberian Migration that led to the so-called Indian population and the European Invasion led by Columbus.

Chapter Five discusses the heart of darkness in Barbados where White Supremacy is born and slaves are worked to death, thereby creating the model for the southern states in North America.

In Chapter Six the Columbus invasion is examined, along with introduction of white slaves, indentured servants.

Chapter Seven reveals another side of George Washington, the side in which he is a land speculator deriving wealth from stealing Indian lands. It also explores his role in instigating the French and Indian War that benefitted his brother's private enterprise, the Ohio Company, that made its fortune by way of Indian lands. This war was so costly, England prohibited new excursions for taking Indian lands. The Proclamation Line was a prime motivator for rebelling against England.

Chapter Eight delves into the concept of Settler Colonialism in which settlers eat away at Indian lands.

Chapter Nine shines a bright light on the James Somerset case in England that provided a lightning rod igniting the American Revolution.

Chapter Ten suggests the American Revolution was more of a Secession than a revolution.

Chapter 11 brings us to the Industrial Revolution, another wealth generating proposition making some rich and others slaves.

Chapter 12 contemplates the charge of Genocide in the Removal of Indians.

Chapter 13 takes up the Civil War. This is not about battles. Battles are a means to an end. But what if the victorious fail in winning the peace?

Chapters 14 and 15 consider the Post Civil War and how Slave Masters, the moral narrative, and their worldview lived on to fight another day. America needed a new Constitution, emphasizing human rights, instead they sought to amend the Constitution that was written for property rights.

Chapter 15 brings us to the modern day in Post World War II America, a country on the brink.

Chapter 16 makes salient America's aggression against foreign lands.

Chapter 17 discusses the World Wars and the insurgency formed by power elite.

Chapters 18 and 19 examines the Civil Rights Movement and the Vietnam War.

Chapter 20 takes on the financial crash of 2008 and its implications.

Chapter 21 discusses America on the brink of its end.

PART ONE

Foundation for the Charges

Opening Statement

THE UNITED STATES OF AMERICA represents an on-going criminal enterprise. Christopher Columbus opened a path for invasion and occupation of the Americas by foreign powers, including Spain, France, the Dutch, Britain and Russia. This invasion, under the banner of the Doctrine of Discover, 1452 and 1493, was an illegal invasion and an illegal occupation. Issued by the Vatican, the Doctrine did not represent an international accord, recognized by a valid international authority, and was, therefore, a contrived justification for perpetrating Crimes Against Humanity.

The American Enterprise, placed under scrutiny and in dramatic contrast to the America represented in typical high school textbooks, is founded upon Crimes Against Humanity. The evidence indicates genocide, invasion, murder, rape, torture and raw brute force theft. The pieces of evidence are astounding based on the sheer depth and long-term existence of this criminal behavior.

The evidence will show the accused willfully intended to apply brute force in obtaining people, lands and resources for their personal gain, wealth and power. The evidence also reveals the Doctrine of Discover, that provided the alleged legal, moral and spiritual foundation for the invasion, was merely a thinly veiled disguise of the real agenda, averting attention from the murderous and tortuous invasion and occupation.

The evidence is founded upon research by renown academicians, using the rigorous standards of the historical, science and journalism professions. Their research, vetted in peer reviewed journals and books, provides detailed accounts of the crimes alleged.

The evidence illuminates the amoral goals of the accused, unrestrained by any sense of right and wrong. There were no boundaries. If indigenous peoples represented an obstacle in seizing occupied lands or the resources to be found on those lands, the invaders murdered. Multiple orgies of bloodletting will be revealed, including genocidal attacks upon women and children.

The evidence makes salient enormous wealth and power derived from these crimes. The lands provided some of the richest soil on the planet, producing wealth generated by sugar, tobacco, cotton, oil, gold, silver and a range of other commodities in high demand. Enslaved people provided the labor essential for extrapolating money-making commodities. Labor was provided under duress with tortuous sanctions including witnessing the rape and murder of loved ones. Wealth and power derived from the invasion and occupation catapulted the United States to the richest most powerful nation in the world, all the product of illegally gotten gains. This includes the enterprises that grew from the invasion and occupation; banking and finance, law and professional services, insurance and investments services, universities. Each and every part of contemporary U.S. commerce is founded upon the wealth developed by way of invasion and occupation and all of the associated crimes.

Context will accompany the allegations presented. Wealth and power are relatively new to the Human Experience. We will present evidence of a time when our species existed without property, possessions, ideological ideas and political objectives. These emerged with the Neolithic Period, about 10,000 years ago as humans discovered agriculture. For an estimated 200,000 years prior, our species existed without the carnage that emerged with agriculturalists. Our ancestors did, indeed, exhibit aggression before agriculture, but not to the depth that emerged later. This change in Human Existence introduced ideas of wealth, power and dominance, establishing a world environment ripe for the invasion and occupation of the Americas. Greed is at the heart of the alleged crimes.

The evidence will show the indigenous peoples originated in Asia and migrated across frozen lands into North America, establishing themselves over 20,000 years throughout the Americas. They were not invaders; they were people following the herds in search of sustenance not dominance. About 600 hundred years ago, Europeans invaded.

The West Indies became a focus of attention for the invaders as sugar was prolific. These islands stretching across, North, South and Central America created enormous wealth. Obtaining that wealth required intensive labor. The invaders obtained enslaved people from the indigenous peoples, criminals from their homelands, and people purchased on the Atlantic Slave Trade. The entire slave enterprise represents a massive crime against humanity.

Each time an initiative emerged to moderate brutishness, the invader-occupier, Slave Masters, responded with more brutishness and recalcitrance. When England attempted to reign in the attack upon Native lands, the occupiers refused compliance and angled for war against England. When England was forced to confront slavery in a court case involving an American enslaved black man, the Slave Masters reacted in organizing a war for separation from England. When the United States attempted addressing the intolerable crime of enslavement, the Slave Masters went to war against their own country.

When defeated, they continued resistance, forming guerilla operations, known as the Ku Klux Klan, in continuing their fight for dominance.

They continue resistance up to the modern day with an objective of overthrowing the U.S. government so they may return to power. There is no evidence of contriteness.

This is the real America: no principles, no honor, and no integrity. From the beginning of European occupation of the American landmass, immoral brute force ruled the land. The American Revolution, the Founding Fathers, the Constitution, and the Declaration of Independence are utterly irrelevant. The Doctrine of Discovery; Protestant-White Supremacy imported into South Carolina from Barbados; the French Indian War; Proclamation Line; James Somerset case; Industrial Revolution; Louisiana Purchase; and Rebranding Slavery under the disguise of Jim Crow are the significant events in American history, not the fanciful tale of America.

This dichotomy between the advertised product and reality is stark; for many it is the height of hypocrisy. Political leaders claim they are a voice speaking for the "American people," while embracing political agendas aimed solely at the power elite. While claiming to be a voice of the people, political forces have focused on interests of wealth and power, beginning with gold and silver, followed soon thereafter by rice, indigo, sugar, tobacco, cotton, and oil.

The political, social and cultural characteristics of the United States represent an accumulation of values instituted by European invaders arriving 600 years ago. Spain's Queen Isabella implanted a stake in the heart of the land when she commissioned Christopher Columbus' journey to go forth and conquer. This mission established legitimacy for invading lands; brutalizing and enslaving native peoples; and exploiting natural resources in service of the power elite. The ensuing political, social and cultural institutions produced by the

Queen's initiative established the Americas and adjoining islands as a place for creating dominance, wealth and power for the few by way of resource exploitation and human slavery. This, however, has been obscured by tales of freedom and justice.

History is typically addressed as a series of individual discrete events. Individual events, however are merely parts of one continuous event, all connected, helping explain how we arrived at the here and now.

Beware of the bright shiny object. It distracts and obfuscates, disguising true motivations. Bright shiny object events capture attention. All too frequently history focuses on these events because they are spectacular.

But what if the real agenda is hidden without documentation that could implicate the actors? Consider The Gulf of Tonkin, a contrived attack, used to justify the Vietnam War by claiming it was an unprovoked attack. Or the notion that the Revolution was caused by taxation without representation and a tyrannical King, as opposed to the private agenda for re-opening attacks on Indians to steal their lands and resources, along with a threat to slavery as evidenced by the James Somerset case. The Revolution was about taxes not the massive wealth producing taking of Indians lands, worked by enslaved peoples extracting wealth producing resources. No, it was the tax on tea, a much better public relations campaign justifying the American Revolution, in contrast to the hidden agenda. And let us not forget a wall, a wall, we must have a wall to halt the psychotically contrived tale of invaders from Mexico used as a ploy to distract from the corrupted Trump regime.

The Art of History works best when digging deep for the hidden agenda, revealing true motivations, usually unveiling sheer brutality in service of wealth and power for the few at the top of the power hierarchy, often removed from public scrutiny.

The United States of America represents the accumulation of events beginning with the European invasion of America, blessed with the Doctrine of Discovery. The invasion and ongoing occupation of the land, where riches derived from the soil by way of enslaved human sweat, represent a crime against humanity, a criminal enterprise, an on-going criminal enterprise.

You be the jury. This is my case.

For man, when perfected, is the best of animals, but, when separated from law and justice, he is the worst of all; since armed injustice is the more dangerous, and he is equipped at birth with arms, meant to be used by intelligence and virtue, which he may use for the worst ends.

Aristotle, Politics, Book I, Part 2
***NICOMACHEAN ETHICS* (350 BC) by Aristotle**

Emergence of Wealth and Power and Monotheism

"A great deal of the world's history is the history of empires. Indeed, it could be said that all history is imperial – or colonial – history, if one takes a broad enough definition and goes far enough back. Since this short book is trying to say something about the entire history of humanity, from the earliest times and right around the globe, the only sensible place to start is with today's newspapers." Stephen Howe, *Empire: A Very Short Introduction*[1]

IT ALL BEGAN IN A world wind of rock and dust. Through a process of accretion, a solid formed making our 4.6 billion years old planet. Life on earth, however, starts just over 500 million years ago and doesn't emerge above water until 375 million years ago. Our Ape family ancestor emerged about 25 million years ago. Humans—*homo sapiens*—became a distinctive life form about 2-300,000 years ago, a relative newcomer on the planet, although humans dominate it today.

This is a difficult concept for most people to integrate into their worldview. It is just as difficult recognizing that our species existed

EMERGENCE OF WEALTH AND POWER AND MONOTHEISM

for thousands of years without any notion of property, possessions, or political ideologies.

Before we—humans—became "civilized" about 10,000 years ago, we had no concept of wealth, racism or religious hate. We existed for an estimated 200,000 years without any of that. But something happened about 10,000 years ago changing human existence. Before "civilization" graced us with a variety of mechanisms for hating each other, humans operated cooperatively for survival. The rugged individual did not have a place, because operating alone meant exposure to hyaenas and other animals of prey. Working with a team protected the so-called "rugged individual."

So, how did we alter the human experience of our homo sapiens species from a relatively cooperative existence for basic survival into a greedy and dominating existence filled with warfare, human butchery and hate? Understanding how we got here requires understanding from whence we came.

Earth is 4.6 billion years old. Our species is but a speck on that timeline. American history exists within the context of global and human history. America's emergence as a nation-state occurs within a broader narrative, fitting into patterns in which humans become predatory against each other, creating empires of extraordinary wealth and power for the few, at the expense of the many.

Our very young species began as a member of the Ape family dating back millions of years. Darwinius Masillae emerged somewhere in Germany about 20 million years ago opening a branch on the Ape Family tree eventually evolving into another family branch represented by us humans, when we emerged as a separate species in Africa about 200,000 years ago. The milestones of our evolution led to homo sapiens, the humans, as we know them, with a mental capacity for world domination. It's difficult for humans living in the here and now to contemplate a broader human experience. Imagine what we were like before evolving into the being we are today. Humans did not magically appear. We evolved, mutated, or developed, over millions of years.

Our brain developed, long before our species evolved, from a primitive brain stem 500 million years ago, known as the Reptilian Brain. About 120,000 years ago, our brain evolved or mutated into the Mammalian Brain that added the limbic system to the Reptilian Brain. Our New Brain, the brain we function with today, emerged an estimated 35,000-100,000 years ago, adding the Neocortex into the mix, providing us humans with billions of neurons allowing us to think, plan and strategize, separating us from the rest of the animal kingdom.

Neolithic Period

The past 10,000 years, defined as the Neolithic Period, however, established contemporary existence. Using our New Brain with the Neocortex, humans discovered agriculture thereby changing everything of Human Existence and unleashing the dark heart of greed. Agriculture and animal husbandry set in motion an array of interconnected events, instead of following herds in search of food and water, a sedentary lifestyle emerged, tying humans to a spot. Taking control over food supply and using animals for work in plowing fields provided many advantages. Excess food production, properly stored, provided security from the uncertainty of hunting and gathering. It also created an excess of food, that could be stored and used for creating wealth. Indeed, excess food was the first marker of wealth.

Excess came with a price, however. When the environment did not cooperate with agricultural needs on the spot where someone set their roots and when they exhausted their excess reserve, it meant no food. And when starving agriculturalists looked to neighbors for help and neighbors refused to share their excess, the hungry attacked.

Excess equated to wealth. Refusing to share with starving neighbors equated to greed and power. Fighting to protect excess wealth from starving neighbors gave birth to warfare and consequent slavery. To be sure, it was greed that produced warfare, slavery and empire building that created every greater and more horrific warfare and draconian slavery.

Greed, ever greater demands of more wealth and more power, and empire expansion provided the heart and soul of the forces creating the United States of America. Understanding America's founding requires understanding how our species transformed its existence from hunter-gather to civilized nation-states.

As Noah Harari tells us in *21 Lessons for the 21st Century*, "As humans gained ownership of land, animals, plants, and tools, rigid hierarchical societies emerged, in which small elites monopolized most wealth and power for generation after generation. Humans came to accept this arrangement as natural and even divinely ordained. Hierarchy was not just the norm but also the ideal."[2]

Reza Aslan in *God: A Human History*, adds: "Then, sometime around 12,000 to 10,000 years ago, we inexplicably swapped our spears for plows and transformed ourselves from foragers to farmers. We ceased scavenging for food and started producing it. Rather than hunting for animals, we began to breed them."[3]

Our ancestors had no concept of the forces being unleashed with civilization. Humans stepped away from being a part of nature to dominating nature. Somewhere in the Middle East, perhaps in the Cradle of Civilization, humans recognized that edible plants were grown from seeds. This led to human transition, but this came with risks. If crops failed for whatever reason, the agriculturalist couldn't simply revert to hunter-gatherer techniques for obtaining food.

Discovery of agriculture and animal husbandry, defined as the Neolithic Period, altered human existence from egalitarian communal living to stratified societies with extravagantly rich and desperately poor. The wealthy created a protective edifice of warriors for defending against attack. And when other greedy barons emerged with their protective edifice, "defensive" wars emerged in defeating potential enemies before they grew too strong. This led to Empires, the first born near the Cradle of Civilization, the Akkadian Empire, 2300 BCE, about 4,500 years ago.

Transcendence

This led to blowback from those fighting for empire expansion as the bloodshed and mayhem of empire building warfare exposed the folly of dying for the emperor. This blowback was impotent, however, as the emperor had all the power. Still ideas about morality, right and wrong, continued to stew and spread. It may be argued that within 3-400 years of the Akkadian Empire, these ideas forced a change in religion, leading to the ideas of the Bible, thereby positioning religion as the centralizing force against the greedy.

Before agriculture and civilization, humans sought transcendence, a force greater than themselves, to help in making sense out of human existence. They believed in multiple gods, each with a specific task or duty such as providing rain or sunshine. The pagan gods were transactional. Humans made sacrifices to the gods who in turn granted wishes for sun, rain, or innumerable other natural occurrences necessary for survival. When humans became aggressive with each other, fighting wars for the wealthiest to get wealthier, new ideas emerged

EMERGENCE OF WEALTH AND POWER AND MONOTHEISM

organically stipulating right and wrong, a moral code. These ideas ultimately became codified by religion in the Bible.

Abraham set off a tectonic shift in the human experience when he introduced the concept of one God around 4,000 years ago, within a 3–400-year range of the Akkadian Empire. Replacing a wide range of pagan gods with the idea of monotheism, One God, and thereby replacing the multiple gods. This was a radical change in how humans related to transcendence. This dramatic change came along with adoption of a moral code that replaced sacrificial rituals. The world did not change at a moment's notice. It took thousands of years for monotheism to take hold. Today, the way we view religion and God is dramatically different than the view of 4,000 years ago.

The juxtaposition of the Akkadian Empire and Abraham circumstantially suggests a cause and effect. It took thousands of years for monotheism to become embraced. But more importantly, the ideas of morality took root, backed by the power of an all knowing and all-powerful God, countering the brutality of Empire building. Of course, emperors learned the art of manipulation and spun wars for empire into defensive wars, "just wars" and wars with God on our side.

Abraham's ideas of Monotheism were revolutionary and were followed about a thousand years after by Moses and his ten commandments; and Moses was followed about a thousand years after that by Jesus with a message for expanding upon Moses' efforts; and that was followed about five hundred years later by Mohammed with a message encapsulating the words of Abraham, Moses and Jesus. Similar messages came from Hindus, the Buddha and Confucius. Although powerful, the forces of greed persisted, even into the modern day. It is unmistakable; however, that Monotheism with an all-powerful God and a moral code designed for pleasing God represents action by the powerless against the power of Empire.

Understanding human dominance requires understanding how wealth and power emerged in the human experience. America's dominance is not unique; it is merely a chapter in the multiple volumes of human depravity. If we, the human species, desire a sustainable existence and future, we must begin with a clear and honest reflection on our past, our history. If not, we are destined for self-destruction.

"It's just human nature to be greedy," is a frequently expressed refrain when confronted with depraved action by the powerful. It is a means for accepting the unacceptable by the powerless, providing a laconic resignation to powerlessness. It suggests a "be calm" response for enduring a hostile and threatening environment fostering a sense that "we will survive this." Don't be so sure. Hundreds of millions of people did not.

Ironically forces advocating for morality, establishing restraints against the powerful, were themselves co-opted or corrupted by the forces of wealth, frequently enlisted in support and in defense of the most depraved acts by the wealthy.

DNA

Religious texts suggest a higher power magically created humans. Scientists in the 1980s, however, endeavored to find a more real-world answer by exploring deoxyribonucleic acid (DNA), the source of our genetic code. Results of their efforts, the Genome Project, represent a monumental discovery for science, but it also represents a substantial discovery for history and social science.[4]

The Genome Project established that humans are descendants of the Ape family and that our species, homo-sapiens, began in Africa with melanin infused skin, now related to as black. Changes in skin appearance coincides with human migrations out of Africa into colder climates, clearly evident in DNA and its code mutations that emerged as humans moved into new lands.

Perhaps American History does not have a start date. Perhaps it begins with World History, when *homo-sapiens* split from the Ape Tree and established its own branch and root system. Consequently, American History must be viewed within the context of World History.

Where does American History begin? Does it start with migrants traversing the Chukchi Sea 15,000-20,000 years ago? Or does it start with the European invasion 500 years ago? American history, the history of North, Central and South America, must be viewed within a context of two distinctive Eras:

- The **Siberian Migration Era**, in which humans driven by environmental pressures traversed across Russia into Alaska and North America, moving across the plains and the south, ultimately into Central and South America;

- The **European Invasion Era**, in which humans driven by greed and conquest, equipped with new technology, traversed the ocean in search of new lands providing power and wealth.

Recognizing two distinct Eras of America, which includes North, South and Central America, is essential in understanding American history, because it is a history dominated by aggression against indigenous people across the continent and brutalization of slaves, white and black, during specific phases of American slavery.

Understanding American history requires beginning at the beginning of what we know of human existence. Modern humans (*Homo sapiens*) began about 200,000 years ago; a branch rooted in the hominid species. Modern humans emerged on the African continent remaining domiciled there for over half of its existence. A volcanic eruption at Lake Toba about 80,000 years ago threatened the survival of humans as weather patterns were altered by massive volcanic ash and cloud cover. The human population depleted to about 2000 people, but managed to survive.

Agriculture produced excess and excess produced wealth. When the wealthy did not share their excess, warfare emerged and warfare produced slavery. The wealthy developed a protective edifice and subsequently used it to fight other wealthy and powerful people before they became too powerful. These battles led to Empires causing those fighting war to contrive ideas about morality and a higher power that could serve as a counterweight to the wealthy emperors.

Slavery

Roaming the countryside, in search of food sources, consumed the daily life of humans, as it still dominates the lives of our closest relatives, the chimpanzees in the wild. As our species evolved, making a new branch on the Ape family tree, survival still hinged upon finding food sources, just as before.

As the story unfolds, one day, somewhere in the Middle East, a woman observed sprouts on a spot for discarded food. That observation signaled a mechanism for taking control over food sources, giving birth to agriculture. The human experience changed dramatically with the introduction of agriculture as hunting and gathering tasks were replaced by planting and harvesting tasks. Shortly thereafter, humans lassoed and harnessed animals for work in planting and harvesting, adding animal husbandry into the mix of agricultural

EMERGENCE OF WEALTH AND POWER AND MONOTHEISM

enterprise. Soon this concept of harnessing animals for work would be applied to humans.

This enterprise spread over thousands of years; eclipsing hunter gatherer means for survival. As noted previously, however, agriculture came with risks. If the environment failed to cooperate and crops failed, hunger resulted. Reverting to hunter gathering was not a viable option, because that life required traversing the countryside following sources of food. Agriculture required remaining fixed on a spot for planting and harvesting. As a consequence, when desperate for nutrition, the hungry could not simply catch up to the herd and, instead, simply attacked neighboring agriculturalists. The victorious emerging from the attack, then confronted what to do with the vanquished. Over thousands of years, enslavement of the vanquished became the answer.

Enslavement is the original sin, not biting an apple. Placing a human in chains, ripping children from their mothers, raping a person before an audience of their loved ones, all equates to one thing: a crime against humanity.

Little is documented about the beginning of slavery as a part of the Human Experience. Biblical references are inadequate, because the Bible is not a historical document, but more importantly, slavery begins long before the Bible. Researchers suggest it begins after the advent of agriculture and is a by-product of attacks by starving people against agriculturalists. The prevailing force in those attacks was then faced with what to do with the vanquished. Some killed off the defeated. But then, the slavery concept provided a mechanism for using the muscle and sweat of the defeated in building more excess, and thereby avoiding execution, while offering a pathway to citizenship so the defeated could eventually emerge as a member of the victorious side.

Slavery means different things based on time and place. It begins as an alternative to summary execution, but then, like a virus, it mutates. Today, many people assume slavery relates solely to people of color. A student once asked me, "why did they only enslave the chocolate people? Why not the others?" My answer was that they did enslave the others. To be sure, the first empires reside in the Cradle of Civilization. The Slavic Nations were named as such because they were a source of slaves. The bitterness, resentfulness and rage exhibited in contemporary warfare in the Balkans, 1990s, is deeply rooted in the brutality and enslavement dating back thousands of years, beginning 8-10,000 years ago and reaching a fevered pitch 4-5,000 years ago.

White skinned Europeans enslaved other white skinned peoples. Indigenous peoples in North America enslaved other indigenous people. Black skinned people in Africa enslaved other black skinned people. The Egyptians, Chinese, Romans and Greeks had slaves. The first code of law produced by Hammurabi prescribed death for anyone who helped a slave escape. Slavery had become an integral element in Antiquity; it is estimated that during certain periods only 5 per cent of the world's population was free. Human progress came with a price tag that included war, prisoners and slaves.

In *The Fortunes of Africa: A 5000-Year History of Wealth, Greed, and Endeavor*, Martin Meredith argues "enslavement was an organized activity. It was frequently the result of wars of expansion or civil wars. In some cases, rulers of an expanding state regarded enslavement of a conquered population as a useful means of increasing their wealth and status and building armies; in other cases, slaves were simply a by-product of political conflict which could be turned to profit. There was consequently a large market in slaves readily available to passing seafarers with goods to exchange."[5]

Emergence of religion, as we know it today, established rules for handling enslaved peoples, but it still remained a brutal and depraved domination of other humans. Enslavers knew the slavery enterprise was morally bankrupt. They contrived rationalizations and justification for their depravity. There is much debate about when and how racialization began, but there is substantial evidence of racialization used in the 9th century in Africa, as enslaving African emperors deflected criticisms of enslaving their own people, arguing they were not enslaving their own, they were enslaving the lighter skinned or darker skinned people.

On the lands we know as America, enslavement began long before Columbus. Indigenous people occupied the land 10-15,000 years before discovery of agriculture. Enslavement emerged in the Native peoples with the advent of agriculture, just as it did across the globe. Historian Karen Armstrong in her highly acclaimed *Fields of Blood: Religion and the History of Violence*, "As a result, the human population increased so dramatically that in some regions a return to hunter-gatherer life became impossible. Between about 8500 BCE and the first century of the Common Era— a remarkably short period given the four million years of our history— all around the world, quite independently, the great majority of humans made the transition to agrarian life. And with agriculture came civilization; and with civilization, warfare."[6]

European enslavement practices differed from the Natives. European slavery was more draconian, growing ever darker as the Europeans seized control. Indeed, the New World for the Europeans opened a path for discarding restraints imposed by religion.

Slavery and racism serve as the core of America. The European invasion of the Americas, driven by expansion of wealth and power, depended upon forced labor in exploiting the lands and extracting the land's resources, albeit gold, silver, tobacco, sugar or cotton. Systemic racism, used as a tool for rationalization and justification of slavery, is painfully obvious, even though slave masters deny it and claim themselves as stalwarts of freedom and justice, making a mockery of these characteristics.

The American tale stands in stark contrast to reality. Enslaved labor rationalized with bigotry exposed the selfish and inhuman soul of the powerful, but their power provided them with a megaphone for redefining reality, making a lie into a stated fact, so-called alternative facts. Tragically these tactics played out before a receptive audience with its own characteristics of bigotry.

Seizing control over a human being, coercively forcing them into an existence of serving the interests of the enslaver, gives meaning to the words inhumane, cold blooded and diabolical. Cognition of slavery terrifies all humans. Indeed, it is so terrifying that psychological defense mechanisms kick in for shielding the psyche; somehow viewing the enslaved as not human, as a separate species removed from real humans. It is a phenomenon best encapsulated in concepts of "us" and "them."

Constraints upon slavery imposed by monotheism became the equivalent of modern-day regulations, prompting slave masters to balk at moral restrictions. These restrictions included rules for the managing of enslaved people and rules for "no slaving zones" because those areas were inhabited by followers of the faith. This equated to restriction on the slave market. By doing so, the sources of slaves became more constricted, compelling those, who wanted slaves, to expand the search for sources of slaves. Expanding the search for slaves was costly causing slavers to seek alternatives and, thereby, causing a decline in slavery.

The Portuguese initiated rebranding of slavery within the African Slave Trade, the slave trading within the African continent as opposed to the Atlantic Slave Trade that followed later involving the international trade in slaves. Slaves were concentrated on the gold coast of

Africa where they were used in mining operations. Gold was needed for trade, which emerged from the global trading business initiated by the Europeans. When Africans wanted more European goods, slaves were offered for trade, initiating the international trade.

In the mid-15th century, the Portuguese obtained African slaves for domestic services in Portugal, the first shipment of slaves arriving in Lagos, Portugal in 1445. European traders considered bypassing slave traders by invading the continent and seizing slaves. African resistance, a harsh environment and exposure to deadly diseases, however, dissuaded the Europeans of that idea.

This was just the beginning, however, followed soon thereafter by what became known as the Atlantic Slave Trade. Herein are the roots of Slavery and Colonialism, manifesting wars, slaves and a world in which humans are the greatest predator and the most formidable threat to Humans.

In the African Slave Trade, slavery mutated from a punishment with a pathway for joining the society into a commercial enterprise in which the enslaved were little more than a commodity. Enslaved peoples were uprooted from their homes and families, moved across the continent in service of industrial level mining operations and later shipped off to foreign lands. This displacement from homelands is a significant milestone, driven by the salt mining industry of the 8th century. It may be argued that this was the first industrial revolution, only humans served as the machinery instead of the mechanized systems of the 18th century. To be sure, salt was exploited on a mass production scale. [7]

In the 15th century, Europeans explored a new concept for deployment of slaves, representing another mutation, by creating plantations off the African coast designed for mass producing agricultural products. This plantation business model, beta tested and refined off the

African coast, was transported to the New World after new navigation tools opened the oceans for travel. Upon arrival in the so-called New World, slavery mutated once again, tossing off religious restrictions imposed by faith while introducing new ever more harsh slave rules.

The African continent provided enslaved peoples for the New World, but it also provided normalization of displacing the enslaved from their home lands and families and providing normalization of racialization, along with the plantation business model.

The Atlantic Slave Trade has become the focus of considerations about slavery, but slavery began thousands of years before the Atlantic Slave Trade. The African Slave Trade took shape around the 9th century and established the template for slavery in the New World, about 600 years later.

Triangle Trade

A financial system emerged, the Triangle Trade of the 16th century, later maturing into Capitalism, representing banking, investments, insurance and legal services. The roots of capitalism remain murky, but the Triangle Trade highlights conversion of multiple services into a system for profit and loss. This system results in enormous wealth and power. It has no conscience or moral compass. Humans operate the system and stand behind it, even when inhumanity is revealed.

Beneficiaries of the system revere the system as if it were a God. Call it free market capitalism, war capitalism or something else, if you wish, but in the end, it is the same old system. Take raw materials wherever you find them; kill anything that gets in the way; feed those minerals, raw materials, into the industrial machine; mass produce goods for sale; retain a monopoly over the market; and rake in the profits. Use a portion of the profits in purchasing ruling authorities so governing rules protect the system and maintain an ominous protective edifice for squashing any and all threats to the system, an institutionalized and systematic means for obtaining wealth and power. There are no boundaries in what those with wealth and power will perpetrate in defending the system. There is no place in the system for those left behind and brutalized by the system. They, the environment and the very existence of society are merely collateral damage. Reasoning for the Common Good has no effect as domination in service of wealth and power reigns supreme.

Racism evolved as a tool for protecting the system. It provided rationalization and justification for the system and diverted attention from the human abuses of the system. It also created fear and hate for controlling mass populations and compelling them to protect the system against forces for regulation of the system.

In contemporary discourse, this is known as systemic racism and institutional racism, a key tool for system preservation. Religious, ethnic and nationalistic themes are also tools for control of the mass population. The same institutional mechanisms are used in societies, where race is not an issue, but other distinctions are applied such as caste or other wedge issues. Many relate to the system as capitalism, but capitalism is not inherently inhuman; it only becomes inhumane when mixed, as in a laboratory, with greed, insatiable, ravenously immoral, greed.

In the New World, slavery, natural resources, and no monotheistic restrictions, opened a path for wealth and power heretofore unimaginable. Spanish explorers opened the path to the New World for taking riches and wealth. The circumstances were ripe for unlimited gain at the expense of other humans. The new geography of the Caribbean meant this escapade in human depravity could rewrite the rules, establishing a new code for managing slaves, and creating a rationalization and justification making human exploitation acceptable. White supremacy was born.

The Spanish enslaved indigenous peoples in the New World exploiting them in mining operations. This slave enterprise, however, involved direct enslavement of natives, along with purchasing of native slaves from other native nations. The natives were not one homogeneous group of people; they represented hundreds of individual autonomous nations. These nations engaged in warfare with each other and established a slavery infrastructure for dealing with the vanquished in war. Europeans skillfully exploited divisions within the indigenous peoples and used the natives for enslavement of other natives in service of Spanish interests.

The British also used native slaves, but their plantation operations required significantly more human labor compelling them to expand suppliers of slaves. They began their North American adventure with indigenous slaves, but quickly embraced indentured white slaves as a labor source, followed shortly thereafter by slaves purchased in the Atlantic Slave Trade.

Examining American History requires attention to the individual European invaders of the Americas and how those experiences merged into the United States. It did not begin with the British colonies; it begins with the conglomeration of all European invaders and the country that emerged from consolidation of the invaders.

Consider slavery as a virus. It begins with the vanquished in warfare that are later integrated into society. The virus is constrained by religious restrictions evidenced by no slaving zones and rules for handling slaves. The virus mutates and slaves are traded, moved away from home lands and family for service to slave masters. Global expansion and invasion open new lands free from religious restrictions and the virus mutates again based on new and ever more inhuman rules. Industrialization creates demand for resources for feeding industrial machinery producing enormous wealth and power. The virus mutates again into another depth of depravity.

Slavery established the cornerstone for American Capitalism. As the Industrial Revolution, beginning around 1750, began to take shape, cotton took center stage as the world's key commodity. The Louisiana Purchase of 1804 provided the fledgling America with the rich fertile soil of the Mississippi Delta, a soil well suited for growing cotton. A separate chapter on the Louisiana Purchase will delve more deeply into the topic. The point here is that America's house of cards was built on a foundation of slavery.

Investors in England recognized the potential financial boom, placing their bets on American cotton by way of mortgage-backed securities. To be sure, this represented a massive transfer of capital. Since enslaved black people were deemed property, they, too, were mortgaged. So, investors purchased mortgage-backed securities for the land and the labor that produced hefty returns. And they pumped millions into railroads for moving cotton to market. Nothing is more American than investing in morally bankrupt enterprises that provide a handsome return on investment.

Siberian Migration Era

TODAY THEY ARE LABELED "ILLEGAL immigrants." They, however, may be the only legal inhabitants of the Americas. Humans led by nature to lands uninhabited by other humans are not exactly illegal; they are merely migrants. So-called European explorers, in contrast, are more appropriately designated "invaders," which makes them illegal, if you have a sense of justice.

The spin of American History presents European invaders as pioneers exploring new lands, implying that these "new lands" were virgin lands untouched by human feet. Brave pioneers searched for a place where they would commune with nature, work hard in the fields and reap rewards from their labor. This spin is a testament to the human spirit with freedom and decency interwoven into the tale.

This spin has always been complicated by the presence of indigenous peoples, so-called Indians. Within the context of the spin, Indians were not people; they were savages, ripe for saving by the pioneers who would bring them God and civilization. This spin is further evidence of the mental gymnastics required for avoiding admission of the brutality unleashed against other humans in service of personal gain. Understanding American History requires un-spinning the spin.

The Indians, the indigenous peoples, also known as Natives, lived in the hunter-gatherer world. Climatic changes forced them to migrate, following the herds that instinctively moved toward sources of food and water. They adapted to the harsh and demanding environment of Siberia as the herds led them into North America across the Bering Straits that had frozen over. Nothing about their entry into North America can be deemed illegal. Indeed, they were the first humans here in North America. Those who followed, not following herds, but on a quest to conquer, are quite different.

Historian Alan Taylor in his masterpiece *American Colonies: The Settling of North America* tells us "Most scholars believe that the first Americans migrated from Siberia in northeast Asia. Genetic and skeletal (especially dental) evidence suggests special affinities between Native Americans and the peoples of Siberia...[8]

...About fifteen thousand years ago the inhabitants of Siberia lived in many small bands that ranged far and wide in pursuit of the roaming and grazing herds of large and meaty (but dangerous) mammals, especially mammoths, musk oxen, and woolly rhinoceroses...

...But between about twenty-five thousand and twelve thousand years ago, a colder global climate— an Ice Age— locked up more of the world's water in polar icecaps, which spread southward as immense glaciers, covering the northern third of North America. The enlarged icecaps lowered the ocean levels by as much as 360 feet, creating a land bridge between Siberia and Alaska. "

David Stannard in *American Holocaust: Columbus and the Conquest of the New World* also adds, "Where the first humans in the Americas came from and how they got to their new homes are now probably the least controversial of these age-old questions.' Although at one time or another seemingly all the corners of Europe, Asia, the Middle East, and Africa fancifully have been suggested as the sources of early populations in the New World, no one any longer seriously doubts that the first human inhabitants of North and South America were the descendants of much earlier emigrants from ancestral homelands in northeastern Asia…"[9]

This land bridge between Eurasia and the American continents opened a path for peoples of Siberia to follow migratory herds into North America. Their journey continued into lands of South and Central America. Today in North America their offspring are known as "illegal immigrants."

Sophisticated Society

Siberian migrants, so-called savages, populated the continent, establishing sophisticated societies including elaborate trading centers. They were not one homogenous society; they formed over 500 Nations during their 20,000-year history. Advanced societies emerged known as the Inca, the Maya and the Aztec civilizations. Later invading Europeans would characterize them as uncivilized savages, so they could rationalize and justify clearly uncivilized acts of brutality and enslavement.

Cahokia, established long before the arrival of Columbus, around the 10th Century and located along the Mississippi River near St. Louis, became a center for trading, ceremonies and political events. This was a planned development, engineered in accordance with spiritual beliefs for aligning the development with the spirits. Cahokia is symbolic of an advanced society in which multiple independent nations interacted for trade and internation relations.

Native populations differed from the Europeans who were soon to invade. Property was an alien concept. There were designated hunting grounds, but land was not a thing to own; it belonged to nature and everyone had a right to use the land for obtaining sustainable food. Invading Europeans held a different view, particularly British invaders. In Britain land ownership was a key for wealth and power. They brought this idea with them, along with the Doctrine of Discovery of 1493, a special blessing from the Vatican authorizing invasion of these lands, later codified into U.S. law by the Supreme Court. Their acts of aggression were also rationalized by the concept of "use it or lose it."

Historian Alan Taylor explains these conflicting views, "European Christians insisted that humanity had a divine charge to dominate and exploit the natural world. In the first book of their Bible, God ordered people to "subdue the earth and have dominion over every living thing that moves on the earth." As a result, colonizers regarded as backward and impious any people, like the Indians, who left nature too little altered. By defaulting in their divine duty, such peoples forfeited their title to the earth. They could justly be conquered and dispossessed by Europeans who would exploit lands and animals to their fullest potential. "[10]

Bernard Bailyn in *The Barbarous Years: The Peopling of British North America: The Conflict of Civilizations, 1600-1675* also adds how indigenous peoples viewed land, "No one possessed—"owned"— land. "Ownership"— exclusive possession, with the publicly approved right to sell as a commodity or otherwise alienate and use as one saw fit— was unknown. Land was held and used communally, by the "larger corporate groups, and ultimately the tribe, that discharge a proprietary or controlling function over territory and thus resources."[11]

The Natives did not react to the invading Europeans as a threat. They sought ways for interaction so they could obtain benefits of trade consistent with their culture. They did not expect an assault for domination.

Black Plague

About a hundred years before Columbus sailed the ocean blue, a silent and invisible killer descended upon Eurasia. A crippling sickness stopped people in their tracks as their bodies became disfigured with swollen growths filled with bilious fluids and fevers rendered them helpless.

It was mysterious sickness, some thinking it a punishment from God. This inexplicable horror terrified Eurasia. What could this invisible monster be? Perhaps it was punishment for following Christendom and not sacrificing to the pagan Gods. The death toll was enormous, some estimates suggesting half of Europe died, as a result of what we now know today as the Black Plague. After the plague ran its course and faded, Christendom fractured, making way for new Christian faiths. There was widespread belief that the plague was an expression of God's anger, a punishment for sins they could only imagine. Some broke away and formed a new sect of Christianity: Protestantism. Simultaneously, Catholicism was engaged in battle against Islam, provoking the Vatican to encourage Catholics to "kill the infidels."

The European invasion of the Americas coincided with the post Black Plague episode of the 14th Century.

The Plague fractured the bond between Christendom and its followers. As a result, Catholicism needed replenishment of believers. When new technologies emerged opening navigation of the ocean, the Vatican seized upon the opportunity for replenishment of its population by issuing the Doctrine of Discovery. It provided the legal, moral and spiritual foundation for the invasion, occupation and theft of new lands, along with murder, rape and kidnapping of indigenous peoples. It may be the world's most severe sin.

The European explorer, discoverer, invader then arrived in the New World and it all changed.

In *The Other Slavery: The Uncovered Story of Indian Enslavement in America*, Andrés Reséndez, writes:

"The first Europeans in the New World found a thriving archipelago: islands large and small covered by lush vegetation, teeming with insects and birds, and alive with humans. The Caribbean was "a beehive of people," wrote Bartolomé de Las Casas, the most well-known of the region's early chroniclers, who accompanied several expeditions of discovery.

Bartolomé de Las Casas, who arrived in the New World in 1502, averred that greed was the reason Christians "murdered on such a vast scale," killing "anyone and everyone who has shown the slightest sign of resistance," and subjecting "all males to the harshest and most iniquitous and brutal slavery that man has ever devised for oppressing his fellow-men, treating them, in fact, worse than animals."[12]

Spanish invaders wanted gold, but soon discovered an abundant source of silver. They enslaved indigenous people forcing them to work in mines extracting riches. Queen Isabella opposed enslavement, except if it was a product of warfare, and, only then, if it was a just war. Spanish invaders easily established the pretense of just war and brutalized the native population in service of wealth producing enterprises. Redefining aggression as a defensive act in a justified war became a model for rationalization and justification for invasion and brutality serving the world's bullies for the past 600 years.

PART TWO

The Charges

European Invasion Era

HE DREAMED OF THE DAY when he would get an opportunity to exercise his technical prowess. The navigator's astrolabe opened a door for application of navigational skills heretofore unimagined. With support of Queen Isabella and a special blessing from the Vatican, the Venetian navigator Christopher Columbus set sail with the power of Spain at his back.

Sail the ocean, find new lands, and conquer for power and for glory. The so-called "explorer" Columbus was presented as a gallant man boldly taming the ocean in search of a New World. He set forth under the Spanish flag on a quest for empire expansion, just as others had beginning with the Akkadian Empire 4500 years ago.

Columbus started a new chapter, however, by expanding across the oceans, elevating empire and conquest on an industrial scale. Lessons learned from this new chapter in Empire building provided a template for international colonialism ultimately leading to worldwide warfare in the 20th century. To be sure, raw brutality in service of wealth and power was the driving force for invasion of the New World. Disguising it as some sort of mission for God or just war, the New World invasion represented a death sentence for indigenous peoples, while lawless invaders plundered the people and the land.

EUROPEAN INVASION ERA

Traditional history books quickly skip past Spain's butchery in the 15th and 16th centuries jumping ahead to the British colonial enterprise, because the British settlement became the most dominant. The Spanish, Dutch, Russian and French expeditions were formidable, however, and must be considered when evaluating U.S. history.

North America was not a British colony; it was invaded by multiple Europeans with diverse and sometimes conflicting agendas. The settlement of North America was a part of a much broader epic in human history, invasion of the New World.

This New World colonial exploration seemed to just emerge. It was uncoordinated and unplanned. By the 15th century, the Neolithic revolution, spawned by agriculture and animal husbandry, was at the center of the Human Existence, having existed for roughly 8-10,000 years. During that time, people of wealth and power established massive armies—the protective edifice—and navies for control of the seas. Aristocrats became Kings and Queens with special blessings from God, nation-states emerged and warfare contaminated the planet. This was brute force warfare, undisguised by some contrived spin of fighting for freedom and justice. No, the warfare was naked aggression for seizing lands, resources and so-called "booty," the accumulated stuff and wealth of the people under attack.

Genocide did not start with the Holocaust in the 20th century. Genocide represented the far extreme of not only killing an adversary, but killing everyone connected with the adversary; women, children and their sources of food. Even though the Bible is not a historical document, as Norman Naimark tells us in *Genocide: A World History*, as God led the Jews in the desert to the land of Israel, God wanted punishment for those attacking the Jews. [13]

The exodus of the Jews from Egypt, their wandering in the desert, and their conquering of the land of Israel serve as the central narrative trajectory of the Old Testament. As their God led the Hebrews on this journey, he demanded obedience from his chosen people in exchange for supporting their claims against more numerous and powerful enemies who sought to bring them harm. Most prominently, the Amalekites, a semi-nomadic people of the desert, earned the wrath of God by attacking the Israelites. The Amalekites became a target and God wanted them vaporized, but Saul was reluctant to go to that extreme. Saul got a visit from Samuel with a message from God. [14]

"Samuel explained that God, "according to Naimark, "ordered Saul to attack and kill the Amalekites because of their transgressions against the Israelites when the latter had escaped from Egypt. "Now go and smite Amalek, and utterly destroy all that they have, and spare them not; but both man and woman, infant and suckling, ox and sheep, camel and ass."[15]

The world was an extremely dangerous place. Our New Brain provided us with the intelligence for creating agriculture, taking control of food sources for a steady flow of nutrition. The potential of our New Brain, about 35,000 years old, proffered an idyllic Human Experience. But instead, a select group of humans applied this new brain capacity for greed, transforming the idyllic potential into a cauldron of brutality for the select few to accumulate enormous amounts of wealth.

The first half of the Neolithic Period, 10,000 BCE-4,000 BCE, was somewhat tame according to historians, based upon limited evidence. But by 4,000 BCE, emperors became more aggressive. As indicated previously, the first empire formed around 2,300 BCE. It may be suggested the brutality of empire building led to the ideas of the Bible and the notion of one God, as attributed to Abraham, 2,000 BCE.

Mind you, this bloodletting and brutality began before nation-states formed, before religions as we know them today formed, before concepts of racism and ethnicities formed. Each of these would become

EUROPEAN INVASION ERA

tools for the powerful in agitating the populous to fear and hate the adversary, gleefully charging off to war. Nationalism, racism, religious antagonisms and ethnic hatreds became tools for the powerful, clearly evident in modern times. There is a private agenda for the wealthy, hidden from public consumption. That agenda is greed, stealing resources, such as oil, sugar, cotton, lands and more, serving enhancement of their wealth and power. Racist troupes, religious antagonism, homo-sexual hate along with nationalism are merely public relations tools for inciting the populace to fight.

In contemporary world events, raw brutality is clearly on display as Russia attacks neighboring Ukraine, a horrific attack placing the world on the brink of nuclear war with the potential for killing everything. Recent bloodletting in the Balkans, 1990s, also exemplifies the butchery of the past 10,000 years. Indeed, my argument is that the bloodletting of the modern day is rooted in the aggressions of the past 10,000 years.

When Columbus used his brain and intelligence in traversing the Atlantic Ocean, it was an enterprise with lethal consequences for the inhabitants of the New World. The slaughter of indigenous people was not something new. It removed obstacles to the real agenda.

The Spanish were on a quest for power and gold under the disguise of missionary zeal. The Dutch sought new business enterprises, constantly angling for control of a commodity, serving a monopolistic enterprise. The French wanted trade. And the British were splintered; unwilling to financially sponsor colonial settlements; England issued corporate charters to adventurers who went their own separate ways, but were still subject to British rule. The Russians stayed close to home establishing fur trading operations in the northwest.

Spain led the invasion of North America followed by the French and the Dutch. The British came later but they were fractured and never connected with each other behind a common set of principles and beliefs; indeed, each British corporate settlement was independent and had no connection with the others. When England did enter the fray, however, it became the most aggressive in populating its colonies, quickly outnumbering the other colonies.

Blessed by the Vatican, and with God on their side, the Europeans invaded, muscling aside indigenous peoples, taking lands and riches at will. Columbus' invasion set the stage connecting events from the 15th century through contemporary times. The arrogant mindset of the invader occupier is clearly on display in the 19th century colonization of Africa, India and China. That unquenchable thirst for ever greater wealth and power connects Empire building colonization with contemporary events. including the residue of hate playing out between the haves and have nots. Empire building did not begin with Columbus, but the industrial scale of Columbus's enterprise established his invasion as a new chapter in the saga of domination.

"According to the centuries-old Doctrine of Discovery," says Roxanne Dunbar-Ortiz in *An Indigenous Peoples' History of the United States*, "European nations acquired title to the lands they "discovered," and Indigenous inhabitants lost their natural right to that land after Europeans had arrived and claimed it. Under this legal cover for theft, Euro-American wars of conquest and settler colonialism devastated Indigenous nations and communities, ripping their territories away from them and transforming the land into private property, real estate. Most of that land ended up in the hands of land speculators and agribusiness operators, many of which, up to the mid-nineteenth century, were plantations worked by another form of private property, enslaved Africans. Arcane as it may seem, the doctrine remains the basis for federal laws still in effect that control Indigenous peoples' lives and destinies, even their histories by distorting them."[16]

EUROPEAN INVASION ERA

Columbus led the way to the New World. It has been presented as an innocuous venture in search for new trade routes and spices. Columbus is depicted as brave and heroic exploring for new trade markets. But the Charter that authorized his mission is very clear that his objective was to conquer.

> For as much of you, *Christopher Columbus*, are going by our command, with some of our vessels and men, to discover and subdue some Islands and Continent in the ocean, and it is hoped that by God's assistance, some of the said Islands and Continent in the ocean will be discovered and conquered by your means and conduct, therefore it is but just and reasonable, that since you expose yourself to such danger to serve us, you should be rewarded for it. *Privileges and Prerogatives Granted by Their Catholic Majesties to Christopher Columbus : 1492* [17]

Before Columbus set sail, Spanish and Portuguese traders established an infrastructure along the African west coast. Blocked from opening plantation operations in Africa, they awaited an opportunity to do so elsewhere. Columbus afforded them that opportunity. When a path to the west opened, the Spanish led the way on a straight line from the African coast to the Greater and Lesser Antilles. These islands beckoned with rich soil, coastal ports and indigenous peoples for enslavement. Jamaica, the Bahamas, Barbados and many more became the target of European invaders.

Early occupations of the Antilles used indigenous peoples for enslaved labor. This was supplanted by indentured slaves, people displaced from common lands in Europe. Many of the displaced migrated to urban centers in search of new beginnings. Disillusioned they descended into crime and when they were caught or when they

INDICTING AMERICA

were unable to pay off debts, they were then sentenced to indentured servitude and shipped off to the colonial settlements, where slave labor was in high demand. Few survived to live out the term of the indenture. Still, this was not enough to meet labor demands.

Soon demand for labor skyrocketed, outstripping the supply of enslaved labor provided by indigenous peoples and indentured white slaves. By the turn of the 16th century, the African Slave Trade was well established, quickly becoming the supplier of forced labor. The first Spanish ship with a cargo of enslaved humans arrived in the Caribbean in 1510. The Dutch made fortunes transporting enslaved people from Africa to the Caribbean. The French and British also entered the slave trade enterprise.

Martin Meredith says "In the second half of the fifteenth century, according to modern researchers, the traffic in slaves taken by sea merchants from the west coast of Africa amounted to about 80,000. In the first half of the sixteenth century, when other European merchants became involved and the trans-Atlantic trade began, the number rose to about 120,000."[18]

Sven Beckert's award winning *Empire of Cotton: A Global History* says, "Christopher Columbus's landing in the Americas in 1492 marked the first momentous event in this recasting of global connections. That journey set off the world's greatest land grab, with Hernán Cortés attacking the Aztec Empire in 1518 and establishing vast territorial claims for the Spaniards in America, spreading into South America and also farther north."[19]

The Spanish focused on gold and silver in their New World enterprise. They established a pervasive dominion over the Americas to such an extent that today Spanish is spoken through South and Central America, along with Mexico. The cultures of the indigenous peoples were overwhelming by the Spanish. By the close of the 16th century, however, the French, Dutch and British entered the fray with a focus on sugar and fur trading. Caribbean islands were ripe for sugar production.

Beckert adds, "Europeans invented the world anew by embarking upon plantation agriculture on a massive scale. Once Europeans became involved in production, they fastened their economic fortunes to slavery. These three moves— **imperial expansion, expropriation, and slavery**— became central to the forging of a new global economic order and eventually the emergence of capitalism.

> Instead, private capitalists, often organized in chartered companies (such as the British East India Company) asserted sovereignty over land and people, and structured connections to local rulers. Heavily armed privateering capitalists became the symbol of this new world of European domination, as their cannon-filled boats and their soldier-traders, armed private militias, and settlers captured land and labor and blew competitors, quite literally, out of the water. Privatized violence was one of their core competencies. While European states had envisioned, encouraged, and enabled the creation of vast colonial empires, they remained weak and thin on the ground, providing private actors the space and leeway to forge new modes of trade and production.
>
> Beckert, Sven (2014-12-02). **Empire of Cotton: A Global History** (Kindle Locations 905-909). Knopf Doubleday Publishing Group. Kindle Edition.[20]

More importantly, the Europeans brought with them the template for slave operations established in the African Slave Trade beginning in the 9th century in which slaves were treated as mere commodities, stripped of home and family roots, moved thousands of miles away for work in slave enterprise systems, based upon a rationalization and justification centered on skin appearance. The plantation business model, tested and refined on islands off the African coast, also provided a blue print for slavery in the New World now subject to invasion and occupation by European empires.

The American history curriculum of the birth of the United States is a contorted tale designed for making America's origins noble. The narrative centers on British colonies in North America, suggesting that America was born from English peoples who came to America seeking freedom and opportunity. The idea of indentured slaves is spun as people who entered indentured servitude to pay for their transportation. This is distorted, bearing slight resemblance to the real story. The story suggests that English men and women disillusioned by the lack of freedom in Britain made a conscious decision to take a risk and move to the New World where they could better themselves. It is a tale of the human heart yearning for freedom and opportunity, thereby distracting and obfuscating the real events of human butchery in service of wealth for a select few.[21]

The first British foray into the New World arrived at Roanoke Island off the North Carolina coast where they were welcomed by natives and disease. It did not fare well. Undeterred they tried again in the Chesapeake Bay in the Tidewater Region establishing a foothold along the James River. They were aided by the kindness, generosity and humanity of natives. British corporate settlements eventually survived in the form of the Massachusetts Bay Company and the Virginia Company, while the relationship with the crown remained ambiguous.

The English invaders depended upon Britain's military might for protection, but when the motherland asserted a degree of authority and control, thereby threatening the wealth creation enterprise, England's colonial leaders decided it was time to sever ties. It was not driven by noble thoughts of freedom and justice; it was driven by greed facilitated by genocide against the Native peoples and exploitation of enslaved humans.

It is important to separate the Siberian Migration Era from the European Invasion Era, because the manipulative tale of America simply relegates the indigenous population to the status of savages, a designation suggesting something less than human. But they were not savages, whatever that may mean; they were humans and must be recognized as such. When they are recognized as humans, then the question must arise about the legitimacy of European invader claims to the land.

The European Invasion Era establishes a record of arrogance, immorality, depravity and greed that cannot be denied. It is vital for understanding American History. It is estimated that more than 100 million Natives died due to the invasion.

America is charged with an illegal invasion of occupied lands, the beginning of the criminal enterprise, murder, rape, theft, kidnapping and torture. It is a Crime Against Humanity, Genocide and an on-going criminal enterprise.

Barbados

A SEGMENT OF THOSE WITH wealth and power never seem to have enough, investing time and energy in finding new opportunities for expanding their wealth and power. The New World unleashed wide ranging opportunities and they were poised for taking advantage.

Their thoughts quickly contemplated unimaginable sums of wealth potentially derived from enterprises, fueled by enslave labor. This represented the ultimate prize for the powerful and for those aspiring to join their ranks.

Restrictions imposed upon them by religion, however, made them feel hemmed in. Religious institutions, still advocating for a modicum of humanity in managing enslaved peoples, imposed limitations on slave management, requiring a minimal level of humane treatment. If they—the Slave Masters—could just unshackle themselves and their business enterprises from the stranglehold of religious restrictions, they could open the flood gates of money that would pour into their coffers.

A glimmer of hope, peeked through at the close of the 15th century as Columbus unveiled the New World. The slavers envisioned a new land where new rules took precedent, free from encumbrances imposed by religion. As they approached the New World, they hammered out the details for operating without religious restrictions. New religions spawned by the Black Plague became established without rules for handling slaves. The slavers would embrace these new faiths, proclaiming themselves free from what was the equivalent of government regulation.

After setting sail from Africa, the New World invaders waited anxiously for validation of Columbus' finding. As they sailed west, they scanned the horizon seeking a glimpse of land as they voyaged across the ocean. Then specs of sand arose indicating that Columbus might just be right. They appeared as little more than small islands, little dots on the vast Atlantic Ocean off the North American continental coast. A century later, these small islands took their seat at the head of wealth producing properties where sugar cane thrived. Indeed, these islands, in what became known as the West Indies, produced unimaginable wealth, dwarfing the value of all of the other colonies on the North American continent

As Spanish and Portuguese sailors, following the lead of Columbus at the turn of the 16th century, approached the New World, they came upon this group of islands in the Lesser Antilles, southeast of the North American continent. Although this was a gateway to North America, the West Indies would become central to British interests in the 17th and 18th centuries, as sugar—sweet tooth gold—thrived across the landscape. The island named Barbados became the crown jewel outpacing all others in the proliferation of sugar and the profits attendant to it.

Control of the island changed hands several times between the Spanish and Portuguese. Eventually England entered the scene, 1625, forming a permanent settlement in 1627. The English settlers entered with a goal of making a bundle of profits and then returning to England. This equated to a focus on profits at the expense of the human toll. The English legacy established in Barbados, planted the roots of what would become racial animus in North America.

Barbados gave birth to White Supremacy in the 17th Century, later exporting it into South Carolina. Barbados set the template for the southern slavocracy in North America. To be sure, it is here in Barbados where the enslavement virus mutated once again, working slaves to death in harvesting and processing sugar, a key commodity for European aristocrats. It starts in Barbados quickly spreading across the Americas.

The Black Plague of the 14th Century that fractured Christendom, plays a key role in the Barbados story. This fracturing created turmoil for religion and was an impetus for the Doctrine of Discovery of 1452 and 1493, authorizing Spain and Portugal to conquer news lands and convert anyone found on those lands to Catholicism. The Barbadian slave masters, took advantage of the Discovery Doctrine, but balked at conversion.

Slave masters obsessed with unburdening themselves of religious constraints, declared themselves free from regulation under the banner of Protestant Supremacy. Conversions were banned, because they did not want the old rules of not enslaving fellow believers. For slave masters this New World represented an opportunity to break free from religious restrictions. They declared Protestant Supremacy that meant the old rules need not apply.

Protestantism, an outgrowth of the Black Plague, represented the break with established religious order. When slavers arrived in Barbados, they recognized the chance to rid themselves of religious boundaries. This new religious institution, Protestantism, came without rules restricting slavery. Indeed, overtime, this new religion would be used for validating slavery, even creating a Slave Bible supporting enslavement. In Barbados, as the slave population became darker skinned due to use of the Atlantic Slave Trade, Protestant Supremacy was transformed into White Supremacy.

Columbus' "New World" represented unencumbered opportunities for lavish luxuries, wealth and power. Europeans seeking fortune poured through the door opened by Columbus, paving a way for the greedy, unrestrained by rules and regulations. Brute force enabled these invader colonists for seizing control, enslaving indigenous peoples and obtaining riches derived from gold, silver and other products in demand such as sugar and tobacco.

The New World ignited intensive competition between European powers. All felt themselves specially endowed by their creator to take lands, peoples and resources. Such inhuman and immoral action required some sanction, some authority. The Vatican filled the void with the Doctrine of Discovery. By fulfilling God's wishes, bringing civilization and Christianity to the nonhuman savages, the Europeans were doing God's work in saving these savages, while also unleashing the darkest of human's hearts.

And it was here in Barbados, about 50 years after the Jamestown settlement, 1609, that King Charles II focused his attention on the British colonial enterprise in North America. The colonial settlements created by the adventurers operated independently of the Crown's leadership. King Charles asserted his authority taking control by assigning Governors, clearly establishing British dominance. The Massachusetts Bay Company, settled in the northeast, was fractured by religious differences. The Virginia Company set its roots in the Tidewater region, but it had no connection with the northeastern settlements. It remained ambiguous as to what North America offered the crown, but King Charles was not about to let the Spanish, French or Dutch establish a foothold on land that he felt should be claimed for England. And so, King Charles decided to assert his authority.

As the Crown consolidated power, its counterparts in France, Spain and the Netherlands also were maneuvering for control of the New World. The British had an edge, however, as they aggressively populated their colonies with indentured slaves.

European monarchs were eager for control, keeping a step ahead of each other. The Spanish established a strong foothold across the south and west; the French set roots in Canada and on down through the Mississippi Valley; the Dutch settlement in New York was becoming a central point for commerce; while the British remained fractured along the eastern seaboard.

King Charles bullied the Dutch from New York with a show of British naval forces in New York Harbor taking control of what became the Mid-Atlantic States. He also directed attention to what was to become South Carolina where the Spanish and the French were encroaching from Florida and Louisiana.

The King wanted South Carolina inhabited and claimed for the Crown. But the appetite for new adventures by the aristocrats and militarist explorers had waned by this time, as stories of disease and native beheadings became widely known. If the King wanted to settle South Carolina, he had to provide some enticement.

In March, 1663, King Charles II made an offer they couldn't refuse. He offered free land, a land grant, if the Lord's Proprietor, a selected group of aristocrats, took the lead in settling South Carolina.

In the northern part of the territory, the area of North Carolina, the Virginians had established an infrastructure for settlement, but the territory of South Carolina was merely inhabited by "savages and barbarians," as they were called. Consequently, the aristocrats, Eight Lords Proprietor, were charged with settling South Carolina.

Settling South Carolina converged with events in the Lesser Antilles where British slave plantation owners feared for their lives.

In Barbados, British colonial invaders established a slave environment that reached new depths of human brutality.

Historian Katherine Gerbner tells the story of black man named Lazarus who was baptized in an Anglican church in 1651. "Lazarus," Gerbner writes, "who was described only as 'a negro' in the church register, was the first Afro-Caribbean to receive baptism in the Anglican Church on Barbados." Gerbner adds, "Lazarus's baptism challenged the emerging culture of slavery in the Protestant Atlantic world. The Anglican Church in Barbados was exclusive, the domain of slave owners and government officials. While most historians have downplayed the relevance of Christianity in the seventeenth-century Protestant Caribbean, viewing the sugar colonies as islands of depravity, the Anglican Church was central to the maintenance of planter power in Barbados and elsewhere.2 The planter elite believed that their status as Protestants was inseparable from their identity as free Englishmen."[22]

Catholics, intent on replenishing their ranks depleted by the Black Plague, advocated for conversion of the indigenous peoples to Christianity; the Protestants did not. Barbados was settled by Anglicans and Dutch Reformed believers and they mounted a concerted effort against conversion to Christianity. This effort is known as Protestant Supremacy, directly aimed at thwarting application of religious restrictions on slave management. They also adopted new slave codes making salient a slave environment unrestrained by religious doctrine. Dutch and Danish colonies shared the Barbadian views of conversion. The stalwart prohibition against conversion, however, waned as African slaves became predominant as the slave population.

"Protestant Supremacy," Gerbner writes, "was the predecessor of White Supremacy, an ideology that emerged after the codification of racial slavery. I refer to "Protestant" Supremacy, rather than "Anglican" or "Christian" Supremacy, because this ideology was present throughout the Protestant American colonies, from the Danish West Indies to Virginia and beyond."[23]

Market demand for sugar outpaced the supply of indentured slaves, so plantation operators turned to the African Slave Coast for slave resources. This was a critical juncture in the history of slavery, which dated back to antiquity. But in Barbados a new slave code was established. Sugar cane required intensive labor. When harvested, sugar cane needed quick processing. In Barbados slaves were worked to death. Plantation operators rationalized that it was cheaper to procure new shipments of slaves than to treat existing slaves humanely. Indeed, humane treatment may not have been an option, because production demanded timely conversion of sugar cane into molasses and sugar.

South Carolina

Free Land, on a spot that once was a spot on Pangaea, adjoining the Scottish Highlands, was too enticing for the Lords Proprietor to turn down. One day their names would be etched into South Carolina history. Indeed, the Ashley and Cooper Rivers are named for Anthony Ashley Cooper, 1st Earl of Shaftesbury. Settling this land that is sought after by Spain and France and is infested with savages and barbarians represented a formidable challenge.

The Lords Proprietor were uncertain of what to do with South Carolina. They agreed they wanted a place with religious freedom. A state religion, such as the Anglican Church in England, was fraught with too many conflicts. But what else did they want? Perhaps a return on whatever they invested for development of this free land?

Exploitation of enslaved peoples came to mind because that was the rule of the day and had been for thousands of years by the 17th century. They needed skilled and experienced Slave Masters for this enterprise. Then a recession hit, impacting the plantation operators in Barbados. This converged with an increasingly hostile environment in Barbados where working slaves to death provided an incentive for slaves to wish to kill the Slave Masters.

In response to the land grant provided by King Charles, the Lords Proprietor deployed William Hilton (Hilton Head) to scan the South Carolina coast for prospective settlement locations. The coastal lands and southeastern region were swampy, but there was a natural port area good for shipping. Moving north and west, hills and mountains took shape, resembling the Scottish Highlands. It seemed the lower part of the area had a potential for plantation operations.

Barbadians Slave Masters seemed ripe for the picking. The environment they had created in Barbados was hostile and life threatening. Coinciding with the economic downturn in the late 17th century with efforts for establishing a South Carolina colony, the Lords Proprietor seized the opportunity recruiting the Barbados plantation operators for South Carolina.

Barbados was a money maker, but conditions were untenable. South Carolina provided an escape mechanism for setting up shop in an environment that would not be as threatening as Barbados. Barbados was a small island without scapegoats for displacing anger away from the plantation operators. In South Carolina, there was more room for evasion from a slave uprising and there were natives who could be used for deflecting and channeling animosities away from plantation operators.

By early 1670, Captain William Sayles led an expedition transporting Barbadians to Albemarle Point, later renamed Charles Towne in honor of the King and even later renamed Charleston. South Carolina Governor John Yeamans (namesake of the Yeamans' Golf Club) escalated recruitments in 1672. Over the next two decades over 50% of the white people in South Carolina came from Barbados.

Copying the wedge issues techniques employed by Virginia in response to Nathaniel Bacon, the Barbadians in South Carolina became skillful in playing natives against slaves. Had the natives and black slaves joined forces, the white skinned occupiers would not have been a match for them. But the occupying force succeeded in keeping the natives and slaves divided and hostile to each other. Indeed, they also succeeded in manipulating one native tribe against another, so as to divert attention from themselves.

Rice and indigo emerged as key crops for South Carolina. Cotton was also added to the mix. The Barbadians were stymied by the swamp lands. Fortunately for them, however, their African slaves had experience and skills with such landscapes, teaching the Barbadians about rice and indigo. Unfortunately for the African slaves, they were not rewarded for their skills and experience; they were enslaved. If this is not a crime, it should be and is therefore added to the list of crimes alleged in this presentment.

The Barbadians were cold and calculating. They never gave ground, never admitted wrong, and embraced a win at any cost determination insulating them from any scintilla of conscience that might moderate their practices. They brought with them a draconian slave law that made Barbados notorious and they adopted a management style of all stick and no carrot. Soon they would also turn on the Lords Proprietor who had made their money through rents charged to the plantation operators. When the plantation operators, in the 18th Century, refused to pay their Quitrents, the King simply acquiesced.

Barbadian plantation owners became centered in Goose Creek, just outside of Charleston. The Goose Creek men, as they became known, quickly became engaged in conflict with the colonial settlement created by the Lords' Proprietors, who advocated for religious freedom. No, no, no, the Barbadians were Anglicans. By 1702, they pushed governing authorities to prohibit non-Anglicans from holding office and established the Anglican Church as the colony's official church, supported by taxes.

That, of course, wasn't enough. Within 20 years, they forced a restructuring of government, pushing out the Lords' Proprietors, replacing them with royal governors. This meant England would have to take the lead in fighting Indians and Spanish encroachment.

Eugene Sirmans in his historical work titled *Colonial South Carolina* says, "In a move that foreshadowed the history of South Carolina politics for the next four decades, the Barbadian immigrants in the colony showed an early desire to take over the provincial government. The Barbadians, who by 1671 constituted nearly half the population, were ambitious, experienced, and occasionally unscrupulous men who had little interest in Lord Ashley's dream of erecting a perfect society in Carolina."[24]

The Lords' Proprietors received land grants for settlement, but then they had to invest their own funds in subsidizing the start-up. "The proprietors had sunk nearly £ 10,000 into Carolina without seeing a penny in return," according to Sirmans. "If the colonists could ignore the palatine's instructions on debts, Indian trade, and land distribution, the proprietors could never be sure that any of their orders would be obeyed. Thus, by the end of the first decade of active settlement the proprietors faced nothing less than the collapse of all their plans for Carolina. Their only choice lay between writing off South Carolina as a total loss or trying to revitalize the colony through drastic action of some kind."

The Lords Proprietor opened the path to South Carolina for the Barbadians and in doing so unleashed a monster. It is here in South

Carolina in the 1660s that North America recruited the most brutal slave operators known to history. It was a monumental point in American history because the Barbadians were brutal, inhuman, and mean spirited; win at any cost people who would treat humans with the same contempt and disdain they received when they were cast into the gutters of London and sentenced to indentured servitude. By understanding where they came from, it is possible to understand what they became. The oppressed had become the oppressor.

And by understanding what they became, it becomes possible to understand the society and culture that emerged in South Carolina; a bitter, hateful and spiteful culture, later defined as "Fire-eaters" that grew into a political entity that would not cooperate; that would give new meaning to recalcitrance; and that would set in place a political thorn that would debilitate the American government for centuries to come, right up to the modern day. Donald Trump may be a direct product.

Slavery in the New World, however, took on characteristics uniquely harsh and brutal. Since antiquity, rules for handling slaves provided a mechanism for slave treatment and integration into the society, out of slavery. Over time and space, the rules changed, but essentially the rules for handling slaves provided some limitations on the slave owner, affording slaves, at least, a modicum of humane treatment. These rules may be found in the Old Testament, New Testament and the Quran.

In Barbados the treatment of slaves was so despicable, slave operators feared for their lives and made great efforts to isolate themselves from slaves for fear of attack. They built mansions on top of hills in central Barbados far removed from slave quarters, but their fears grew deeper and for good reason. Conditions were brutal and plantations' operators were mindful of their vulnerability should the slaves revolt. Fear of slave reprisals compelled the plantation operators to tighten security; enact stiffer and more brutal Slave Laws; and isolate themselves as far as possible from the slave population. Fear of slaves grew more intense in subsequent years. Indeed, it was a key in motivating colonists to join a fight for independence from England and is prominently displayed in the Constitution, to be discussed in later chapters.

This culture, imported from Barbados, established itself in downstate South Carolina and spread across the southern states. The example of plantation operations in South Carolina set the standard for Georgia, overshadowing James Oglethorpe's dream of a colony for debtor redemption, 1732. And when the Louisiana Purchase, 1804, was concluded, prospective plantation owners, weaned on the human exploitative techniques employed in South Carolina, continued the example established by South Carolina into what became Alabama, Mississippi and Louisiana. The root of the so-called "Southern way," however, is in South Carolina, transplanted from Barbados, and germinated in the gutters of London.

To understand the political attitudes of truculence and no-compromise that became endemic to the south in North America requires focusing upon its roots in Barbados; then, and only then, can the determination to never let go of slavery be understood. To be sure, the predisposition of the south for intransigence toward compromise is a direct offspring of London's outcasts who found riches in the convergence of the fertile soil of the Mississippi Delta; the products it produced; a market that would take all it could make; and the lynchpin of the entire operation: Slavery.

Harsh and give no ground slavery established itself deep inside the emerging culture; a culture that would never compromise, never accept defeat and never be affected by reason. When northern colonists issued entreaties to join for an initiative to split with England, the South Carolinians were disinterested. Their biggest customer was

INDICTING AMERICA

England and they were not inclined to tamper with the goose that laid the golden egg.

That is until British Abolitionists instigated legal actions that threatened slavery; then, and only then, would they agree to meet and discuss a split with England. (See the case of James Somerset, 1771-72, in later chapter.)

Still, they were reluctant and proceeded with the hope that the Crown would give in and provide assurances for protection of slavery. The Crown had given in before to the recalcitrant colonists over tariffs and quitrents, but this time King George said no. This set the colonists on a road to war; one that the South Carolinians did not want; a road that meant joining with the other colonies which they also did not want; and forming a relationship that they did not embrace in any way.

They had a choice: risk a threat to slavery or join, however tentatively, the other colonies in a fight with England. If they were to join with the other colonists, however, they would do so at arm's length. The dregs of Barbados embraced no one and they had no intention of giving up their independence by joining with other colonists.

Columbus and Queen Isabella started the enterprise; the Barbadians in South Carolina refined it. Slavery—human exploitation—in service of personal wealth was rationalized and justified on the basis of racial superiority and a special blessing from God; sanctioned by a Slave Code inspired by the Doctrine of Discovery and insulated from the restraints of monotheism; designed for reaching new depths of depravity in South Carolina soil later grafted and planted throughout the Mississippi Delta; and created for the darkest chapter yet in the long history of slavery.

The Barbados-South Carolina story is a pillar of American History establishing the deep racial character of America based on white supremacy, bully politics and recalcitrance against any and all initiatives for forming a government based on human spirit, both black and white. South Carolina spread its Barbadian ways, like a virus, across the southern states where that rich Mississippi Delta soil could be transformed into wealth and power on the backs of black people. Exploiting humans in this way required mental gymnastics rationalizing sheer brutality, including blessings by God. This, the mental gyrations contrived to make honorable the clearly despicable, became the central theme of American political discourse from the founding of the United States in 1789 up to the modern day.

"In the antebellum United States," Gerbner tells us, "Protestantism was a core feature of proslavery ideology and Southern planters claimed that their plantations were modeled on the slave-owning households of the Old Testament."[25]

The Barbadian influence continues haunting America. The aristocracy of the 21st century remains hostile to concepts of a government serving Common Good as envisioned by Montesquieu, the 18th century philosophical theorist whose ideas of three equal branches of government became an inspiration for the U.S. Constitution. Conflict between government serving Common Good versus a government establishing ground rules for maximization of personal gain is still clearly evident in contemporary affairs.

Government actions for Common Good, in the modern day, infuriate aristocrats who have formed a political insurgency within the Republican Party under the guise of Libertarian orthodoxy, arguing for dismantling of government and its Common Good initiatives. Those initiatives were politically unpopular, however, and fighting for elimination meant operating by stealth so the electorate did not use the power of the vote to thwart their efforts. Leadership of this political force came under control of businessman Charles Koch, an uncompromising persona molded from the cast of Barbados.

INDICTING AMERICA

"Every man in the room looked to Charles Koch," reports Nancy MacLean in *Democracy in Chains: The Deep History of the Radical Right's Stealth Plan for America*, "when talk turned to funding an infrastructure of "professional libertarians," for who else could? The Wichita CEO was willing to commit the resources needed, he said, but with one condition: "that libertarians must remain uncompromisingly radical." They had to forswear "the temptation" to "compromise" with those currently in positions of power. Any such conciliation, Koch warned, would "destroy the movement." [26]

No compromise America has rendered American government impotent. It is a product of wealthy and powerful people operating by stealth with a goal of dismantling the American government. Today they are referred to as Movement Conservatives and Christian Nationalists. They are anything but conservative; they are radicals, angry, bitter, resentful radicals, cut from the cloth of Barbadians.

Virginia and Bacon's Rebellion

As events played out in South Carolina, Virginia remained anxious and hypervigilant about the threat posed by enslaved people, both white and black, and both held in indentured servitude. They also feared indigenous peoples who became increasingly hostile against the invaders who took things that didn't belong to them, such as hunting grounds and women.

Nathaniel Bacon wanted natives forcibly removed from lands Europeans wanted. He implored the English to become more aggressive and attack Indians who attacked him. In 1676, Bacon led a rebellion because he was angered by England's reticence in killing Indians. Bacon organized the lower classes, white and black, to rebel against

British authorities. Bacon died and his rebellion fizzled, but, more importantly, it made salient the need to drive wedges between those on the lowest rung of society. To do so, the House of Burgesses in Virginia passed legislation stipulating different rules for slave masters when handling white and black slaves. Wedges were essential for dividing the poorest of the poor, because if they knew how many of them existed, they might turn their rage against the masters.

D. Jordan in his history, *White Cargo: The Forgotten History of Britain's White Slaves in America*, argues "to this day, Nathaniel Bacon remains a paradox. He was an aristocrat from one of England's most illustrious families yet he almost sent Britain packing from America a hundred years before George Washington."[27]

Bacon joined in Indian wars, according to Jordan, "after a servant on his plantation was killed. Within weeks, he emerged as leader of the most violent settlers who favoured total extermination of the indigenous population. This set them at loggerheads with the Governor, who counselled conciliation, distinguishing between 'bad' tribes who should be destroyed and 'good' tribes who behaved."

Bacon exposed the vulnerability of the European invaders highlighting the power of joining whites and blacks against the power structure; indeed, had indentured white slaves joined with black slaves and with the Natives they would have formed a coalition of overwhelming power. Bacon's Rebellion made salient the need for driving wedges between the underclass, pitting whites against blacks against Indians. This is a key for understanding racial and ethnic animus in the contemporary political environment.

The actions of the House of Burgess provided a social structure in which blacks were placed at the lowest level, establishing a standard for human misery that the rest of society permitted and accepted. Keeping black people down was a key for offspring of indentured servitude, because no matter how bad conditions were for them, it was, at least, not as bad as conditions for blacks.

The status of black slaves as indentured servants with the possibility of freedom at the end of slavery was already tenuous by the time of Bacon's Rebellion. In 1640, John Punch, a black indentured slave, attempted to run away with two white slaves. They were caught. The two whites were simply returned to their master, but Punch was treated as property and punished by the state.

Jordan says, "They played the race card. The status of the European servile class was upgraded and a sense of racial superiority instilled. Meanwhile, the process of degrading non-whites was accelerated. Law after law deprived Africans and Native Americans of rights, while bolstering the legal position of European servants. In the space of twenty years, non-whites lost their judicial rights, property rights, electoral rights and family rights. They even lost the right to be freed if their master wanted to free them. In parallel, whites gained rights and privileges. Masters were forbidden from whipping their white servants 'naked without an order from a justice'.

Colin Calloway in *The Indian World of George Washington* adds: "As Virginia Indians struggled to adjust to the new world that English invasion and colonialism had created, the English increasingly consigned them to a separate world reserved for inferior races. 28 In 1691 the Virginia Assembly passed a law forbidding white people to marry "Negroes, Mulattoes and Indians" on pain of expulsion from the colony."[28]

The concept of White Supremacy, given birth in Barbados and imported into South Carolina, became codified into Virginia law. Calloway adds: "In 1705 Virginia declared Indian slaves, along with black and mulatto slaves, to be "real estate" and forbade them, as it did blacks, to hold office, testify in court, sue white people, or strike a white person, even in self-defense."

At the end of the Civil War, 1865, Andrew Johnson, Lincoln's Vice President who replaced Lincoln, expressed the thoughts of poor whites from whence he came, as he opposed Reconstruction. A. Gordon-Reed in her acclaimed work *Andrew Johnson (The American Presidents)* reports: "All of his talk about states' rights, limited government, and low taxes were sideshows compared to his real concern, which was to ensure that "the people of the South, poor, quiet, unoffending, harmless," would not be "trodden under foot to protect niggers."[29]

America is charged with the morally bankrupt crime of human enslavement, torture, illegal imprisonment, rape, murder and theft—the theft of uncompensated labor.

New World and White Slaves

OVER THOUSANDS OF YEARS, HUMAN existence transformed as a living organism from a member of the Ape Family, most closely associated with chimpanzees, into a separate branch on the Ape Family tree, *homo sapien*. This organism, equipped with a brain capable of planning and strategizing for survival, discovered a means for controlling food sources ushering in the Neolithic Age, the age of agriculture.

After adapting to the world of agriculturalists, some pursued ambitions as a leader, an emperor. Others eschewed a life of fame and fortune, opting instead for a simple life, finding contentment in planting and harvesting food, raising a family and being a good citizen. Farming and family were deeply intertwined, giving meaning and purpose to their life.

When land ownership—property—became a thing, the farming population rarely held ownership of their land. By custom these lands were considered common lands for use by the farming population with landowners extracting rent for use of the land they owned. This was a profitable arrangement for the property owner, catapulting some to the rarified status of aristocrat. The farmers, on the other hand, were considered Commoners.

New uses for the land emerged as the human population expanded, creating demand for new products and services. Wool used in making clothing became profitable, more profitable than the rents derived from commoners. In Scotland, the Highland Clearances introduced industrial strength farming, in part, so more food could be produced for industrialized England. Removing the common farmers so the land could be used for grazing sheep and other purposes would not be easy, however.

Displacement and relocation of Commoners from England, Scotland, Wales and Ireland, albeit as punishment or forced relocation, represented a traumatic life altering event. Sudden disintegration of the norms, mores, worldview of the displaced resulted in a bitter, angry, yet powerless, people who would carry those feeling into the New World. The people who found meaning and purpose farming lands that their ancestors farmed were now kicked out. Stripping them of their dignity and self-worth was crushing. In the modern day, Rush Limbaugh may be considered the voice of that anger and bitterness stewing for hundreds of years and never resolved. It helps to explain the inexplicable of modern-day politics.

The cruelty of the massive relocation of people from the British Isles to the New World, however, is not uplifting. And so, the story must be spun. It is described as freedom seeking people with hopes for finding a land where they could reap the rewards of their toil, worship as they pleased and raise a family with decency and integrity, unencumbered by hierarchical powers dominating Europe.

As the story is told, they adventured across the oceans, risking everything—family, possessions, home—in search of a promised land. This is an inspiring, yet crafted, tale for patriotism, love of country and a model for people around the globe to dream about. This is a story of a "bottom up" colonialism, centered on British "immigrants," in search of virgin lands offering new beginnings. Native peoples are invisible in this tale.

As the Barbadians settled into South Carolina, however, tensions escalated between colonial powers and native populations. Spanish settlements expanded from the Caribbean islands into South, Central and North America focused on gold and silver mining, while converting natives to Catholicism. The French established themselves in Canada expanding their fur trading interests south along the western side of the Appalachians and along the rivers feeding the Mississippi. The British pushed the Dutch aside carving out their niche along the eastern seaboard. It was the British, however, who were the most aggressive in populating their new land holdings using the mechanism of Indentured Servitude.

Yes, Columbus and the Spanish led the invasion, but traditional American history skips ahead to the Jamestown settlement, 1607, and the arrival of the Mayflower, 1620, with a boatload of Pilgrims. Many consider the British arrival as the real beginning of America, because the British were the most aggressive in populating their colonial adventure, quickly dominating the other European "adventurers," invaders, and the Native peoples due to their sheer numbers. By 1700 there were 200,000 settlers and by 1770 over two million.

A key for populating the colonies with indentured slaves and other adventurers was Enclosure. It began in the 12th century, but expanded considerably in the 17th and 18th. Parliament passed the Enclosure Acts, whereby common lands were privatized by the landed gentry, who discovered more profitable uses for their land. Yeoman farmers who had farmed the common lands for centuries were cast aside. The very foundation for their existence was shattered and they were cast adrift. These people became the source of indentured slaves, eventually shipped off to the colonies by way of the Transportation Acts.

But soon the white indentured slave was not enough to meet needs of the plantation and so plantation owners, compelled to seek other able-bodied people, turned to the Atlantic Slave Trade. Consequently, slaves for the New World were supplied by three sources: indigenous peoples, white indentured servants and the Atlantic Slave Trade.

Henry Wiencek writes in *An imperfect God: George Washington, his slaves and the creation of America*, that "White indentured servants greatly outnumbered black slaves in seventeenth-century Virginia. (Washington's great-grandfather established himself in Virginia not by buying black slaves but by importing white servants.) In 1671 Governor Berkeley reported to the Board of Trade that Virginia's population was 40,000, of which 6,000 were indentured servants or "Christian servants for a short time" who had immigrated to Virginia in "the hope of bettering their condition in a growing country." (Others had been kidnapped and sent against their will, and still others were convicts.) "[30]

Virginians spoke out against the jailbirds sent from England, according to Wiencek. Perceiving England to be overpopulated by poor people, the British government encouraged the transportation of the indigent, unemployed, and criminals. Some landowners paid for relocation of the displaced to the New World.

It started in the 16th Century, "…in 1597 under Queen Elizabeth I, it did pass the first official act that sanctioned the transportation of rogues and vagabonds to the English colonies," according to Anthony Vaver in *Bound with an Iron Chain: The Untold Story of How the British Transported 50,000 Convicts to Colonial America*. He continues, "This statute did not institute a system of forced labor in the colonies—merely deportation—so even though it made the act of reprieving felons in order to send them to work in the fields of Virginia possible, the use of convict labor for colonization ultimately failed to take hold, since there was no official place to send them."[31]

INDICTING AMERICA

At the turn of the 17th Century Virginia was struggling. "Governor Thomas Dale asked King James I to send across the Atlantic all of the convicts who were both being held in prisons and sentenced to die in order to furnish his colony with able men," according to Vaver. In 1615, the Privy Council authorized forced labor in the colonies. "As punishment for idleness or misdemeanors, the Council created a system for transporting convicts by granting reprieves on condition that the felons remove themselves to one of the colonies," writes Vaver.

Indentured Servitude has been spun as a means for America's pioneers to join colonial adventures. This is a spin. Yes, there were some who agreed to work as indentured servants in exchange for transportation to the New World, but a sizeable contingent was physically forced on board ships for dispatch to the New World as enslaved people under contract that would free them when the contracted duty was fulfilled, meaning four to seven years of enslavement, if they behaved and did as their master instructed. If not, the length of servitude could be extended.

As Jordan and Walsh indicate in *White Cargo: The Forgotten History of Britain's White Slaves in America*, by the 16th Century "life in the mid-sixteenth century was pitted and disfigured by poverty. Recurring harvest disasters, the enclosures and economic depressions had left hordes of peasants and labourers dispossessed and on the margins of survival."[32]

The significance of Enclosure, and subsequent indentured slaves, must not be minimized. The people of England who populated the American colonies have been described as people seeking religious freedom and opportunities for realizing the fruits of their labors, the noble frontier people. The journey from England to America, however, was very different.

English yeoman farmers embraced a subsistence living growing crops and grazing livestock on lands shared by everyone in their community. These lands were Common Lands. English aristocrats owned the lands and were paid rent by the common farmers, but they wanted those lands for sheep herding in service of wool and textile trades. The Enclosure Acts seized the lands for the aristocrats, shoving aside the people who used the Common Lands as their ancestors had used them for centuries.

Displaced, demoralized, angry and bitter they were refugees in their own country. They drifted into urban centers offering them criminal opportunities for survival. Crime and unpaid debts condemned them to indentured servitude on another continent, leaving them with a bitter and poisonous anger that continues infecting the United States of America. This must be understood for reconciling the uplifting narrative of a nation born in freedom with the bilious anger expressed by Rush Limbaugh, Father Coughlin, and Donald Trump. It is rooted in Enclosure.

Historian Peter Linebaugh, author of *Stop, Thief!: The Commons, Enclosures, and Resistance*, says Parliament passed the Acts when it was composed of landlords. "They called it "improvement," and today they call it "development" or "progress." Just as the emperor has no clothes, these words are naked of meaning. The "greater villains" aim to take land. In the Ohio valley, in Bengal, in the English midlands, in west Africa, in Chiapas, in Borneo, Indonesia. Why? They want what's underneath: gold, coal, oil, iron, what have you. They also create the proletariat, i.e., you! This taking, this expropriating the common, is a process of war, foreign and domestic."[33]

Enclosures upended the social, political and economic world of common people, the people who survived by way of subsistence farming. Their world, passed down from generation to generation, of communal farming, disintegrated leaving them with few options. Displaced farmers filled with wrath embarked on a journey inevitably resulting in imprisonment. Landed gentry won the contest for control of lands, but also came to live with fear, as the displaced became enraged.

"The terrible economic situation in England during the 18th century," according to Vaver, "generally offered the unemployed two choices: They could either sell themselves into indentured servitude in America or steal for their subsistence and risk being transported to America anyway. Many chose to gamble with their futures by taking up a life of crime in a desperate attempt to maintain their freedom in England as long as possible—and lost."

England did not have a robust prison system for incarcerating the many displaced common land farmers who appeared in urban centers, perpetrated crimes and required punishment. Parliament then passed the Transportation Acts, which sounds like some sort of logistics network. Instead, it was a legal mechanism for offloading convicts to colonial lands, thereby solving the problem of what to do with criminals and, secondly, how to populate colonial lands with British subjects. Characterization of the pioneers must be replaced with a defeated common lands farmer, embittered by collapse of the social structure resulting from greedy instincts of the landed gentry, ultimately forced onto a ship and sent off to foreign lands.

Before the Transportation Acts, England executed her criminals, but when executions became unmanageable, London turned to banishment, thereby sending criminals to the so-called New World. This solved two problems by unloading the prisoners to foreign shores and by populating the lands in which England staked its claim.

The wealthy and powerful in position to write the rules of the game crafted laws for their self-interest, at the expense of the Common Land farmers. Critics of such a hierarchical system argued for a more equal playing field, lamenting the loss of the hunter gatherer egalitarianism of the past. These critics became voices for the Common Lands people and became known as the Commonists, a label later refined into Communists.

Enclosures coincided with a population expansion in England. According to Alan Taylor, the population grew from three million in 1500 to four million in 1600 and five million by 1650. The economy failed to keep up with this growth, severely impacting people at the lower strata. Most people lived in farming communities, working the Common Lands. When displaced by Enclosure, they entered a life of homelessness, uncertain of where to find food, an early version of food insecurity. [34]

They sought relief in urban centers along the coasts. As Enclosures displaced people, London's population exploded from an estimated 120,000 in 1550 to 200,000 in 1600 and 375,000 in 1650. As a result, London was overwhelmed. While the upper class enjoyed new riches, displaced workers found themselves in a city infested with poverty, high crimes, plagues and filth. [35]

This population of displaced people, however, "was available to serve as settlers in the North American British colonies," says Roxanne Dunbar-Ortiz, "many of them as indentured servants, with the promise of land." The land dangled before them, however, was usually occupied by Natives. That was a minor inconvenience, "they were free to squat on Indigenous land and become farmers again. In this way, surplus labor created not only low labor costs and great profits for the woolens manufacturers but also a supply of settlers for the colonies, ..."[36]

The system given birth by the Triangle Trade was to be maintained and operated, regardless of who it may hurt. "By the time Spain, Portugal, and Britain arrived to colonize the Americas," Dunbar Ortiz argues, "their methods of eradicating peoples or forcing them into dependency and servitude were ingrained, streamlined, and effective."[37]

INDICTING AMERICA

According to Bailyn, England's emigrants dwarfed the other colonists, using whatever means necessary in feeding the system. "The result," says Baylin, "was a further scattering of half-organized, socially inchoate clusters of strangers drawn disproportionately from certain segments of English society, seeking, in the crude, stump-filled tobacco farms of this subtropical lowland, to re-create a world they had known."[38]

The most vulnerable were targets for incarceration and shipment to the New World. "The company's coercive power was directed mainly at the most vulnerable element in Jacobean society," adds Bailyn, "the vagrant children. How many hundreds of children and petty criminals the company managed to collect from the streets and public institutions of London is not precisely known, but some of the numbers were recorded. Between August 1618 and August 1620 the company obtained from Bridewell Hospital, a detention center and jail for vagrant children, "idle wastrels, petty thieves, and dissolute women," at least 337 of its charges to be sent to Virginia as "apprentices." This equates to child abuse and kidnapping.

Poor houses were also targeted. Churchwardens were directed by aldermen to visit poor houses and inquire if they were overburdened with children and, if so, agree to ship those over 12 to Virginia. In return, the children would receive a good education.

The victims of Enclosures attempted to fight back and reclaim the life of Common Lands. They became known as the Commonists, the Communists. Their ideas coincided with the views of Native Americans who were victims, too. The Haudenosaunee, or Iroquois confederation, were influenced by Marx and Engels in understanding concepts of private property, patriarchy, and the state, according to Linebaugh.

"The destruction of the Iroquois commons," says Linebaugh," was at the specific order of George Washington, known in the language of

NEW WORLD AND WHITE SLAVES

the Haudenosaunee, not as the "father of his country," but as "Town Destroyer." In 1779 George Washington ordered Major General John Sullivan to terrorize the Iroquois. Accordingly, Sullivan deliberately destroyed the crops, uprooted the orchards, burnt the houses, and massacred every man, woman, and child of the six nations of the Iroquois confederacy until September 15, when he was exhausted by the effort not far from Letchworth Gorge."[39]

Some indentured slaves came by way of their own choice. In An Imperfect God, Henry Wiencek writes

"if you hated the squalor and stink of London or the tedium of your father's pig farm in Yorkshire, America beckoned. If you were too poor to buy passage to the New World you could get there by signing a contract selling your labor to a planter for seven years. The labor and the conditions might be harsh, but at the end of your term you would get your freedom back and some cash, and you would be in the New World with the sky as your limit. [40]

Vaver was shocked to learn about the vast scale of indentured slaves, "… more than 50,000 convicted felons were forcibly shipped across the ocean and that they played a significant role in performing needed work in colonial America, I was shocked. How could I not have known more about this form of punishment and the people who were subjected to it? Apparently, I was not the only one who had such a gap in my knowledge of American history. When I mentioned my budding interest in convict transportation to family and friends, their immediate response was almost always, "Right, Australia," not realizing that our own American shores had served as the first major destination for British convicts."[41]

The **Enclosure Acts** displaced common land farmers setting them on a path to urban centers seeking work for sustenance. Eventually they engaged in crime and indebtedness. To deal with this problem,

INDICTING AMERICA

England passed the **Transportation Act** so they could dispose of these criminals and dead beats. This became the source for populating the English colonies not the characteristic yeoman farmer pioneer.

"Between 1718 and 1775," says Vaver, "more than two-thirds of all convicted felons at the Old Bailey in London were sentenced to transportation, while only one-sixth received the death penalty during the same time span."[42]

Indentured servants caused problems for the colonial leaders, because most came from the bottom rungs of society. Between 1700 and 1775, a total of 585,800 immigrants arrived in the 13 colonies from all over the world. About 52,200 of these immigrants were convicts and prisoners (9%). Slaves by far constituted the largest group (278,400; 47%), followed by people arriving with their freedom (151,600; 26%) and indentured servants (96,600; 18%). Note that almost three-quarters of all the people arriving in the American colonies during this time period did so without their freedom, according to Vaver.[43]

> There were a few indentured servants, however, who learned the game and benefitted from it. Indentured servants were promised 50 acres and a small amount of money when they completed their service. The plantation owner who purchased the indenture would be entrusted with land to be granted to the servant upon completion of the agreement. If the indentured servant died, however, before completing service, the plantation owner would take the land promised the servant. In many cases the freed white slave simply sold off the 50 acres for ready cash.
>
> Maintaining control over the slaves was an obsession for the ruling classes. Their fears became manifest with Bacon's Rebellion in 1675, a rebellion that gave sustenance to the

notion of white supremacy. Indeed, animosity between white and black slaves is rooted in Virginia's response to Bacon's Rebellion, 1675.

This episode highlighted the need to drive wedges between the lesser people. Virginia's House of Burgesses passed laws stipulating different rules for handling white, black and Indian slaves. The strategy worked and continues to separate the lesser people. Indeed, it is a key for understanding the contemporary political events.

The effect of the indentured servants cannot be overstated, because it has become a central core of the American culture. The indentured slaves were desperate people, many from the bottom rungs of society. They were poor and miserable, but they could feel a bit better about themselves, if there was someone worse off than they. The black slave served such a purpose. After the Revolutionary war and up to the modern day, there are many white Americans who still believe a black person is inferior to them. Even if the white person is still in a desperate situation, it seems easier to retain the illusion of being better than the blacks, because the alternative of confronting the power elite for a better standard of living is just too daunting.

The intensity of white's with deeply rooted racial hatred may be found in the hearts of the offspring of indentured servants who needed someone to look down upon, rather than fighting with the powerful for a better existence. This phenomenon continues to baffle social and political analysts who feel indentured servants share common ground with African slaves, but act against their own self-interest merely to keep black people at a lower status.

INDICTING AMERICA

"Even as they struggled with the exploitation of sweatshops and slums," says Heather McGhee in *The Sum of Us: What Racism Costs Everyone and How We Can Prosper Together*, "becoming "white" afforded them a civic and social esteem that could constantly be compared against the black second-class citizens one rung below them." She adds, "In a hierarchical system like the American economy, people often show more concern about their relative position in the hierarchy than their absolute status."[44]

A Georgia officer fighting in the Atlanta campaign during 1864 wrote his wife that "in two months more we will perhaps be an independent nation or a nation of slaves." If we lose, "not only will the negroes be free but…we will all be on a common level." Historian James McPherson quoting from confederate soldier's letter in a speech given by McPherson on April 12, 2011 in Charleston, S.C.

He quotes another Texas Private, "we are fighting for what matters real and tangible…our property and our homes…they for matters abstract and intangible…for the flimsy and abstract idea that a negro is equal to an Anglo American."[45]

Much attention has been directed to the depravity of slavery as it related to African slaves. Much less attention, if any, has been focused on the white indentured slaves. This is another pillar of American history because it is the off spring of indentured slaves who joined the fight in the Civil War to keep black people enslaved; who refused to accept the result of the Civil War, fighting for the so-called "Lost Cause;" and who remained receptive to racist political rhetoric aimed at exploiting their predisposition in keeping black people at a status level below them. Dog whistle politics and racial hatred are rooted in the phenomenon of white indentured servitude.

America is charged with Crimes Against Humanity, conspiracy to kidnap, enslavement, illegal confinement, torture, rape and murder.

French-Indian War (1754-1763) and Proclamation Line

Ohio River Valley

DREAM OF RICHES DANCED IN the imagination of George Washington's half-brother Lawrence. The Ohio River Valley, encompassing lands in Virginia, Pennsylvania, North Carolina and Maryland, represented Indian occupied lands that Britain could claim as its own. This is how the system worked: Britain selected specific lands, declared them part of the colony, auctioned them off to aspiring aristocrats, who would then divide their lands into parcels for resale. This is the essence of colonization.

Colonization is, indeed, a euphemism for brute force invasion and occupation of lands already occupied. Greed drove colonial leaders in taking more and more lands inhabited by those Siberian migrants, killing them when they resisted, while fending off other invaders. This is an open and shut case. North American and West Indies lands were money makers. In some regions of North America, the fruitful lands enjoyed over 40 feet deep of top soil. The invaders wanted riches

INDICTING AMERICA

and the lands were the means to the end, along with enslaved labor. Obstacles had to be removed at any cost.

People in contemporary times resist what is obvious; it shatters their worldview. Upper middle class and the very wealthiest, by and large, believe they earned their privileges. They live in nice homes and in nice neighborhoods, with sufficient resources for affording nice cars, designer clothes and good schools, even tutors, if needed. The tale that they enjoy this comfortable lifestyle because pilgrims bravely crossed the ocean in search of freedom and justice makes for an inspiring narrative in support of that worldview. This House of Cards, however, comes tumbling down, when a real history is presented, prompting state governments across America, in the modern day, to stipulate, under penalty of law, prohibitions against teaching real history. Indeed, well healed organizations recruit protesters in a drive to intimidate school boards and universities into adopting curricula supporting the Pilgrim tale. Even selected books are banned from libraries and librarians are muzzled by law.

Nothing speaks to the fabrication of a tale in defining a nation's history better than that nation passing laws prohibiting teachers from presenting contradictory information based on attributed facts. The governing leaders frame their laws in a pathetic way so as to somehow disguise their purpose, such as prohibiting lessons that make a student feel uncomfortable. Clearly they are ashamed of their nation's past and they do not want their children exposed.

The real history reveals, however, that the British were insatiable. By the 18th century their North American population had grown to more than a million. Their colonies—occupied lands—were arrayed along the east coast. As they looked west, they saw more inviting lands, but those lands were occupied by some 500 Indian nations. Their objective: take those lands, push the natives out or kill them.

FRENCH-INDIAN WAR (1754-1763) AND PROCLAMATION LINE

Transform the lands into profitable enterprises, thereby expanding wealth and power for the powerful. Maintain control of the million people population by giving them a small piece of the prize, while keeping the embers burning for fear and hate of Indians and African slaves.

Slaughtering Natives, now called ethnic cleansing, became rehearsal for the fight against Britain.

"The Anglo-American settlers' violent break from Britain in the late eighteenth century," according to Roxanne Dunbar-Ortiz *Loaded: A Disarming History of the Second Amendment* "paralleled their search-and-destroy annihilation of Delaware, Cherokee, Muskogee, Seneca, Mohawk, Shawnee, and Miami, during which they slaughtered families without distinction of age or gender, and expanded the boundaries of the thirteen colonies into unceded Native territories." Dunbar adds "both the seasoned Indian killers of the Revolutionary Army and white settler-rangers/militias using extreme violence against Indigenous noncombatants with the goal of total domination."[46]

This agenda was not unique for North America. The same template applied to Asia and the Middle East. The British Empire was a juggernaut of violence, expropriation and enslavement. After defeating its major competitors, Britain then "peacefully" invaded, occupied and exploited new lands, a period known as Pax Britannica, beginning around 1815 and lasting up till World War One. Before then Britain was engaged in conflicts with France and Spain; King William's War, 1689-1697, Queen Anne's War, 1702-1713, and King George's War, 1744-1748.

Multiple factors converged resulting in the French Indian War. The English and French engaged in adversarial relations for many years. Britain, and France were the powerhouses competing for dominance, followed by Spain. By the mid-18th century, Britain claimed eastern

INDICTING AMERICA

coastal lands, while France claimed New France from Canada to the Gulf of Mexico, even though their presence was concentrated in the north. Both wanted control of the Ohio River Valley. Conflict in the Valley was preceded by conflict in Canada.

Alan Taylor tells us "The peace of 1748 proved short-lived, as both the French and the British overreacted to local aggressions as if they were part of some grand power play by the other empire. In Nova Scotia, the British established a fortified town and navy base at Halifax in 1749 to counter nearby Louisbourg. Alarmed, the French promptly built two new forts at the head of the Bay of Fundy to hem in Nova Scotia to the west, which the British resented as an intrusion on their colony."[47]

In North America, the colonists salivated over the west, the other side of the Appalachian Mountains. The Ohio River Valley beckoned. The river traversed lands we know today as Illinois, Indiana, Ohio and Pennsylvania. It also connects with the Mississippi River. In taking lands, England conducted surveys, mapping out chunks of land that would then be declared part of the colony and auctioned to speculators. Speculators divided up the parcels and sold them to individuals.

This was a profitable enterprise. Magically, England somehow made the land's inhabitants invisible. It was as if the lands were unoccupied and England merely declared the lands as part of the colony. This required rendering the natives invisible as if they just didn't exist. And, if they resisted this expropriation of their visibility, the British attacked, along with local militias organized for fighting Indians and controlling enslaved people.

Before the American Revolution, the attacks on native peoples were plentiful. Killing native peoples began with the arrival of Columbus. All of the invading countries participated in the killing. This is what invaders do. To make the native peoples invisible, the invaders perpetrated massacres. And when the native peoples fought back, the invaders escalated their assault to genocide.

Not so invisible were the French who had interests in the Ohio River Valley. The French had a meager population in their North American colonies, estimated at under 100,000. Their interests involved fur trading and they had relatively good relations with the native peoples.

Soon, conflict emerged between these competing interests. Lawrence Washington, George's older half-brother, was keenly interested in the Ohio River Valley, even forming the Ohio Company in anticipation of Ohio lands being auctioned off to speculators. George Washington, in conjunction with his militia troops, conducted surveys of lands in the valley so his brother would know the quality of prospective parcels in preparation for anticipated land auctions. George was astonished at the rich black earth he found in the valley. This was more than fine agricultural land; it also contained an abundance of minerals including coal.

French Indian War

In England, the Industrial Revolution was in its infancy, a byproduct of discovering coal off its coast. Coal burned more efficiently and at higher heat than wood burning fires. This was followed by discovery of steam and its ability for driving mechanical systems. Machines driven by steam, with efficiently burning coal, opened a path for mass production. This new capacity drove England into becoming the textile supplier for the globe. But for all of it to work, England needed raw materials and markets.

China, India and the Middle East drew attention as sources of raw materials and as markets for finished products. So, when colonial leaders wanted attention to their particular needs, Britain had other interests, except that is in the West Indies, where sugar was abundant and profitable. Other colonies, however, were of a lower priority.

George Washington was ambitious. He wanted land and he wanted credentials. Leading a militia into the Ohio River Valley served both objectives. Accomplishment as a military leader provided him with credentials while he scouted new lands for his personal portfolio.

As a militia leader, Washington, lobbied the British Governor Dinwiddie to take action against the French who were encroaching upon British interests in the Ohio River Valley, around Pittsburgh. Historian Robert Middlekauff in his work, *The Glorious Cause: The American Revolution, 1763-1789*, says "…the wilderness between French troops and American colonials led by young George Washington, whose description of the affair revealed that his interest in war lay in the opportunities it offered for honorable and gallant action."[48]

It appears George also had additional interests, however. Along with earning credentials as a soldier, he wanted Britain to act against the French encroachment to protect the interests of he and his brother. Dinwiddie agreed to send George and his militia into the Ohio regions with a letter for the French warning against encroachment upon British interests. He also admonished Washington to not engage in battle.

But George found a way to incite a fight, allegedly firing the first shot, eventually leading to a retreat. The retreat was an embarrassment for Britain requiring a retaliation. Britain sent General Braddock to fight the French and their Indian allies. Of course, Washington proudly joined Braddock in the battle, as he was seeking a commission in the British Army.

About a decade later, when the British became even more reticent in fighting Indians, Washington betrayed his duty to Britain, turning rebel against the Crown. Taking Indian lands and the wealth derived

FRENCH-INDIAN WAR (1754-1763) AND PROCLAMATION LINE

therefrom ranked at the top of Washington's priorities; not duty, honor and country. This priority also ranked at the top of the list for the many other Founding Fathers, who were also land speculators seeking wealth by stealing Indian lands, extracting natural resources, and using enslaved peoples. Wealth and greed were the driving force, not valiant notions of freedom and justice.

After his failed attempt at delivering a message without starting a fight, Washington was sent back to the area of confrontation to build a fort, thereby announcing British determination. The French were not itching for a fight. After some skirmishing the British abandoned the fort.

This did not play well in England. Jack Rakove in *Revolutionaries: A New History of the Invention of America* says "But the reaction that mattered most took place in distant London. Within weeks of learning of the debacle, the British government adopted an ambitious plan to send additional regiments to North America, appoint Braddock to command royal forces there, and launch multiple attacks on French positions, not only in the Ohio Valley but also from northern New York to Nova Scotia."[49]

The French Indian War should be named the Real Estate War, in honor of America's first significant business, or better yet, it could be named George Washington's War, because he played a central role. Instead, the war had several names: the French and Indian War; and the Seven Years War.

The Real Estate enterprise needed land for sale and that equated to killing Indians and stealing their lands, a central theme in the story of the United States. A key factor driving colonial leaders for Revolution was England's resistance to Indian Wars.

Nothing encapsulates the North American colonial enterprise better than the French Indian War. It was all about Native American

INDICTING AMERICA

lands; the rich fertile soil of the Ohio River Valley coveted by English gentry determined to achieve aristocratic status. This was the path to wealth and power.

About 250 years after Columbus arrived in Hispaniola, the Spanish, French and British remained unstable in their colonial settlements. By the 18th century the Spanish focused on South and Central America, including Mexico and western North America, searching for gold and silver using enslaved Indians for mining operations. The French embraced fur trading operations from Canada to Louisiana. The British colonies operated independently of each other engaging in agricultural enterprises and plantation businesses growing tobacco, rice and indigo.

The Europeans continued elbowing each other from lands they wished to claim, while maneuvering around the indigenous peoples who they did not view as having any legitimate claim on the territory. The French established friendly relations with the Native peoples, but the British were viewed skeptically by the natives who suspected them of plotting to take their lands.

Native culture did not accept the notion of land ownership. English white slaves came from Common Lands similar to the Native American culture, although distinctively, the Common Lands were rented in England. Still, the lands were used for the community, not for an individual. Those with wealth and power, however, derived their status by way of land ownership. Aspiring aristocrats needed land.

England aggressively populated her colonial settlements in far greater numbers than the French or Spanish. They needed land for sustenance. Indentured slaves, sent for populating the colonies, were promised 50 acres upon completion of their servitude, also known as the Headright System. Where was that land to come from?

Colonial invaders did not consider the lands of North America as under the domain of the native peoples; the uncivilized savages who

FRENCH-INDIAN WAR (1754-1763) AND PROCLAMATION LINE

had occupied the space for over 20,000 years. Colonists patronized natives making dubious deals for taking control over property, often making treaties and purchasing land in the process, even if the natives making the deal didn't have control over the territory. When the natives recognized their fate, it was too late and the colonists held control.

"Washington, more than most," writes Colin Calloway in *The Indian World of George Washington*, "had a hand on the scales and was instrumental in the dispossession, defeat, exploitation, and marginalization of Indian peoples. He rarely used the term "Indian country"— he called it "wilderness," "the frontier," "the Ohio country," "the West"— but he lived his whole life with one eye on it and one foot in it."[50]

Lawrence Washington was the first chairman of the Ohio Company. The board also included Thomas Lee of Virginia who developed his wealth by way of land speculation, too. "As Henry Wiencek in *An Imperfect God* tells us: "In 1744 Lee journeyed from Stratford to Lancaster, Pennsylvania, to negotiate with the Iroquois for the purchase of an enormous inland empire—territory that would form the future states of Kentucky, Ohio, Indiana, Illinois, Wisconsin, Michigan, and part of Minnesota—all for about $400 in cash and gifts. With a group of other Virginians Lee founded the Ohio Company to settle and exploit this tract. Thereafter, Ohio Valley land speculation became the dream and the bane of Virginians, including George Washington." [51]

Combine the land with enslaved peoples and you have wealth, massive wealth. Calloway add, "From cradle to grave Washington inhabited a world built on the labor of African people and on the land of dispossessed Indian people. Indian people were not as ubiquitous in his daily life as the enslaved men, women, and children who planted, tended, and harvested his crops, cut his wood, prepared and served his food, washed his laundry, cleaned his house, and attended to his every need. Nevertheless, Indian people and Indian country loomed large in Washington's world."[52]

Land speculators were not alone in the thirst for native lands. Former indentured servants, essentially homeless people after completing their servitude, wanted native lands for squatting. Most sold their promised 50 acres when servitude ended, but then ventured off into native lands where they became squatters. Restive speculators reacted to the squatters encroaching on native lands, because they wanted to beat the squatters to it. England tried to restrain them because they could not afford Indian wars. There was wealth and power in those lands, however, and greed would not be quieted.

While English colonists salivated over the Ohio River Valley, the French also made initiatives for staking their claim. This set-in motion a series of actions and reactions ultimately leading to the French Indian War in which the French allied with native peoples in conflict with English claims for territory.

Virginia Governor William Gooch permitted the Ohio Company to expropriate an estimated 200,000 acres of land near the Ohio forks. When Lee sent people to survey the lands, the native peoples suspected something was up. They joined with the French to fend off the anticipated assault upon the land.

Proclamation Line

The British won the fight, but it created an enemy in the French that would come back to haunt them in the coming years as the French decided to fight a proxy war against the Brits by way of the American Revolutionaries. In the wake of the war, however, England decided it did not want additional wars. The **Proclamation Line** was established

FRENCH-INDIAN WAR (1754-1763) AND PROCLAMATION LINE

restricting colonists from expanding west into Indian lands. It didn't mean they could never take Native lands; it meant there would be a planned and orderly process implemented. This would surely delay the speculators and place their profits at risk. George Washington found himself recalibrating his loyalty to Britain and considered action for splitting from the Crown. Instead of fighting Indians as an English soldier, he would now initiate collaboration with natives as a revolutionary at war with England.

The Proclamation Line, October 7, 1763, issued after the end of the French-Indian War, represents a declaration prohibiting colonists from invading and stealing Indian lands. This, in conjunction with the James Somerset case, propelled colonial leaders to move toward secession from England. I make a distinction between the leaders and the led. The leaders have one agenda; the followers are incited by incendiary rhetoric crafted by the leaders.

"The Royal Proclamation of 1763," says Calloway, "was Britain's first attempt to administer the new American empire it had won. Its guiding principle was to restore and maintain order on the frontier. Indian relations must be directed from London by a government with an imperial vision of American affairs, not by individual colonies pursuing local agendas. It organized the newly acquired territories into four new colonies— Quebec, East and West Florida, and Grenada— and it established the Appalachian Mountains as the boundary between Indian and colonial lands, reserving for Native peoples a vast territory stretching from the Appalachians to the Mississippi."[53]

Engaging in battle with France created a financial crisis. Parliament decided colonists benefitting from the war needed to help in defraying costs. A stamp tax was considered a palatable means for taxing, because it primarily applied to the upper classes of the colonial settlement, those benefitting the most from land speculation.

France also buckled under the financial strain of the war. Wars are costly. Roots of the French Revolution may be found in the French Indian War, along with other costly battles. It also led to the Haitian Revolution and the warrior years of Napolean. No one ever really wins a war.

Calloway says "British taxpayers were staggering under the costs of a long global war, and British ministers thought it only reasonable that the American colonies should pay their share. In 1765 Parliament passed the Stamp Act, a measure that is often considered the first step in the imperial crisis that led to the American Revolution."[54]

The stage was set for a confrontation with colonists who felt they were independent; somehow immunized from taxation. A series of actions and reactions were set in motion ultimately leading to the American Revolution; a revolution that was not inexorable and planned, but one in which the colonists stumbled into a fight with England.

The governing relationship with England was ambiguous, at best. The crown merely issued charters for the invasions under its banner. Colonists felt themselves independent. There was not a cohesive connection between the individual colonies, as the colonial leaders wanted riches for themselves with few collaborators to share in the bounty.

"The colonies had been founded under the authorization of the Crown, and governmental authority in them had always been exercised in the king's name, though rather ambiguously in the three proprietary colonies, Maryland, Pennsylvania, Delaware, and tenuously in Rhode Island and Connecticut, the two corporate colonies," according to Middlekauff. "What had lasted long apparently seemed best left unchanged."[55]

War costs compelled Parliament to consider taxing the colonists, particularly the upper classes who benefitted from the war. To finance the debt incurred by the French and Indian War, the British imposed taxes upon the colonists. The Stamp Act was adopted that taxed stamps on legal documents. Since the upper classes were more likely to work with legal documents, this seemed appropriate because they were beneficiaries of the war. The colonists objected claiming that Britain could impose **external taxes**, such as tariffs on foreign trade, but they could not impose **internal taxes**, such as a tax on stamps applied to legal documents.

Rakove writes "While testifying before the House of Commons in favor of repealing the Stamp Act, Franklin hinted that Americans might not object to all taxes levied by Parliament. **"Internal" taxes**, such as the stamp duty, were improper, but **"external" taxes**— such as duties on trade— might be acceptable. That was the loophole Charles Townshend, chancellor of the exchequer, proposed to exploit with his duties on paint, paper, lead, and tea. In his Letters, Dickinson argued that it was the purpose of the tax, not its form that mattered. If the Townshend duties were designed to raise a revenue— and not, say, operate as a protectionist tariff—then they were clearly as much a tax as the detested Stamp Act, and equally impermissible."[56]

The British acquiesced and repealed the taxes, except for a tax on tea. Parliament also passed the Declaratory Act of 1766 stipulating that acts of Parliament took precedence over colonial legislatures. This set the stage for conflict. According to Rakove "When Parliament adopted the Declaratory Act back in 1766, affirming its power to govern the colonies "in all cases whatsoever," that ominous phrase stated only a broad principle, not a plan of action."[57]

Those benefitting from the war, however, dug in for a fight. These leaders needed public support and that meant creating a conflict the masses could understand. The leaders were angry with King George for not reigning in Parliament. So, they crafted a campaign around fighting a tyrannical king. But in actuality, they wanted a tyrannical king to keep Parliament inside its boundary and not allow it to declare itself governing powers over the colonies. That was too complicated. Agitating the masses against a tyrannical King was much more effective.

> The history recounted in a recent book on the Constitution's origins, by Eric Nelson, a political theorist at Harvard, raises that disturbing possibility. In *The Royalist Revolution*, Nelson argues that the standard narrative of the American Revolution—overthrowing a tyrannical king and replacing him with a representative democracy—is mistaken. Many leaders of the patriot cause actually wanted George III to intervene in their disputes with parliament, to veto the bills it passed, even to assert that he alone had the right to govern the American colonies. In short, they wanted him to rule like a king. When he declined, they revolted.
>
> As they framed their appeals to the king, Nelson demonstrates, the patriots reached back to the debate leading up to the English civil wars. In the 1620s, the Stuart monarch Charles I feuded with his parliament, which feared that he would usurp its authority to approve taxes, and reign as an absolute monarch. Both sides claimed to be working for the common good. The parliamentarians insisted that only a legislature—a miniature version of the people as a whole—could represent the people's interests. Royalists responded that legislators were mere creatures of their constituencies, bound to cater to voters' whims instead of tending to the kingdom's needs. Only a monarch, they argued, could counterbalance legislative parochialism and look to the long term.
>
> Applebaum, Y. (2015) "America's Fragile Constitution," **The Atlantic** October, 2015.[58]

FRENCH-INDIAN WAR (1754-1763) AND PROCLAMATION LINE

The French-Indian War resulted in the Proclamation Line and taxes to pay for the war. The Proclamation Line limitation infuriated land speculators, Washington, Jefferson, Patrick Henry, Franklin and others, the leaders. The war also produced taxes to pay for the war. This became a tool for ginning up the broad population for war.

Perhaps the time has come for reconsidering George Washington. His father died when he was 12 years old. His brother Lawrence assumed a parental role educating George and preparing him as a land surveyor, a logical career direction considering Lawrence's involvement in the Ohio Company, a land speculating company. George learned the value of rich fertile land. He becomes a militia leader promoting British action in the Ohio River Valley to pushback against French encroachment on the territory. This leads to the French Indian War with George fighting for the British for the purpose of gaining control over Indian lands. The British win but it costs them and they restrict colonists from starting new Indian wars. George then turns against the British, joins a revolution freeing colonist from restrictions on taking Indian lands. What remains consistent is George's focus on taking control over Indian lands. When the war was over, Washington took ownership of close to 10,000 acres along the Ohio River; some 23,000 acres along the Kanawha River, an Ohio River tributary; 200 acres in Pennsylvania near the Great Meadow; 5,000 acres in Kentucky; and 3,000 acres in what was called the northwestern territory.

American textbooks frequently highlight the tale of Benedict Arnold who participated in the revolution, but then betrayed the revolution, serving as a spy for the British. Arnold has been labeled a traitor. What about Washington? He wanted a commission in the British military. Was he a traitor to Britain? Indian lands and the riches they represented were Washington's focus and he would fight on whatever side advanced his drive for personal success and wealth.

America is charged with conspiracy to steal Native lands, murdering the peoples occupying the lands, genocide, and fraud by presenting George Washington as a man who couldn't lie, without adding his deeds as town destroyer who ordered genocidal massacres.

America is charged with invading occupied lands, murdering natives defending those lands, and theft of resources derived from the land.

Settler Colonialism

BITTER, ANGRY, HATE FILLED WHITE slaves, the residue of Enclosure Acts, Transportation Acts and Highland Clearances, and the dregs of society known today as white trash, squatters, and mudsills, became the invaders and occupiers of foreign lands, right here on the North American Continent. The victims became the victimizers. They came as prisoners to England's penal colony in North America. And when they got their freedom, they wandered off to other lands, unclaimed by their former slave masters. They squatted and claimed the land for themselves. But these were lands already occupied by the more than 500 nations of Native peoples.

There is a distinction to be made between colonialism by a nation-state and colonialism by settlers from the nation state who move against contiguous lands outside the boundary defined by the invading nation state. The settlers—the peoples forced, coerced or enticed—to the colonial occupation, acting without sanction of the colonial invader, take it upon themselves to venture off into other lands that they will fight for and occupy. This is settler colonialism.

While in the clutches of their slave masters, they learned their lessons well. Brutality, free from any moral constraint, ruled their world and they unleashed a fierce brutality opening a path for Native people genocide. They weren't alone. The aristocrats, Thomas Jefferson, Ben Franklin, George Washington, Patrick Henry, also joined in the slaughter. They didn't squat on lands; they purchased them at auction from the Crown; they were land speculators.

The phenomenon of a European invader, establishing a colony under the authority of the Doctrine of Discovery, established the colonial settlements. These were invaded territories, occupied by the invaders, euphemistically called "colonies." Once the so-called colonies were established, then the colonists initiated another phase of invasion and occupation. Today historians refer to this as Settler Colonialism. Those who settled in the colonies, albeit under the umbrella of Indentured Servitude or some other mechanism, then invaded and occupied other lands contiguous to the colony, but inhabited by Native peoples.

Colonialism involved foreign powers invading lands and establishing control, almost operating in parallel with the political leadership of the indigenous population. Settler Colonialism involves colonial settlers displacing and/or killing indigenous peoples so they can occupy and take control of the lands, essentially eliminating the indigenous population.

"The form of colonialism that the Indigenous peoples of North America have experienced," says Dunbar-Ortiz, "was modern from the beginning: the expansion of European corporations, backed by government armies, into foreign areas, with subsequent expropriation of lands and resources. Settler colonialism is a genocidal policy."[59]

Historian Patrick Griffin adds, "A Moravian missionary named John Heckewelder, who visited the Ohio Country in 1773, encountered a frightening world. Men formed themselves into gangs to "rove through the country in search of land, either to settle on or for speculation." Others "destitute of both honour and humanity" became a "rabble." These believed "that to kill an Indian, was the same as killing a bear or a buffalo, and would fire on Indians that came across them by the way."[60]

Land speculators were a key force in Settler Colonialism. Those leading the American Revolution were noted land speculators. Indeed, the Proclamation Line restricted their land speculation initiatives. In essence, England refused to use its forces for fighting Indians and seizing new lands for speculators. At the same time, speculators competed against squatters, former indentured servants, who occupied Indian lands.

"Getting American colonists to accept the proclamation was another matter," according to Calloway. "Many frontier settlers simply ignored it. Those who had crossed the Appalachians were now squatting illegally on Indian land and might be removed by British troops. Squatters were used to that, however, and the proclamation had limited effect on them, especially as there were no courts beyond the line and the British army lacked the resources to patrol and maintain the line." [61]

Law abiding George Washington directed the law be violated.

The speculators feared that common squatters were taking the best lands while the Proclamation deprived gentlemen of the legal standing to prosecute and evict intruders. In 1767, George Washington directed his land agent "to secure some of the most valuable Lands in the King's part . . . notwithstanding the Proclamation that restrains it at present & prohibits the Settling of them at all, for I can never look upon that Proclamation in any other light (but this I may say between ourselves) than as a temporary expedient to quiet the Minds of the Indians & must fall of course in a few years." His agent dutifully marked and claimed 25,000 acres.

> Taylor, Alan. **American Revolutions: A Continental History, 1750-1804** (p. 75). W. W. Norton & Company. Kindle Edition.[62]

The Proclamation Line along with the squatters hit the buttons of the Founding Fathers. They wanted the speculation business to proceed because it meant wealth, riches and power. With the squatters openly violating restrictions on taking western lands, the Founding Father Speculators felt these lands slipping away.

Calloway adds "…'settler political theory' that included the right to acquire property by dispossessing and supplanting Native peoples without restriction or interference from the imperial center; for many, the restrictive new policies threatened their rights as settlers and constituted the first step in their alienation from the empire."[63]

England's assertion of political control over the colonies was spun by colonial leaders as an assault upon the colonist's freedom. The word freedom is used throughout American history. It is the freedom to invade, kill, steal lands, exploit enslaved humans; it is a freedom for depravity. Manipulation of the word, freedom, is used extensively by those wishing dismantlement of the United States in the modern day.

The idea that taxation was a prime motivator for the American Revolution simply does not compare with the antagonism incited by England's reticence in fighting new Indian wars. Of course, the colonists did not want to pay for war, just as the super wealthy in America today do not want to pay for roads, bridges, communications networks and all other forms of infrastructure vital for their business interests. They just want what they want and they want it paid for magically by someone else, whoever that may be.

Washington became one of the richest men at the time by way of land speculation. Taxes were not important; blocking the land speculation enterprise most certainly was important.

Calloway says, "Washington, Jefferson, Arthur Lee, Patrick Henry, and others denounced British interference as tyranny and demanded freedom. It included the freedom to acquire and sell Indian land at will."[64]

The British faced a dilemma. Squatters, speculators and native peoples had competing interests sure to erupt in warfare that Britain could not afford. Lands west of the Appalachian Mountains were seductive. Indeed, the herds leading Siberians into North America instinctively followed their nostrils sniffing out the immensely rich and fertile soils of the Mississippi Delta. With navigable rivers, a favorable climate and a worldwide marketplace just waiting to be exploited, these lands represented wealth and power that could be extracted from them; Britain be damned.

Despite Proclamation Line constraints, colonists—squatters and speculators—plowed ahead. Legendary Tom Quick of Pennsylvania continued his one-man assault upon Native people. In the French Indian War, his father was killed. Quick vowed to kill 100 Indians in retaliation. His killing spree was prolific. Quick was but one example of the colonists' attitude favoring genocide.

Colonial leaders needed an incendiary theme for their hostility against Britain. Virginia's Governor, Patrick Henry, a wealthy land speculator and slave master, made the freedom argument. A slave master, who became rich stealing Indian lands and the brutality that went along with it, made the "freedom" argument. The assault on Native peoples also continued throughout the Revolution.

Squatters attacked the Indians, even those who were considered friendly. Brutality was normalized. Griffin tells us. "…by the early

1780s. Settlers no longer killed because they could ill afford to wait for civility to transform Indian societies. In part, they now killed because, in an increasingly violent state of war, most believed that the civility model was fundamentally flawed."[65]

"While militiamen from frontier counties were killing women and scalping children," Griffin tells us, "Indians were acting with great reserve. Indians and whites, therefore, had turned the civility equation on its head. In these circumstances, after decades of disorder and as violence escalated, settlers rejected its premises. Behavior no longer betokened development or human worth. Color did."

Racism became an integral factor in the fight against Indians as America moved west. Griffin adds, "Racist violence, in other words, was becoming the new basis of society in the West. The frightening, even modern, vision of the way the world worked would provide the social template for the West, one that speculators, military commanders, and officials in the West would either come to accept or have to tolerate."[66]

Indians were not without blame in the bloodshed. Pontiac's War unleashed a consortium of Native Nation's against the British and their colonists at the close of the French Indian War. In essence, Pontiac wanted a return to 1491 before Columbus arrived. Colonization was catastrophic for native peoples and Pontiac somehow wanted to change it all. He led attacks against British forts and against colonists. Britain and the colonists also attacked. All are rationalized and justified as defensive actions, not acts of aggression. When did it all start? When was the first attack? 1492, perhaps?

Pennsylvania Paxton Boys earned fame for killing Indians. Operating under a Presbyterian banner, they slaughtered 20 unarmed Indians who they suspected of plotting an attack. Such attacks are usually reasoned as defensive, not aggressive, even though the Indians were merely suspected.

Colonists strategically formed alliances with selected Indian tribes, thereby driving a wedge between Indian nations. Driving wedges was an essential tactic in conquering the New World and transforming it into a slave plantation society.

"The New English also exploited their alliance with the powerful Mohawk Indians (one of the Iroquois Five Nations), who lived to the west' according to Taylor. "In return for colonists' presents, the Mohawk escalated their destructive raids on their old enemies the New England Algonquians."[67]

Native peoples also had antagonisms with the French. In 1729, the Natchez attacked the French in Louisiana killing over 200 men, women and children. They also took women and children as captives. The cycle of violence continued when the Choctaw attacked the Natchez, about a year later, destroying their villages. [68]

The French and Choctaw chased after escaping Natchez, killing hundreds and enslaving at least five hundred. When it served their purposes, the French massacred and enslaved natives just like the British.

Settlers

Indentured servants, white slaves, forced to North America as punishment for crimes committed in England, worked off their obligation over a period of four to seven years, some longer, and when freed were given 50 acres and some cash. The 50 acres were entrusted to the colonist who held the indentured contract. Most indentures, however, simply sold off the 50 acres and wandered off to set up a self-sufficient existence as squatters on uninhabited land. But this was outside the scope of permissible settlement on lands claimed by the crown. They became known as the "crackers" and "squatters".

INDICTING AMERICA

"The "Adam" of American wilderness," says Nancy Isenburg in *White Trash: The 400-year untold history of class in America*, "had a split personality: he was half hearty rustic and half dirk-carrying highwayman. In his most favorable cast as backwoodsman, he was a homespun philosopher, an independent spirit, and a strong courageous man who shunned fame and wealth. But turn him over and he became the white savage, a ruthless brawler and eye-gouger. This unwholesome type lived a brute existence in a dingy log cabin, with yelping dogs at his heels, a haggard wife, and a mongrel brood of brown and yellow brats to complete the sorry scene."

Isenburg adds: "Both crackers and squatters—two terms that became shorthand for landless migrants—supposed stayed just one step ahead of the "real" farmers, Jefferson idealized, commercially oriented cultivators. They lived off the grid, rarely attended a school or joined a church, and remained a potent symbol of poverty."[69]

The French Indian War makes salient the land speculators appetite for Indian lands. The resulting Proclamation Line restricting speculators from encroachment on Indian land was a significant agitation provoking Revolution. Former indentured slaves also wanted native lands where they could become squatters and simply claim the land for themselves.

The Proclamation Line agitated colonists who wanted more of the native lands. It was a central antagonism fueling the revolution.

Washington pursued properties across the Ohio River Valley, damn the Proclamation Line. He owned significant properties along the Ohio River, Kanawha River and southeastern Pennsylvania. He wanted more but the Proclamation Line constrained his reach.

The California Gold Rush triggered more genocidal acts against Native peoples. It will be discussed in subsequent chapters.

America is charged with invading occupied lands, killing natives occupying the lands and theft of natural resources.

James Somerset

HE WAS A HANDSOME AND likeable guy, carrying himself with an air of dignity and grace. His charm engaged his Slave Master, Charles Steuart, who decided he should accompany him on a trip to London. This trip set in motion a series of events, establishing the second of two key pillars underpinning the American Revolution; the Proclamation Line represents the first pillar and James Somerset case the second.

Buried deep in American History shelves in American libraries is the story of James Somerset. It is hidden because it reveals the heart of the Revolutionary leaders. The broader population may have rallied to themes about taxation, tyranny and the like, but for the leadership, there were two over riding issues: The Proclamation Line and James Somerset.

Many historians refrain from such a claim, instead continuing the taxation-tyranny theme. Indian lands and enslaved people made the colonial leaders wealthy so they could live a life of luxury. Taxes pale in comparison. Suggesting that a threat to their wealth producing enterprise was not the driving force, but ideas about democracy, freedom and justice were the key issues, is ludicrous and absurd. A

INDICTING AMERICA

threat to slavery sent electric shock waves through colonial leaders. The "founding fathers" were slave masters. Rape, murder, whippings, stealing children from their mother and father were perfectly fine, but ideas of freedom and liberty suddenly touched their souls.

There are historians, however, who have provided the research for connecting the dots. Perhaps one day secondary school textbooks will cease perpetrating the spin, of taxation without representation and the tyrannical king, which are catchy marketing phrases, but not much more than that.

By the mid-18th century, slavery-based enterprises thrived. The Industrial Revolution was underway in which machines, driven by steam, produced finished products on a massive scale, faster and more efficiently than hand made products. Demand for raw materials for feeding the industrial machine was gaining momentum, growing more intense as industry expanded. Extracting raw materials required mineral rich lands and enslaved labor for planting, harvesting and mining operations. The road to wealth was clear and straightforward. Extract raw materials in demand, from lands muscled away from the legitimate occupants, with inexpensive slave labor, and feed them to the industrial machine. Better yet, do so with a monopoly.

North American colonists could not predict the Louisiana Purchase still to come at the turn of the 19th century, but they were certainly aware of the fertile soils that awaited them as they pushed westward. France claimed the lands known as Louisiana, even though Native peoples occupied the area. Still, the Europeans plowed ahead, making the natives invisible.

This audacity was not lost upon Native leaders. As Taylor tells us: "Rejecting the transfer made by the Treaty of Paris, a Creek chief, Yahatatastonake, warned British officials that natives were 'surprized how People can give away Land that does not belong to them.'"[70]

JAMES SOMERSET

In England, slavery instigated political turmoil. Christian evangelicals understood the hypocrisy of the inhumanity of slavery and the teachings of their faith. Those accumulating enormous wealth cared nothing about hypocrisy, simply ignoring the contradictions of their business practices and their faith. English evangelicals, however, remained determined to fight.

Moral considerations were secondary concerns for British colonists. Slave rebellions in the West Indies, however, were another matter altogether. Whereas the British colonists of North America did not want British troops to fight their battles, depending instead on militias, the colonists in the West Indies did, indeed, want British troops to muscle natives and enslaved people. They even agreed to foot the bill for British troops, if need be. These plantations were enormously profitable, but the enslaved labor force was not happy and rebellions were spreading. West Indies colonists were frightened. But England was stretched thin as it embarked upon China, South Asia and the Middle East. They didn't have the troops to police the Americas. They considered arming enslaved people to serve as a defensive force, an idea that fell flat with colonists.

Evangelicals, inspired by John Newton's *Amazing Grace* and operating as Society for Effecting the Abolition of the Slave Trade continued their activism against slavery. Granville Sharp, Tom Clarkson and William Wilberforce, a member of Parliament, organized strategies for abolition of slavery. Sharp hunted for legal actions that would force a court to rule on the legality of enslavement.

Granville Sharp served as the orchestra leader organizing legal action before Lord Mansfield, Chief Justice in the court of the King's Bench. The initiative challenged slavery on English soil, because Parliament had not established by legislative action a legal foundation for slavery. The Somerset case provided an opportunity to sue under a *writ of habeas corpus* for the slave master to show the legal basis for holding Somerset against his will.

In North America, as resentments stemming from the Proclamation Line stewed, British abolitionists, across the ocean, were organizing, planning and plotting a means for advancing their cause. Granville Sharp, a Christian evangelical, led a loose coalition of other evangelicals, political leaders and lawyers in crafting a plan for bringing a legal action in British courts. Their opportunity emerged in 1771 when an American colonist, Charles Steuart, brought one of his slaves with him to England. The enslaved—James Somerset—became the center of a monumental legal action threatening slavery in the colonies.

After arriving in London, Somerset decided to flee captivity. He ran away. He was captured and sold off to a slave trader for shipment to the West Indies where grueling plantation labor awaited. Before his ship could sail, however, attorneys working with Sharp filed a legal action under *a writ of habeus corpus* to show the law supporting Somerset being held against his will. This became the center of the Somerset case.

The case was scheduled for hearing before Chief Justice Mansfield, a highly respected jurist. Lord Mansfield looked to the law, reason and justice in deciding cases. He recognized that slavery existed on shaky ground, because there was nothing in English law that established the institution of slavery. He also recognized that something so profound—the loss of liberty—was so severe that it required something more than mere Common Practice; it required Positive Law, an act of Parliament.

Lord Mansfield understood the implications of ruling in favor of the petitioners in that it could be deemed a ruling outlawing slavery across the British Empire. He encouraged plaintiff and defense to negotiate a settlement so he would not have to rule on the case. But a settlement was not to be had and Lord Mansfield was forced to rule. He stated that an issue "so odious" such as slavery required positive law, an act of Parliament, and not merely common laws of tradition. Since no positive law existed, he ordered that Somerset be set free. He also said that his ruling was limited to the particulars of the case and should not be taken as a broad sweeping decision.

"Just past ten o'clock," Steven Wise tells us in his *Though the Heavens May Fall: The Landmark Trial That Led to the End of Human Slavery*, "on Monday morning, June 22, 1772, a black man's lawyers shouted into his ear over the din of a celebration in Westminster Hall. What he heard set him racing through central London's dirty narrow streets to Old Jewry, Granville Sharp's home. It must have been a joyful run as, for the first time since he was eight years old, thirty-one-year-old James Somerset was no man's property but his own. Thirty-three months before he had sailed from Boston with his American master, Charles Steuart.' Forty-one days on the open sea later he had taken his first breath of English air. For the past seven months, the African had languished on bail, waiting for the most powerful judge in England, the Right Honorable William, Lord Mansfield, to decide whether that breath had made him a free man or whether he would spend the rest of his short life harvesting sugar cane on a roasting West Indian plantation."[71]

This ruling was so significant it earned a spot in Jefferson's Declaration of Independence, according to Blumrosen & Blumrosen in their scholarly work *Slave Nation: How Slavery United the Colonies and Sparked the American Revolution*. "Jefferson's list of colonial grievances that make up the body of the Declaration is haunted by the Somerset decision in which Lord Mansfield stated that Parliament had the final authority over slavery in the colonies. The king is accused of conspiring with Parliament to enact "pretended legislation" and

INDICTING AMERICA

"declaring themselves invested with power to legislate for us in all cases whatsoever." This is a clear reference to the Declaratory Act, and its threat, after Somerset, to the institution of slavery."[72]

Mansfield said his ruling was to be received narrowly, only applying to the case before him, but if slavery was not legal, it was not legal. Across the British colonies enslaved Africans believed they were on the cusp of freedom. They would be disappointed for the time being as ruling elites resisted the notion of an end to slavery.[73]

The evangelicals persisted pushing England to end the odious trade in human cargo. In 1807, Parliament outlawed the international slave trade. Slavery was abolished on British soil in 1834. Britain also decided to pay reparations—not to the formerly enslaved—but to the slave masters. Payment wasn't completed until 2015.

"The Mansfield decision," according to David Waldstreicher in *Slavery's Constitution: From Revolution to Ratification*, "immediately set off a wave of speculation about the end of slavery in England, fanned by the black community there, who sought to make facts on the ground, and to a significant extent succeeded in doing so. The arguable significance of this event in the history of slavery, however, has obscured its deeper logic, roots, and political implications. Mansfield pushed the envelope on fugitive slaves not because he hated the institution of slavery or thought its legality unproven but rather because it was a matter of parliamentary sovereignty over the local laws and practices of the colonies. He did exactly as he had done in the Stamp Act repeal debates seven years before. He declared the Americans subject to parliamentary statutes regardless of their local laws. "[74]

"The Somerset case had important repercussions in Britain's North American colonies," says Mansfield's biographer Norman Posner in *Lord Mansfield: Justice in the Age of Reason*. "The case was widely noted in colonial newspapers and its perceived threat to the institution of slavery may have provided a stimulus to the desire of Virginia and the other southern colonies to seek independence. Within a year after the decision, slaves in Massachusetts began agitating against the institution. The stark contradiction that many of the "Sons of Liberty" were slave owners gave rise to Samuel Johnson's famous remark: "How is it that we hear the loudest yelps for liberty among the drivers of negroes?"

North American colonists, particularly in South Carolina and Virginia were electrified by the decision. Indeed, South Carolina decided to send representatives to the next Continental Congress, even though it had previously demonstrated no interest in forming any relationship with the other colonists. It has been argued that too much weight is given to the Somerset case, but Somerset's ghost looms large over the Articles of Confederation, the U.S. Constitution, the Fugitive Slave Act of 1793 and the Fugitive Slave Act of 1850. Southern planters were obsessed with protecting slavery and that obsession is evidenced in legislative action.[75]

"Chief Justice Lord Mansfield's ruling in Somerset v. Stewart in 1772," says Calloway, "that an African slave from the colonies who set foot in England became free and could not be returned to slavery, fueled paranoia about impending imperial threats to Virginian planters' property rights. 50 Many began to think radical thoughts and to organize." A revolution was in the offing. This became one of the two pillars providing a foundation for the revolution. It was a central cause of the revolution, even though it remains obscure to most Americans.[76]

> What was this? Did slaves read law reports? How could it be that a judgment rendered in June 1772 by Lord Chief Justice Mansfield in the court of the King's Bench in the case of a

runaway African, James Somerset, recaptured by his master, could light a fire in the plantations?

Mansfield had set Somerset free, but had taken pains not to make a general ruling on the legality of slavery in England. However, the "Negro frolicks" in London celebrating the court decision had swept legal niceties aside. Across the Atlantic word spread, and spread quickly, that slavery had been outlawed in Britain. In 1774 a pamphlet written under the name "Freeman," published in Philadelphia, told American slaves that they could have liberty merely by "setting foot on that happy Territory where slavery is forbidden to perch." Before the Patriots knew it, the birds had already begun to fly the coop.

"Dirty little secret," by Simon Schama,
Smithsonian, May, 2006.[77]

Indeed, Somerset loomed so large, the issue was addressed in the Articles of Confederation; The U.S. Constitution; the Fugitive Slave Act of 1793; and The Fugitive Slave Act of 1850; clear evidence of an obsession for keeping control of slaves. The heart of the issue was the slave holders' right to bring a slave onto free soil and then return to slave soil with the slave. The issue also involved legal authority for retrieval of an escaped slave. For American colonial slave owners, their right to obtain and keep slaves was not negotiable and was central in their understanding of "liberty." Clearly control over slaves loomed large in what was to become the United States of America.

"Slavery had been outlawed in England's home island, though not in its colonies, in the landmark 1772 Somerset decision by an activist judge, who concluded that enslavement was such an egregious denial of rights that slavery had to be specifically authorized by law, and Parliament had never done so," according to Henry Wiencek in

Master of the Mountain. "When there were calls for Parliament to pass enabling legislation for black slavery, the proposal was derided in a widely circulated joke, which was eventually published in The Virginia Gazette: "If Negroes are to be Slaves on account of colour, the next step will be to enslave every mulatto in the kingdom, then all the Portuguese, next the French, then the brown complexioned English, and so on until there be only one free man left, which will be the man of palest complexion in the three kingdoms."[78]

Traditional primary and secondary school social studies textbook claim the cause of the American Revolution was taxation without representation. The threat posed to slavery by the James Somerset case, however, was much more formidable for southern planters than any tax. Parliament's adoption of the Declaratory Act, stipulating that English law took precedence over colonial law, suggested that the Somerset decision would apply to the colonists. Coupling the Declaratory Act, 1766, with the Somerset case, 1771, suggests a perceived threat to slavery, a key ingredient for plantation enterprises. The Somerset case added to resentments caused by the Proclamation Line. The true cause of the American Revolution was not taxation; it was British reticence in seizing Indian Lands and the perceived threat to slavery imposed by the Somerset ruling.

Zong Case

Chief Justice Mansfield was enigmatic. Eleven years after the Somerset case, he presided over the Zong case. The Zong was the name of a ship transporting enslaved Africans from West Africa to Jamaica. The ship's captain lost his way in the Caribbean for an extended period before getting back on course. Water supplies drained during the extended time at sea resulting in an estimated 60 deaths, including 40 who threw themselves overboard and drowned. The ship's captain also ordered another 150 enslaved passengers tossed overboard.

This may seem cold but it gets worse. The Zong's owner filed suit against the ship's insurer seeking compensation for the lost cargo—the humans who died of thirst and those tossed overboard. The case went to a jury that ruled against the insurer concluding that this expenditure of life was a result of normal risks encountered at sea.

The Zong's voyage was grueling. When it got back on course, slaves suffered from dehydration and lack of food. If the Zong docked in Jamaica and slaves died onshore, insurance did not provide compensation. But, if they died while in transit, insurance coverage applied. This suggested, but not proven, that those in the worst condition were tossed overboard for the purpose of insurance. The remaining 200 slaves made it to shore.

The case was appealed with Chief Justice Mansfield presiding. According to Poser, Mansfield did not consider black slaves as actual humans with basic human rights; he thought of them as property. Their owners could do with them as they wished. Notwithstanding his predisposition, Mansfield ordered a new trial on the grounds that the ship's owner did not establish that it was necessary to toss the slaves overboard. Before arriving in Jamaica, it had rained, making it possible for water to be available for the slaves. This suggested that if the Zong's owners could prove water was still insufficient, then the judgement in favor of the ship's owner could be upheld. The trial court judgement was overturned and the insurer's denial of claim upheld.

The Zong case drew the attention of Granville Sharp who lobbied for the ship's captain and crew to be tried for murder. That didn't happen, but Sharp used the grotesque event, tossing humans overboard for insurance fraud, in advancing abolitionism.

Mansfield's disposition is also complicated by the daughter of his nephew, Sir John Lindsay, a British Naval Captain. Lindsay fathered a child with a 14-year-old black slave he met in the West Indies. Lindsay had custody of the child, Dido Elizabeth Belle. His absence at sea, however, meant he needed help in caring for the child. Its unknown as to the status of the mother. Belle was taken in by the Mansfield household where she lived a privileged life and formed a bonded relationship with her new family. Did this experience alter his view of blacks as property? When he died, Mansfield left Belle with cash and an annual stipend. But he never referred to her as his niece.

Post Somerset

The "founding fathers" were obsessed with James Somerset and passed that obsession on to future generations. They would not adopt the Articles of Confederation because the powerful John Rutledge of South Carolina feared a Somerset case, if one of his slaves meandered onto free soil. They were at war with England and desperately needed some governing structure for raising troops and money for fighting the war, but, no, the priority was Somerset. Finally, they adopted the Articles of Confederation, just before the end of the war, making sure that Article Four was a clear part of the compact.

Articles of Confederation: Article IV.

The better to secure and perpetuate mutual friendship and intercourse among the people of the different States in this Union, the free inhabitants of each of these States, paupers, vagabonds, and fugitives from justice excepted, shall be entitled to all privileges and immunities of free citizens in the several States; and the people of each State shall free ingress and regress to and from any other State, and shall enjoy therein all the privileges of trade and commerce, subject to the same duties, impositions, and restrictions as the inhabitants thereof respectively, *provided that such restrictions shall not extend so far as to prevent the removal of property imported into any State, to any other State, of which the owner is an inhabitant; provided also that no imposition, duties or restriction shall be laid by any State, on the property of the United States, or either of them.* (Italics highlight words aimed directly at Somerset and Lord Mansfield)

If any person guilty of, or charged with, treason, felony, or other high misdemeanor in any State, shall flee from justice, and be found in any of the United States, he shall, upon demand of the Governor or executive power of the State from which he fled, be delivered up and removed to the State having jurisdiction of his offense.

Full faith and credit shall be given in each of these States to the records, acts, and judicial proceedings of the courts and magistrates of every other State.

Then came the U.S. Constitution and once again Somerset was addressed. The Constitution is primarily an organizing document assigning tasks and responsibilities to three equal branches of government in a system of checks and balances. Establishing laws fell within the purview of the Legislative Branch. Laws pertaining to slavery should be created by the legislature, once the Constitution went into effect. The Slave Masters, however, would not agree to a constitution, unless it included a Somerset Clause. They also would not agree to a constitution that included requirements that the government serve the common good. That idea of democracy also fell short. Only when constraints were placed upon democracy, such as the Electoral College and a Senate designed for property owners. The Senate also served as a check on the House of Representatives where the number of representatives from each state was based upon population of each state. Each state got two senators regardless of population. This meant slave states could hold in check non-slave states.

Recalcitrance exhibited by the Slave Masters is directly relevant to the modern day. Slavery, racial animosity, bigotry are front in center across the political landscape in the 21st Century. Despite all the efforts at spin and laws preventing distribution of real information, real history, slavery remains the number one threat to America's existence. Ignoring it is perilous.

Excerpt from the Constitution:

Constitution: Article. IV, Section. 2.

The Citizens of each State shall be entitled to all Privileges and Immunities of Citizens in the several States.

A Person charged in any State with Treason, Felony, or other Crime, who shall flee from Justice, and be found in another State, shall on Demand of the executive Authority of the State from which he fled, be delivered up, to be removed to the State having Jurisdiction of the Crime.

No Person held to Service or Labour in one State, under the Laws thereof, escaping into another, shall, in Consequence of any Law or Regulation therein, be discharged from such Service or Labour, but shall be delivered up on Claim of the Party to whom such Service or Labour may be due.

And if that wasn't enough, the slave masters demanded further clarification with the Fugitive Slave Act of 1793. (See Appendix 1)
The following is an excerpt:

SEC. 3. *And be it also enacted*, That when a person held to labor in any of the United States, or in either of the Territories on the Northwest or South of the river Ohio, under the laws thereof, shall escape into any other part of the said States or Territory, the person to whom such labor or service may be due, his agent or attorney, is hereby empowered to seize or arrest such fugitive from labor, and to take him or her before any Judge of the Circuit or District Courts of the United States, residing or being within the State,...

To further solidify their hold on slaves, slave masters demanded another fugitive slave act in 1850 holding police and other officials liable for not retrieving and returning a runaway slave. (See Appendix 2)
This Fugitive Slave Act, 1850, went even further is making sure that their slave was their slave and no one could have them. Just consider this excerpt:

Section 6

And be it further enacted, That when a person held to service or labor in any State or Territory of the United States, has heretofore or shall hereafter escape into another State or Territory of the United States, the person or persons to whom such service or labor may be due, or his, her, or their agent or attorney, duly authorized, by power of attorney, in writing, acknowledged and certified under the seal of some legal officer or court of the State or Territory in which the same may be executed, may pursue and reclaim such fugitive person, either by procuring a warrant from some one of the courts, judges, or commissioners aforesaid, of the proper circuit, district, or county, for the apprehension of such fugitive from service or labor, or by seizing and arresting such fugitive, where the same can be done without process, and by taking, or causing such person to be taken,…

America was born a Slavocracy obsessed with maintaining control of the enslaved. It was the means to their ends. Enslaved labor made them and everyone around them rich, wealthy and powerful. No matter how immoral, inhuman and depraved, they would not give it up.

America is charged with crimes against humanity.

Revolution or Secession?

PROHIBITING COLONISTS FROM encroachment on Indian lands and threatening slavery, along with the riches derived from slavery, enraged colonial leaders, the founding fathers. It was intolerable. But for colonial leaders, fighting back against England required support of the broad population. This would not be easy because the colonists had little connection with each other and the broad population liked being a part of the British Empire. Each colony was separate and distinctive. Indeed, there was an undercurrent of resentments toward each other. How then to galvanize the people to join a fight against England?

Organizing the colonial leaders simply to talk about common antagonisms with England was a sensitive and difficult endeavor. Southerners would likely resist a confrontation because it could threaten their business interests. Talk of war could drive some colonies away. So, at the second meeting, Patrick Henry gave his famous "Give me liberty or give me death." Many thought it premature to call for war. Later Madison communicated with Jefferson about Henry's performance. His reply, "What we have to do…is devoutly pray for his [Henry's] death."

REVOLUTION OR SECESSION?

John Adams and Ben Franklin understood fear, specifically fear of slave uprisings and of aggressive natives. It was a justified fear, because the system of terror, torture and genocide inflicted by the invading and occupying Europeans provided more than adequate provocation for the victims to want to kill their victimizers. Fear permeated the land and fear quickly morphed into hate and, that hate, if properly stoked, could be directed at the English.

Fake News became the tool of choice as they fabricated tales of the English encouraging slave uprisings and native attacks upon settlers. Adams and Franklin used pseudonyms as a cover, publishing news articles circulated throughout the colonies. It worked.

In 2016, Professor Robert Parkinson published *The Common Cause: Creating Race and Nation in the American Revolution*, over 700 pages, examining the run up to war. In 2019, he shortened it a bit under the title *Thirteen Clocks: How Race United the Colonies and Made the Declaration of Independence*. The thirteen clocks referred to the 13 colonies and a comment attributed to John Adams summarizing a key task for those leading the revolution: how to rally the broad population in support of the revolution and to do so in synchronization with each other.

"I argue," says Parkinson, "patriot leaders weaponized prejudice about African Americans and Indians to unite the American colonists and hammer home the idea that the British were treacherous and dangerous enemies."[79]

The founding fathers played the race card, exploiting racial fears against black enslaved people and Native Americans, soon transforming that fear into hate. Racial animus continues providing a powerful political tool in contemporary politics.

Parkinson researched colonial news for the 15 months leading up to the fight. His research unmasked Adams and Franklin as central figures circulating fake news anonymously. Parkinson's work has been widely praised. It significantly counters the traditional narrative that the colonial people, with some exceptions, were united by a spirit of freedom and such. No, it was fear and hate.

"Immediately after Lexington and Concord," says Parkinson, "patriot leaders seized any story they could lay their hands on that hinted British agents might be using Natives or enslaved people to put down the American rebellion. They publicized these widely in weekly newspapers, telling and retelling stories about any involvement between British military officers, royal governors, or any government agents who might be encouraging slaves to rise up against their masters or Natives to slaughter backcountry settlers." [80]

Adams, Jefferson, Washington and Franklin remained skeptical that the ideas of Republicanism would inspire the soul of the colonial population. Something much more provocative was needed. "No matter what they said later on," according to Parkinson, "throughout 1775 and 1776, these men spent a great deal of time, money, and effort broadcasting stories about what the Declaration referred to as "domestic insurrectionists," "merciless Indian savages," and "foreign Mercenaries" working with the king (and therefore against the "common cause") to as much of the colonial public as they could reach."

"Once the war began," he added, "the commitment of patriot leaders to the amplification of these particular stories reveals their conviction that this was the best way to secure American unity. Race made the thirteen clocks chime together; the consequences would last long after 1776."[81]

Preying upon racial animus in galvanizing the broad population was not part of a grand strategy. Indeed, colonial leaders stumbled into the fight with England; it was not a planned action with an objective and a strategy for achieving a goal. There is no event where the Continental Congress decisively voted for war against England, to the contrary, the so-called "founding fathers" merely reacted to events, and before they knew it, they were at war.

It may be argued that voting for the Declaration of Independence was a vote for war, but the war was already underway; they were just catching up. Samuel Adams played an important role agitating for a fight with England. Sam Adams was a corrupted customs agent, frequently performing favors for the smuggler John Hancock. Adams enjoyed his role as England's critic, expressing his antagonistic thoughts in Boston taverns where an intoxicated audience reveled in his commentary pitting England (them) against colonists (us).

Taxes provided a theme for his discourse. It, too, worked. This was to be expected by a society comprised of former indentured servants who retained grievances from their ancestors dating back to the Enclosure Acts. They were victims of unreasonable government action and they were not about to be reasonable now.

The French Indian War was costly and England attempted to tax the colonists to defray costs. The colonists balked and England backed off, but did retain a tax on tea. Smuggled Dutch tea sold for less than English tea so England decided to cut the tea tax making it more competitive against the Dutch tea.

Adams used this as a topic for his discourse before his inebriated audience. As English tea sat on Boston docks, the agitated audience attacked, tossing the tea into the harbor, earning fame in the process as the Boston Tea Party. England reacted by sending in troops, later spreading out from Boston in search of weapons of mass destruction, thereby agitating the population; one action begat a reaction, which prompted another reaction. Before they knew it, they were at war fighting for independence.

From the colonist viewpoint, there were two levels of motivation for fighting the English. On the leadership level, the prime motivators were the Proclamation Line and the Somerset case. For the broad population, the motivation, instilled by provocateurs such as Samuel Adams, was based on issues of taxation, monarchical tyranny, English corruption and, most importantly, Racial Animus.

Slave Owners

American colonial slave owners followed the Somerset case in England fearing it might lead to England outlawing slavery in the colonies, too. The Declaratory Acts of March 18, 1766 passed by Parliament in England established that British law took precedence over laws passed in the colonies. The implications of the Somerset ruling, if it were to be extended to the North American settlements, would have been enormous.

The Declaratory Acts were highly significant. This Parliamentary action followed on the heels of conflict with the colonists over taxation. England relented in these conflicts, but Parliament wanted to send a clear message about power and England's dominion over the colonies. The Act claimed Parliament took precedence over the colonial governments. When the Somerset case occurred just a few years later, the danger antennas of the colonists quickly alerted the leaders that Mansfield's decision could be viewed in the same way as act of Parliament, thereby making an end of slavery. This was speculation, but a reasonable speculation based upon the response to the decision by enslaved black people who believed freedom was awaiting around the corner.[82]

"The controversy, therefore, became too legal not in an abstract sense, but because the procedures or mechanics of constitutional advocacy provided no opportunity for a political solution unless either the British or the Americans surrendered a constitutional principle they thought essential for their constitutional liberty," writes Blumrosen," "...American liberty—the right to be free of arbitrary power—could not be secured under parliamentary supremacy. British liberty— the representative legislature over the crown—could not be secured without parliamentary supremacy.32 Thus, states rights, slavery, and liberty were inextricably linked in the 1774 Declaration of Rights and Grievances."[83]

Judicial decisions may be narrowly defined or they may have far reaching authority. Lord Mansfield said the Somerset decision was a narrowly focused decision that simply said that a *Writ of habeas corpus* applied in the case. He said his decision was not wide ranging and did not outlaw slavery; it simply said that the people holding the slave against his will needed to show why the slave was legally being held.

"In a landmark 1772 decision, Lord Mansfield, the chief justice of England, freed Somerset," says Foner." Since the decision predated the printing of official versions of court decisions, what Mansfield actually said remains a matter of dispute. His ruling appears to have been a relatively cautious one, stating that the laws of England did not allow a master to use force to capture and remove from the country a slave who had escaped. Mansfield tried to rule in Somerset's favor without freeing the thousands of other West Indian slaves present in England or asserting the general principle that slavery could not exist outside the jurisdiction that created it."[84]

The ruling, however, was viewed as wide sweeping by those in the colonies following the case. Slave owners in Massachusetts began transitioning the relationship with their slaves to free labor workers paid for their services. This was plausible in the northern colonies where slavery was not a lynchpin for commerce, but in the south the circumstance was distinctively different. Slavery was essential for commerce, because if the work force was given a choice, it might select something other than the grueling work of cotton picking in the heat of Mississippi. At the time of the Revolution cotton was not dominant but it was emerging.

Slavery was an essential part of the colonial economy in North America driven by cotton, rice, tobacco and indigo. These were labor intensive crops, grown in a forbidding environment, the Deep South, with breath taking heat and humidity. African slaves were an attractive commodity. They were strong and their skin was blessed with a natural sunscreen, melanin.

Fears of outlawing slavery, however, are not what mythic images are made of. Rebelling against tyrannical taxation without representation is much more palatable and marketable as a source of inspiration. As often is the case, history is written by those who wish to cast themselves in the most favorable light. And so, the American culture has it that the colonies rebelled against British rule over the issue of taxation without representation. The institution of slavery, that was at the heart of a lucrative economy and was vulnerable to elimination based on British law, was not the reason for rebellion, as the story goes; it was the price of tea.

In 1768, the Massachusetts legislature urged the colonies to unite in opposition to the Townsend tax, but the southern colonies lacked the motivation. Southern colonists were making substantial profits and their biggest customer was England. They may have balked at the taxes, but they were not about to anger the British. For them to join together for fighting the British took something more motivating than the price of tea. Surely the institution of slavery was much more important.

Before the Mansfield decision, there were several controversies involving English taxes, but they were never substantial enough to

REVOLUTION OR SECESSION?

galvanize the colonists against the English. The Somerset case, however, was serious enough so that the southern colonists became more receptive to the appeal for independence. The southern colonists were reluctant to cause a stir. They wanted things as they were. They were profiting quite handsomely from slavery and they did not want to rock the boat. But the Somerset case caused deep consternation. Perhaps they could coalesce with the northern colonists and pre-empt English action against slavery.

The Continental Congress made initiatives to negotiate with Britain, but King George would have none of it. Several attempts were made to broker an agreement in which the British Parliament and the Continental Congress could work together collaboratively. These initiatives failed, however, because Britain would not budge on the dominant role of the British Parliament.

On one level the landowners, the leaders, motivated by a thirst for Indian lands and protection of slavery, initiated a rebellion; the lower classes on another level also wanted Indian lands for homesteading and they wanted blacks kept at a lower status. Independence provided legitimacy for bullying Indians and maintaining status above blacks.

Those white slaves, the indentured servants, who occupied the colonies in the 17th and 18th century, were also treated inhumanely, and many spent a lifetime as a slave. More importantly, white slaves taken from the lowest rungs of European society and discarded on the shores of North America wanted desperately to find someone who was worse off than they. Black slaves provided white slaves with a relative sense that they—the white slaves—were at least better off than the black slaves. The perceived threat of England outlawing slavery compelled the white underclass to support revolution.

Feeling superior to another is a powerful force, indentured servants and their offspring have continued embracing that sense of superiority up to the modern day. Indeed, the prodigies of indentured servants have fought intensely to keep "blacks in their place" so they—the white offspring of indentures—could continue to be in a position of superiority over black people. A threat to the slave institution seemingly would benefit the indentured slaves, but it was more important to defend slavery thereby keeping black people from freedom and equality. The indentures fought the Brits and later fought the north. Why? It may be argued: to keep "blacks in their place"

The Somerset case was initiated by Christian evangelicals causing a reaction that set-in motion events leading to the American Revolution. Indeed, it seems clear the American Revolution was a direct product of English Abolitionists. More importantly it illuminated internal colonial conflicts that later manifested a Civil War.

A key element of the Somerset decision focused on taking a slave onto free soil. Southern colonists became riveted on this. Although they felt compelled to join the antagonism against England, they also desired maintenance of their independence from the other colonists. But when they found themselves at war with England, they needed a mechanism for joining together, but not too joined together. Answering this dilemma were the Articles of Confederation, a weak and meek document for organizing the colonies and providing some semblance of government. It committed the colonists to "a firm league of friendship."

"In one legal context, the Somerset principle slowly came to be recognized in northern courts," according to Foner. "This concerned the right of "transit"— that is, whether southern slaveholders had the right to bring their slaves into states that had abolished the institution. Until the 1830s, northern states generally recognized the right of transit, although some limited the amount of time an owner could keep a slave within their borders."[85]

The Articles of Confederation, the document for governing during the fight with England were prepared by Delaware's John Dickinson, and were circulated to the leadership for approval shortly after the Declaration of Independence. But South Carolina's John Rutledge stalled action on the document due to concerns about slaves on free soil. Article IV became the James Somerset article stipulating protection for slave owners, but still the articles were not approved until shortly before the war ended. Consequently, the rebels operated without an overarching government for the span of the war.

Americans love the Declaration of Independence, a sonnet to human rights; each year celebrating the Fourth of July, the accepted date for declaring independence from England. Most Americans believe the Declaration is the foundation for their government; it is not. The Constitution provides the foundation for government, but it speaks to property rights, not human rights. The Declaration, however, is so much more inspiring. It may be argued the Constitution repudiates the Declaration. The contrast is stark and continues haunting America in the modern day.[86]

The American story has focused on the British colonies settled by people with new ideas about government dedicated to the cause of freedom. When the British monarchy attempted to reign in this spirit for freedom, the colonists rebelled and, with God on their side, fought the good fight for freedom and won. This belief in the history of the United States is equivalent to a religious belief; a belief based on faith not fact. Indeed, if the American education system was originated to teach history and how to think, not what to think, the cultural myth of what America stands for would be quite different.

The tale of the patriots miraculously defeating the British is presented as the story of a rag-tag Army infused with the spirit of freedom defeating the mighty, better trained and better equipped

INDICTING AMERICA

British professional soldiers. It suggests that a higher power, perhaps God, was on the side of the patriots. How else can it be explained? The Continental Army was no match for the formidable British.

Left out of the tale is recognition that the American colonies were not as important to the British as were the colonies in the West Indies. Indeed, Barbados was a key money maker for the crown. The British were also spread thin as they were making aggressive entreaties in China, Egypt and India. Slave rebellions were pervasive in the West Indies.

"The 1760–1761 revolt in Jamaica," writes Vincent Brown in *Tacky's Revolt*, "was more exemplary than exceptional, because it represented the sum of their fears. Occurring three decades before the 1789–1804 Haitian Revolution destroyed Europe's most profitable colony in the Americas, neighboring French St. Domingue, this Jamaican conflict suspended life as colonists knew it, violating domestic order, halting business, and promising the end of their prestige. It threatened a remapping of colonial America as African territory where white rule would have no sway. The British devoted great energy and spent considerable sums to fortify their society against this prospect."[87]

The British were overwhelmed, compelling them to draft enslaved peoples for military duty in quelling rebellions. This alone terrified British subjects.

"The inadequacy of imperial defense necessitated the arming of unprecedented numbers of people of color and slaves," writes O'Shaughnessy in *An Empire Divided*, "another reason why white island colonists opposed the American War. The planters were unhappy about the necessity of recruiting people of color on such an unprecedented scale. They were more reluctant than other Europeans in the Caribbean to deploy black troops owing to the higher proportion of slaves in the British islands. The acute white manpower shortages necessitating the arming of blacks also posed a threat to the white minority, who lived in constant fear of a slave rebellion. Furthermore, the arming of blacks contradicted the alleged inferiority of subject peoples. It undermined the essential myth of European racial superiority, which justified imperialism and slavery."[88]

After defeating England, the rebels were faced with forming a government. Changes to the Articles of Confederation required unanimous approval. Washington and Madison knew the Articles of Confederation were ineffective for government. They decided to ignore requirements for alteration of the Articles and to simply start from scratch. Although the individual states had not and did not want to embrace each other, it became evident that debts incurred by the rebels must be repaid, because failing to do so would trash the credit worthiness of the new nation. Repaying debts, however, required joining together as one nation. Some embraced the idea of a United States (a singular noun), while others eschewed the notion and viewed States as a plural noun with a constrained view of "united." In contemporary discourse, the "United States" is represented by Blue States and the "united" States are represented by Red States.

Benjamin Franklin met with the Haudenosaunee, the six native nations of the Iroquois Confederacy, to understand how they were governed. To his surprise, Native Peoples formed the first democracy in North America about 600 years before Columbus arrived. Their model of government served as a template for the constitution. In 1988, the U.S. Congress recognized their contribution to the government formed by the invaders of their lands. [89]

"The only thing holding the American colonies together until 1776 was their membership in the British Empire," writes Ellis in *The Quartet: Orchestrating the Second American Revolution, 1783-1789*. "The only thing holding them together after 1776 was their common resolve to leave that empire. Once the war was won, that cord was cut, and the states began to float into their own at best regional orbits."[90]

Historian Mary S. Bilder tells us:

> In September 1783, the Revolutionary War officially ended with the signing of the Treaty of Paris. Congress and the states faced numerous challenges: for example, financial (significant domestic and foreign loans from the war); economic (disagreements over interstate and foreign trade); diplomatic (ongoing negotiations over commercial and other foreign relations and perceived lack of respect from European nations); and political (state legislative disregard of Congress). Although Congress needed revenue, the Articles provided no taxing power except the power to request funds from the states. In 1783, Congress recommended a revenue plan, including a proposal that apportioned the economic burden by population (with the enslaved population being incorporated at a calculation of three-fifths of the white population). The 1783 revenue plan met resistance, and an effort to amend the Articles failed.
>
> Bilder, Mary Sarah. (2015) **Madison's Hand: Revising the Constitutional Convention** (Kindle Locations 322-328). Harvard University Press. Kindle Edition.[91]

Shortly after the revolution and adoption of the Constitution, during the Jefferson administration, the insatiable thirst for Indian lands and for slaves for working lands that created wealth became clearly evident. Napoleon was strapped for cash and decided to sell Louisiana. The advocate of a weak central government and states' rights, Thomas Jefferson, jumped on the deal, abandoning his weak federal government advocacy. In the background the Industrial

REVOLUTION OR SECESSION?

Revolution was underway, England needed cotton and the lands of the Louisiana Purchase were ripe for producing white gold: cotton. Indians had to be removed and slaves were essential for the enterprise to reach fruition.

The Louisiana Purchase opened a pathway for obtaining enormous wealth and power. For Native Americans and African slaves, it was a sentence to hell.

The American Revolution was more Secession than revolution. Little changed. The British were gone, but from the beginning of the British colonial adventure, the British had little involvement with the North America colonies. When Britain attempted to assert authority, the colonists resisted and Britain acquiesced. Removing the British altogether equated to the truculence demonstrated by the Barbadians of South Carolina who turned against the Lords Proprietor who bankrolled the Barbadian invasion of South Carolina.

"The Revolution settlement," adds Griffin, "may have transformed the fortunes of wealthier white men. Elites ensured, however, that women and blacks saw no change in their servile status."

The slave economy of America proceeded ahead, just as it had before the fight with Britain. It was a Secession not a Revolution. The Constitution, written as an organizing document, included protection for Property, not human rights. It solidified slavery and the slave masters. The Declaration of Independence was a public relations spin document, merely a distraction. Just as the Barbadians declared Protestant Supremacy in freeing themselves from religious constraints placed against slavery, the colonial leaders declared themselves independent from British constraints against killing Indians, stealing their lands and exploiting those lands with enslaved labor.

They are charged with conspiracy to murder, sabotage government, and genocide.

INDICTING AMERICA

Industrial Revolution, Cotton, Capitalism and Road to Civil War

As fife and drums heralded birth of a new nation, dark clouds formed on the horizon. World events converged making the ground ripe for ever greater human suffering. The French-Indian war strained France's resources. The American Revolution helped trigger a revolution in French dominated Haiti. Financial pressures provoked the French Revolution for human rights, which later transformed into a blood bath, opening a path for Napoleon and his imperial adventures. More warfare created more financial stress for France, while Napoleon was itching to crush Toussaint Louverture in Haiti. At the same time, Americans salivated over western lands with its rich and deep fertile soil.

France claimed the land mass it labelled Louisiana Territory. The Doctrine of Discovery provided France with the dubious authority to make such a claim. Napoleon needed cash so, he made Jefferson an offer he couldn't refuse. Acting against his stated position opposed to an all-powerful President, Jefferson made the deal. What followed was Indian genocide, terror and torture for enslaved Africans.

The Louisiana Purchase was the opening act of the Civil War. America advertised itself as a country born in liberty and freedom; of course, there was this contradictory problem of slavery and Indian genocide. The advertisement was, indeed, a lie. And as tensions over slavery aligned for conflict, systemic assaults upon indigenous peoples intensified.

Perhaps a Civil War was inevitable from the start of the Constitutional Convention. Many patriots and aristocrats benefitting from the slave society, contrived marvelous mental gymnastics for rationalization and justification for slavery. The same was true for seizing of Indian lands and removing the inhabitants. Some would say the ideas of liberty and freedoms were aspirational; highlighting the goals of the country, as if that somehow negated the lie. Others would argue that America had "flaws" that were eventually rectified, even though they were much more significant than "flaws" and they were never, ever, ever, rectified.

During the fight over the Constitution, arguments highlighted discrepancies between the advertised product and it's "flaws." Southern plantation owners remained intransigent, threatening Civil War. A compromise unfolded preventing Congress from passing legislation altering the slave system until 1808. In return, it was tacitly understood that the goal was for ending slavery so, the advertised product would have some credibility.

At the time of the Constitution slaves were used for agricultural pursuits; production of tobacco, indigo and rice; and for mining enterprises. Virginia had the largest population of slaves. Over time tobacco depleted Virginia's soils forcing slave owners into pursuing other crops not requiring as many slaves. Consequently, there was an oversupply of slaves in Virginia. With a substantial base of enslaved people, Virginians, including Thomas Jefferson, did not oppose the 1808 prohibition against slave laws, because that could be used to end the international trade, thereby enhancing the domestic slave trade. Jefferson thought Virginia could harvest slaves for sale across the country. Virginia represented the center of slavery with over half the slaves in the country domiciled in Virginia, according to Bilder, based on the 1790 census.[92]

Then along came the Louisiana Purchase with England's Industrial Revolution looming in the backdrop. England needed raw materials, specifically cotton. Louisiana's soil, spread across a land mass much larger than the area defined as Louisiana today, was well suited for the crop. Yes, there were Indians on those lands, but George Washington had established multiple precedents in the Ohio River Valley for dealing with that issue.

At the beginning of the 18th century, commerce centered on agriculture, including trading of agriculturally based products and assorted tools for agricultural enterprises. Of course, gold, silver and natural resources, such as wood for generating heat were also traded. Mid-century, England discovered a new source for generating heat when it found an abundant source of coal off its shores.

Mechanical systems were devised for extracting coal, soon followed by steam for driving the mechanical systems. This marks the beginning of the Industrial Revolution. Steam driven mechanical systems, using coal as the source of heat, were applied for manufacturing textiles. Manchester emerged as the center for operating mechanical systems for mass production of textile products for trade across the globe. England had an extensive source of the raw material for driving mechanized systems, coal, but it needed other raw materials, most importantly cotton.

Meeting the demand for this commodity represented an opportunity for enormous wealth. England would take all it could get from suppliers and it would embark upon colonial adventures taking lands and enslaving people inhabiting those lands for extraction of needed natural resources. In addition, England would create an empire in which it would sell its finished products in the colonial lands.

Several events converged providing the infrastructure for King Cotton: England discovered coal off its shore, a source of heat more efficient than wood; England stumbled upon steam as a force for driving mechanical systems, such as a loom; Napolean offered Jefferson Louisiana with its high quality soil; Virginia had an oversupply of enslaved people who could be sold south; technology turned out steam boats and railroads opening up inland properties for production; and

British investors were attracted to mortgage backed securities, even those mortgages embodied by enslaved people who were deemed property.

The lands of the Louisiana Purchase—Mississippi, Alabama, Arkansas, Oklahoma and more—represented prime real estate for cotton planting and harvesting. Tampering with the enslaved infrastructure was anathema to the fortune making potential of the deep south. These lands promised enormous wealth. Slave Masters remained stalwart in demanding slaves. To be sure, forced labor was essential, because given a choice, few people would choose cotton picking for making a living. The environment was grueling. The Mississippi River Delta was a harsh environment and cotton picking was hard. Slavery provided a mechanism for forced labor. Virginia stood at the ready for meeting the need for slaves.

Americans, capitalizing upon this emerging cotton market, needed an enterprise for exploiting the enriched soil of the Mississippi River Delta. As the Industrial Revolution in England expanded, the cotton market boomed. There was a problem, however. Indians had to be removed and a source for supplying slaves had to be available.

During the interim period between the end of the fight with England and construction of a Constitution, under the Articles of Confederation, Congress passed the Northwest Ordinance of 1787. Once again, the Native peoples were made invisible. Arrogant invaders provided a plan for distributing the lands claimed by the native people. This plan would respect the Indians, Griffin tells us, "The utmost good faith," the ordinance read, "shall always be observed towards the Indians, their lands and property shall never be taken from them without their consent." [93]

The act went on to declare, "In their property, rights and liberty, they shall never be invaded or disturbed." The ordinance's goal was to settle the region while maintaining "peace and friendship" with the Indians." The lands were then occupied by revolutionary soldiers and other would-be Indian killers.

At the same time, just as the steam and mechanical systems impacted England, the same technology opened a path for the railroad revolution. Railroads meant that lands far away from the coast could now be exploited. Major cities developed along the coast where goods were traded and shipped. Time was of the essence. If it took too long to extract resources from the land and ship it to the coast for market, that land had limited value. When the railroad arrived, movement of goods sped-up dramatically, transforming inland resources into highly profitable enterprises.

The plan for ending slavery would have to wait, because the convergence of rich fertile soil; England's demand for cotton; new transport services such as steam driven boats and railroads; along with Virginia as a source of slaves; represented a path for wealth and power that was just too irresistible, no matter how inhuman, how immoral and how depraved America would become in the process. Indeed, it was a deal with the devil that cast a dark cloud over the country tarnishing the nation's soul to this very day. The Cotton Plantation South represents a mutation of the slave virus, a mutation producing the darkest hour of slavery.

> The next day it rains hard in the morning, but when it stops the men bring the mules and the plows out. The spongy earth oozes into the plow points. "Fuck this mud," the men mutter.
>
> Fuck. From an Old English word meaning: to strike, to beat. Before that, in an even older language: to plow. To tear open.
>
> The seeds are waiting.
>
> In the sack in the shed. Or maybe safe under the entrepreneur's high bed. The bed where he fucks his wife. Bed brought by wagon from the landing, bed bought with last year's crop.

REVOLUTION OR SECESSION?

Maybe he didn't bring his wife. Maybe the sack is under the bed where he fucks the sixteen-year-old light-skinned girl from Maryland, also bought with last year's crop. Maybe she is the same girl who washes the bloodstains from the sheets in the morning. Who carries the chamber pot to the woods. Who turns it over, brings it back empty, sets it by his side of the bed. Bumps her toe on the bulging sack, full of tiny seeds.
Baptist, Edward E. (2014) **The Half Has Never Been Told: Slavery and the Making of American Capitalism** (Kindle Locations 4617-4624). Basic Books. Kindle Edition.[94]

The Louisiana Purchase contributed significantly to the Civil War, opening new lands for settlement. This represented a threat to the fragile power sharing arrangements between slave holders and northern colonists. If new lands were provided political power, would the balance of power be altered? Compromises accommodating the south during the Constitutional Convention could be overturned, if new lands became available for income producing enterprises, that also resulted in shifting political power. Slave Masters, weened by the Barbadians in South Carolina, demanded political power.

Thomas Jefferson, the man who staked out every position on an issue, inserted a clause in the legislation authorizing the purchase, opening the door for slavery onto the new lands.

"When in 1803 Jefferson acquired Louisiana for the United States and doubled the size of the country," says Wiencek in *Master of the Mountain*, "the question arose: Would we have slavery in this new land? As the Senate began debate on the purchase, President Jefferson sent a secret note to his floor manager, instructing the senator to insert a clause in the bill for establishing a government in Louisiana: "Slaves shall be admitted into the territory."[95]

INDICTING AMERICA

Congressional initiatives for constraining slavery were not supported by Jefferson. In his younger days, Jefferson did support banning slavery in new territories. According to Wiencek, Jefferson authored the Ordinance of 1784, banning slavery in any new territory of the United States: "After the year 1800…there shall be neither slavery nor involuntary servitude." That legislation failed narrowly.

Wiencek says "After the 1784 limitation on slavery failed to pass, as the historian Joyce Appleby has written, Jefferson "backed away from attacking the institution as his power to do something about it increased."16" Ever the chameleon, Jefferson changed colors as the Louisiana Purchase opened new avenues for wealth.[96]

The 3/5's of a person designation for establishing political representation and its consequent power, served the south well providing it with an almost dominant political position. The perceived threat to power represented by territorial expansion was appeased with the Missouri Compromise of 1820, but as America continued its expansion west, the tension for power intensified. Note use of the phrase "expansion west." Blended with "frontier" and "pioneer," it conjures an image of virgin territory, explored for the first time by brave and honorable people seeking opportunity for a better life. The problem is that indigenous peoples, the migrants from Siberia occupying lands now called the frontier, were in the way and needed removal.

"Like King Solomon," says James McPherson in *Battle Cry of Freedom: The Civil War Era* "Congress had tried in 1820 to solve that problem for the Louisiana Purchase by splitting it at the latitude of 36 ° 30′ (with slavery allowed in Missouri as an exception north of that line). But this only postponed the crisis. In 1850 Congress postponed it again with another compromise. By 1860 it could no longer be deferred. The country's territorial growth might have created a danger of dismemberment by centrifugal force in any event. But slavery brought this danger to a head at midcentury."

"At the time of the Louisiana Purchase in 1803 the United States was an insignificant nation on the European periphery," McPherson adds, "Its population was about the same as Ireland's. Thomas Jefferson thought that the empire for liberty he had bought from Napoleon was sufficient," to absorb a hundred generations of America's population growth. By 1850, two generations later, Americans were not only filling up this empire but were spilling over into a new one on the Pacific coast."[97]

In a sense, then, the House and Senate faced a reenactment of 1787, says David Brion Davis in *Inhuman Bondage: The Rise and Fall of Slavery in the New World*, "a ritual underscored by the prominence in the congressional debates of two of the Constitutional Convention's surviving antagonists: Representative Charles Pinckney of South Carolina, who openly defended slavery and now insisted that Congress had no power to exclude slaves, a form of legitimate property, from even the unsettled territories; and Senator Rufus King of New York, the alleged leader of the Federalist conspiracy, who "astonished" James Madison and many other Southern leaders when he announced in 1820 that any laws or compacts upholding slavery were "absolutely void, because [they are] contrary to the law of nature, which is the law of God, by which he makes his way known to man and is paramount to all human control."

Threats of Civil War, just as were threatened in the making of the constitution, surfaced once again, as Davis adds. "Sir, if a dissolution of the Union must take place, let it be so! If civil war, which [Southern] gentlemen so much threaten, must come, I can only say, let it come! ... If blood is necessary to extinguish any fire which I have assisted to kindle, I can assure gentlemen, while I regret the necessity, I shall not forebear to contribute my mite.... If I am doomed to fall, I shall at least have the painful consolation to believe that I fall, as a fragment, in the ruins of my country. ...Henry Clay, the Speaker of the House of Representatives, spoke at one point of returning to Kentucky and enlisting troops. He also told John Quincy Adams that he was certain that within five years the Union would divide into three distinct confederacies."[98]

In spring of 1846, tensions for Civil War heightened as the United States defeated Mexico in America's war of aggression against Mexico, the Mexican War. America's land portfolio expanded considerably to the west, once again threatening the balance of power between free and slave states.

The Compromise of 1850 quieted the drumbeat for war, at least for the moment, but the mutually exclusive notions of a free democratic society and a slave-based society were destined for warfare.

"By the eve of the Civil War," says Foner, "the slave population in the United States had reached nearly four million. The economic value of these men, women, and children when considered as property exceeded the combined worth of all the banks, railroads, and factories in the United States. In geographical extent, population, and the institution's economic importance, the South was home to the most powerful slave system the modern world has known."[99]

The Triangle Trade of the 17th and 18th century matured in the Industrial Revolution. This system of banking, finance, insurance, logistics, law and marketing of finished products established a firm footing by the time of the Louisiana Purchase. It converged with England's need for raw materials, fertile soil conducive for cotton, and slave labor. This system gave birth to American Capitalism. In 2008, Americans became cognizant of Mortgage-Backed Securities when the mortgages backing the securities went into default, crashing financial markets across the globe. In the nineteenth century, however,

REVOLUTION OR SECESSION?

Mortgage-Backed Securities played an important role in the transfer of wealth from London to America in funding the cotton slavocracy.

"The first mortgages," Heather McGhee writes in *The Sum of Us*, "and collateralized debt instruments in the United States weren't on houses, but on enslaved people, including the debt instruments that led to the speculative bubble in the slave trade of the 1820s. And the biggest bankruptcy in American history, in 2008, was the final chapter of a story that began in 1845 with the brothers Lehman, slave owners who opened a store to supply slave plantations near Montgomery, Alabama."[100]

America has touted itself as a melting pot, where a diversified population blended together into a nation of virtues and values respecting human rights and responsible for neighbors. It claimed it was not an imperial power; it was a democracy where common people held power and no one was above the law.

But that stands in contrast to a country built on squatters taking lands occupied by other people, resulting in conflict and warfare. Slavery was and remains an obvious contradiction to support of human rights and support for neighbors. It was rationalized by stating the enslaved peoples were not really people. They were an inferior living organism who needed the help and guidance of intelligent and capable white people. Harsh treatment of slaves was defined as helping them survive the vicissitudes of existence. Indians were labelled savages who needed civilization and saving by God.

The so-called melting pot contained rouge adventurers seeking fame and fortune at any cost; disillusioned and angry displaced Common Land farmers evacuated from their homes and way of life; criminals who perpetrated crimes for survival or borrowed money they could not repay; enslaved people—white and black—captured and imprisoned within a system ruled by brutality and domination

INDICTING AMERICA

of others; and slave masters unrestrained by any sense of compassion or morality. It was a volatile mix, sure to explode at some point.

Then came cotton. This represented untold fortunes. This required a coerced forced labor, trading markets; and slave labor. Over a 40-year-period, exports to Britain expanded from $187,000,000 1811-1820, of which cotton accounted for 157,000,000, to $1,188,000,000. This billion-dollar increase, about 25,000,000 per year or 16% increase each year. Cotton increased from $157,000,000 to $1,235,000,000

The tables below highlight the growth markets attracting investments in mortgage-backed securities. The system designed for making the wealthy wealthier was working. Enslaving human beings and killing people to take control of resource rich land simply were not important. As Milton Friedman put it, the only thing that matters is stockholder wealth.

Consider the impact of cotton on U.S. exports:

Top Exports, 1811-1820	
Value by Country of Destination	
Great Britain	**$187,000,000**
Other European countries	$138,000,000
France	$64,000,000
Germany	$19,000,000
Turkey	$2,240,000
All Other Countries	$183,000,000
Value of Exported Commodities	
Unmanufactured Cotton	**$157,000,000**
Leaf Tobacco	$60,000,000
Wheat & Wheat Flour	$5,000,000
Other Wood Manufactures	$4,000,000

Top Exports, 1821-1830

Value by Country of Destination	
Great Britain	$240,000,000
South & Central America	$117,000,000
France	$93,000,000
Other European countries	$83,000,000
Cuba	$51,000,000
China	$36,000,000
Mexico	$26,000,000
Germany	$26,000,000
Canada	$22,000,000
Brazil	$17,000,000
Value of Exported Commodities	
Cotton	$262,440,000
Wheat & Wheat Flour	$126,300,000
Leaf Tobacco	$57,790,000
Manufactures	$46,900,000
Rice	$20,080,000
Lumber	$16,650,000
Pork, Lard, etc.	$15,080,000
Fish	$9,810,000
Beef, Hides, etc.	$7,540,000
Skins & Furs	$5,950,000

Top Exports, 1851-1860

Value by Country of Destination	
Great Britain	**$1,188,000,000**
France	$280,000,000
Other European countries	$244,000,000
Canada	$214,000,000

INDICTING AMERICA

Top Exports, 1851-1860	
Value by Country of Destination	
South & Central America	$193,000,000
Germany	$107,000,000
Cuba	$84,000,000
Africa (total)	$61,000,000
Brazil	$45,000,000
China	$41,000,000
Value of Exported Commodities	
Unmanufactured Cotton	**$1,235,000,000**
Leaf Tobacco	$141,000,000
Wheat & Wheat Flour	$101,000,000
Meat Products	$30,000,000
Other Wood Manufactures	$20,000,000
Cotton Manufactures	$17,000,000
Naval Stores, Gums, & Resins	$7,000,000
Copper & Copper Manufactures	$3,000,000
Carriages & Parts	$1,000,000

An Illustrated Business History of the United States Hardcover – Download: Adobe Reader, May 21, 2021 by Richard Vague (2021) University of Pennsylvania Press[101]

"When banks create credit by lending out more money than they take in, a small store of value— deposits— gets multiplied into more" explains Baptist. "Through this miracle of leverage, wrote H. B. Trist in 1825, the newly established Bank of Louisiana had "thrown a great deal of money into circulation" by issuing $ 4 million in notes. The bank lent these notes to borrowers, who then made new investments, buying land, supplies, and slaves. "The price of negroes has risen considerably," Trist noted. Borrowers were making calculations much like those of planter-entrepreneur Alonzo Walsh. In 1823, a Louisiana merchant offered him a five-year loan of $ 48,000 at 10 percent annual interest. For collateral, he'd mortgage what he called "from 90 to a 100 [sic] head of first-rate slaves," although some of those slaves would be bought with the money he'd borrow."[102]

"Thus, in effect," he adds, "even as Britain was liberating the slaves of its empire, a British bank could now sell an investor a completely commodified slave: not a particular individual who could die or run away, but a bond that was the right to a one-slave-sized slice of a pie made from the income of thousands of slaves."[103]

This became the system. Banks take in deposits and then lend those funds to entrepreneurs, such as slave masters, in the form of mortgages. After the Great Depression of 1929, banks could not lend out all of their money; they were required to establish and keep reserves, just in case the people they lent money defaulted. Slave masters used the borrowed funds to obtain land and enslaved people in service of churning out cotton. Income from cotton sales was used in meeting mortgages payments.

Banks packaged the mortgages into securities, bonds that investors purchased as investments with a stated return. Packaging these mortgages diffused risk across all of the mortgages. If the cotton market remained strong, the system worked, resulting in handsome profits for the slave master and healthy returns on investment for investors. This explains the financial side of cotton-slave enterprises.

Production required stolen Indian lands and enslaved people forced into labor, hard labor, in the grueling heat of the cotton plantation south. This was the dirty, unholy and immoral side of the enterprise. Finance came away with unsullied hands. Production did not.

The System

The system—the financial system—operates the same way today, by and large. It provides capital for enterprises providing a healthy return on investment. Production may include "free labor slavery," employed people needing a job for survival even if it is a dangerous and miserable job. Production may also involve brutalization of foreign lands in taking resources and pollution of the environment making the planet unlivable. Finance comes away with unsullied hands, while production makes a handsome profit with filthy hands.

Government exists in facilitating this system, albeit using government funded troops for stealing Indian lands or invading foreign lands for stealing resources, or by setting the rules for slavery or free labor slavery. If slavery is upended by a Civil War, simply replace it with Jim Crow slavery by way of government action.

The system, as many learned in 2008, must be protected. And if the enterprises fail, government exists to save the system by spreading the costs across the entire population. Today it is called "free market capitalism." This is not a condemnation of capitalism. How it is allowed to operate by government determines the outcome for society.

America is charged with buying land, Louisiana Purchase, from France, knowing that France had no authority to sell it; it wasn't their land, they were invaders.

Indian Removal/Genocide

WITH VIRGINIA POISED FOR SELLING enslaved people into the deep south and the "Georgia Men" ready to herd them south to New Orleans for sale, the new country—the United States of America—confronted removal of the last obstacle to wealth and power: indigenous people.

While America remained deeply conflicted over slavery, Andrew Jackson, before his presidency, focused on indigenous peoples, killing Alabama's Red Sticks, a subgroup of the Creek Nation, under the umbrella of the War of 1812. Jackson's ascendency to the Presidency represented a clear danger to native peoples and Jackson was not ashamed of it in any way.

Jackson represented something more than an Indian killer. He made salient a key flaw in the American government in that anyone could run for elected office, anyone. Those writing the constitution, led by Gouverneur Morris, set age and citizenship requirements for office, but failed in conforming to Montesquieu's concepts of three branches of government insulated from corruption and dedicated to the Common Good. Instead, anyone could run for office. In 2016 America would feel the full impact of this flaw when the morally and legally corrupted Donald Trump ascended to the Presidency.

INDICTING AMERICA

"Jackson's personal attributes actually disqualified," says Daniel Howe in *What Hath God Wrought*, "rather than qualified, him for the presidency. He possessed a notoriously fiery temper and had repeatedly displayed vindictive anger. Adams partisans reminded the public that Jackson had been involved in several brawls and duels, killing a man in one of them. The "coffin handbill" distributed by Philadelphia newspaperman John Binns called sympathetic attention to the six militiamen executed by Jackson's orders in February 1815." [104]

"As early as 1830," writes Benjamin Madley in his widely acclaimed *An American Genocide: The United States and the California Indian Catastrophe, 1846-1873*, "President Andrew Jackson told the US Congress, in his annual message, that although "humanity has often wept over the fate of the aborigines of this country . . . its progress has never for a moment been arrested, and one by one have many powerful tribes disappeared from the earth." Jackson, unrestrained by respect for human life other than his own, viewed extinctions as a natural occurrence, where one generation simply makes room for the next. [105]

The narrative in justifying theft of Indian lands, as contrived by Jackson, suggested that God created land for human use, but Indians were not using the land properly, therefore, whites were in the right when seizing native lands. The argument is predicated upon the notion that Indians were uncivilized savages, merely using the land for hunting and gathering. The modern world, it was further argued, required application of agricultural operations for meeting food demands; failing to do so results in a shortfall of food for an ever-expanding population. This argument, however, refuses recognition of indigenous peoples exhibiting a high degree of sophistication in managing natural resources.

"Ultimately, this denial that the Indians actually cultivated the land became the white Americans' justification for taking it from them," according to Gordon Wood in *Empire of Liberty: A History of the Early Republic, 1789-1815*. "Drawing from the legal thinking of the sixteenth-century theorist Emmerich de Vattel, political leaders maintained that no people had a right to land that they did not farm. This was one of the most important of the cultural misunderstandings that divided white Americans from the native peoples. Whites expected Indians to become farmers, that is, to move to another stage in the process of social development and become civilized, or to get out of the way of the white settlers."[106]

The cotton enterprise demanded more lands and that meant indigenous peoples had to go, but how best to do it? Squatters took their approach by simply moving onto Native lands and setting up a homestead. Government annexation in exchange for some compensation was another approach, including treaties with the Natives solidifying the deal. Some made deals with tribes that did not have dominion over the lands traded, while others sold off lands without any agreement with the tribes.

Corrupted Georgia legislators packaged and sold Creek occupied lands to investors. The Yahoo land fraud was a complicated affair in which legislators passed law authorizing the land sale even though control of the land was disputed. It conflicted with treaties made with the Natives, but the contracts for sale of the land were deemed legal by the U.S. Supreme Court. Georgia ceded its claims to lands in Alabama and Mississippi, while the new federal government was left with negotiating compensation for the disputed lands.

"Secretary of War Calhoun," Howe tells us, "had been responsible for Indian policy. He had encouraged gradual resettlement of the southern tribes across the Mississippi, while simultaneously promoting the assimilation of some of their members into white society. This dual policy failed to satisfy white settlers eager to seize the Natives'

INDICTING AMERICA

lands; in particular, it led to a conflict between Calhoun and Governor George M. Troup of Georgia. Back in 1802, Georgia had relinquished her claim to what is now Alabama and Mississippi in return for a promise by the Jefferson administration that the federal government would seek voluntary removal of the Indian tribes remaining within her boundaries."[107]

"In the treaty the Creeks ceded two-thirds of the land claimed by Georgia," according to Wood, "but received in return a federal guarantee of sovereign control of the rest. ...Washington backed up the treaty with a proclamation forbidding any encroachment on the Creeks' territory. ...But a corrupt Georgia legislature undid both the president's proclamation and the Treaty of New York. As early as January 1790, six months before the treaty was signed, it had announced the sale to speculators, calling themselves the Yazoo companies, of over fifteen million acres of land belonging to the Creeks. Before the bribed Georgia legislators were done doling out many more millions of acres, which included most of present-day Alabama and Mississippi, they had created the greatest real estate scandal in American history. The consequences of this outrageous land deal reverberated through the next three presidential administrations."[108]

"In the hinterland east of the Mississippi (and west of the Carolinas)," according to Taylor, "the natives remained numerous and powerful. During the seventeenth century, they formed five loose confederations for protection: from east to west, the Catawba, Cherokee, Creek, Chickasaw, and Choctaw. In 1730 about two thousand Catawba lived in the South and North Carolina Piedmont."

"To their northwest, the twelve thousand Cherokee dwelled in the southern Appalachian Mountains. A like number of Creek inhabited the fertile river valleys of what is now western Georgia and eastern Alabama. The twelve thousand Choctaw occupied the hilly pinewoods

152

INDIAN REMOVAL/GENOCIDE

country of east-central Mississippi, while their close kin but bitter enemies the three thousand Chickasaw dwelled to their north," according to Taylor.[109]

Andrew Jackson was determined in pushing the Native peoples out of the way. In a message, in March of 1829, to Creek chiefs and their allies, Jackson, who referred to himself as "your father," said white people and Indian people were living too close together, resulting in endless conflict. He noted that the Natives refused to adapt to white society. So, he proposed an alternative for the Indians to be removed to new lands without white encroachment.

Jackson succeeded in passing the Indian Removal Act of 1830, authorizing land and money for uprooting Native peoples from lands they occupied for thousands of years.

Marc Wortman in *The Bonfire: The Siege and Burning of Atlanta*, says "In the winter of 1834, a first group of 634 Creek Indians departed voluntarily for the West. The exodus proved a disaster when private contractors, paid out of Indian reparation funds, failed to deliver on the government's promised aid. Unprepared for the cold they encountered along the trail and lacking food, scores of Indians froze to death. Many more perished from starvation and sickness. By the time the wanderers reached Oklahoma, 161 had died."[110]

"Few government-guaranteed resources for food or shelter" said Wortman, "ever materialized for those who reached the Indian Territory. In 1832, 21,792 Creeks had lived in Georgia and Alabama. Twenty years after the Second Creek War and the natives' removal beyond the Mississippi River, the tribe had not recovered from the devastation. Just 13,573 Creeks remained alive in Oklahoma—though back east, a few Creeks had disappeared among the Seminoles to fight on in the Florida swamps, while whites enslaved others captured during the fighting."[111]

INDICTING AMERICA

Indian wars continued during the Civil War, growing darker and more ominous with each battle.

"Overall, not surprisingly, Lincoln devoted little attention to Indian policy during his presidency," says Foner. "He allowed army commanders free rein when it came to campaigns against Indians in the West, with the predictable result that the Civil War witnessed events like the 1864 Sand Creek Massacre in Colorado, where soldiers under the command of Colonel John Chivington attacked a village of Cheyenne and Arapaho Indians, killing perhaps 400 men, women, and children."[112]

"The Civil War brought devastation to Native America," says Manisha Sinha in *The Rise and Fall of the Second American Republic: Reconstruction, 1860-1920*. "Even as army regulars stationed in the West were summoned east, volunteers under generals such as James Carleton continued to wage war on the Indian frontier. The gruesome Sand Creek Massacre in Colorado Territory in 1864 saw volunteers of the Third Colorado Cavalry murder nearly four hundred Arapaho and Cheyenne, mainly women and children."

Commanding Officer Colonel John Chivington ordered the massacre. "The report of the Congressional Joint Committee on the Conduct of the War, written by radical Benjamin F. Wade, strongly condemned Chivington's actions and the victims were given forty thousand dollars," according to Sinha. "Congress passed a joint resolution suspending all pay and allowances to Chivington's regiment. Charles Sumner called it an 'exceptional crime,' the 'most atrocious in the history of any country.' Despite congressional inquiries, Chivington went mostly unpunished." [113]

Although Lincoln was preoccupied with the Civil War, he still found time to set the table for expropriation of Indian lands. "Congress, at Lincoln's behest, passed the Homestead Act in 1862, as well as the Morrill Act, the latter transferring large tracts of Indigenous land to the states to establish land grant universities," says Roxanne Dunbar-Ortiz in Not *"A Nation of Immigrants."* "The Pacific Railroad Act provided private companies with nearly two hundred million acres of Indigenous land. With these massive land grabs, the US government broke multiple treaties with Indigenous nations whose people were still living there. It would take genocidal military force to evict them. Most of the western territories, including Colorado, North and South Dakota, Montana, Washington, Idaho, Wyoming, Utah, New México, and Arizona, were delayed in achieving statehood, because Indigenous nations resisted appropriation of their lands and outnumbered the settlers—until they didn't. So, the colonization plan for the West established during the Civil War was carried out over the following three decades of war and land grabs."[114]

California Gold Rush

Meanwhile in the west, gold was found near San Francisco in the new state of California, on land taken from Mexico. The result was genocide. "Between 1846 and 1873," says Madley, "perhaps 80 percent of all California Indians died, and many massacres left no survivors or only small children. Mass death silenced thousands of California Indian voices, but so did California laws and judges: mid-nineteenth-century California courts usually barred and rarely recorded Indian testimony against whites. Outside the legal system, few nineteenth-century writers recorded California Indians' words either."[115]

Greed induced violence, an orgy of blood in service of wealth, exposes the soul of the perpetrators and of the political, social and cultural infrastructure that gave birth to the killers. White skinned

Americans, presuming themselves as special children of God; raised within a landscape of fear and hatred; driven by thirst for fame and fortune; embarked upon a rampage, rationalized and justified by political and religious leaders; perpetrating genocide with a determination for exterminating Native peoples.

Today, America remains incapable of accepting its shame and forthrightly confronting its past. The contemporary refrain "I didn't do it; I wasn't even born then" represents a pathetic response indicative of America's intransigence and truculence. Redemption is not possible without honesty.

Hundreds of thousands of people flooded into northern California in search of gold in the mid-19th century. They followed a path made clear by the Spanish who invaded the continent eager to find gold. The Mexican War opened a new pathway for white people to infiltrate the west and to bring with them a pervasive hatred for native peoples. The assault upon the Indians was supported by state and federal officials who provided funding, laws and logistical support.

Just as Fox News today fans the flames of contempt and disdain, local newspapers played the same role in California. "On December 15, 1850," says Madley, "the Daily Alta California joined the chorus of doom, describing California Indians' destruction as unavoidable, suggesting that they would evaporate "like a dissipating mist before the morning sun, from the presence of the Saxon."[116]

The Natives gunned down in California didn't distract Lincoln as he remained focused on the rebels, paying scant attention to the assault waged against the Natives. Recent studies contend the attacks upon the indigenous peoples meet the standards set forth by international committees for defining genocide. Only in the 21st Century would it receive attention.

Madley writes: "On January 7, 1851— just weeks before special commissioners Barbour, McKee, and Wozencraft began their

INDIAN REMOVAL/GENOCIDE

California treaty-making campaign— Governor Burnett transformed passive acquiescence into active acceleration by inaugurating a new, state-sponsored phase in the destruction of California Indians. During his "Annual Message to the Legislature," delivered two days before he resigned, Burnett prophesied that "a war of extermination will continue to be waged between the races, until the Indian race becomes extinct."[117]

Establishing a predicate for assaulting Indians became something of an art. The so-called Americans provoked Indian attacks warranting a counter-attack, providing justification massacres aimed at eliminating the indigenous peoples.

Charles Drayton Gibbes, son of S.C. Plantation owner William Gibbes, namesake of the Gibbs Museum in Charleston, S.C., suggested an anti-Indian war was brewing in California. According to Madley, "Gibbes's pro-war advocacy and implicit preemptive treaty rejection provide a window into the thinking of war supporters. Gibbes argued that the success of California's mining-based economy depended on subduing its indigenous peoples. Invoking paternalism, naked self-interest, and historical precedent, he concluded, "It is no use to talk about the poor Indians; it has to be done, and has been ever the case since America was first settled, and the sooner done the better for them, and us, too." [118]

And so, war it would be. Superior weaponry inevitably resulted in massive Indian death, with few white people casualties. Washington, D.C. aided and abetted the assault. Arkansas senator William Sebastian told the US Senate, Madley says: "The Superintendent has received information of a character beyond all dispute, that fifteen thousand [California Indians] have perished from absolute starvation during the last season." This was, in large part, due to the Senate's rejection of treaties and state-supported violence that forced California Indians into food-poor areas, and, even in those areas, to continue moving frequently to avoid attacks. In sum, these policies may be considered as "deliberately inflicting on the group conditions of life calculated to bring about its physical destruction in whole or in part."[119]

According to Madley one newspaper argued "What are the lives of a hundred of these savages to the life of a single American citizen?" After all, "Their total annihilation is certain, and it is now but a question of time— whether that event shall not be hastened by a war of extermination waged by the whites."[120]

The U.S. Army was dispatched in the 1870s to move the Modocs off lands desired by the minors. They were to be moved onto lands of the Klamath, which were not inviting.

"God put our fathers and mothers here," said one Modoc according to Madley, "We have lived here in peace [but] we cannot get along with the white people. They come along and kill my people for nothing. Not only my men, but they kill our wives and children." He added, "They will hunt us like we hunt the deer and antelope."[121]

News reports fed the frenzy. Says Madley: "On August 7, the Yreka Mountain Herald called for the state-sponsored total annihilation of all Northern California Indians: "Now that general Indian hostilities have commenced, we hope that the Government will render such aid as will enable the citizens of the North to carry on a war of extermination until the last red skin of these tribes has been killed. Then, and not until then, is our lives and property safe." The editorial continued: "Extermination is no longer even a question of time— the time has already arrived, the work has been commenced, and let the first white man who says treaty or peace be regarded as a traitor and coward." [122]

The extermination-geocide was recognized by the state of California in 2019. The Tolawa had a population estimated at about 1000 people in 1870. It plummeted to 150 due to the mass murder by white militias.

INDIAN REMOVAL/GENOCIDE

A small village, Yontocket, was surrounded by white militia in 1853. At sunrise, the armed militia opened fire against the Tolowa armed with bow and arrow. Madley says "Yontocket may rank among the most lethal of all massacres in US history. Yet, it remains unknown except to a few scholars, locals, and, of course, the Tolowa."[123]

The same happened to the Yuki people. Once again, militia attacked. "Beginning in 1854, however, this bountiful sanctuary became a place of horror, in part because Yuki people did not have firearms. For them, Round Valley became a death trap."

The area of Crescent City was a blood bath of Indian massacres. "In the predawn hours of December 31, 1854, as many as 116 militiamen, accompanied by an unknown number of Smith River Valley whites, quietly surrounded Etchulet and took up concealed positions in the brush. At daybreak, as men, women, and children emerged from their houses to begin the day, the militiamen and vigilantes opened fire. They shot them down as fast as they could reload." Says Madley.[124]

The Yreka Herald," says Madley, "agreed with the Crescent City Herald that this was a "war of extermination," what we would today call genocide. A new era of increasingly lethal state-sponsored Indian killing had begun as the US government, state legislators, militiamen, and vigilantes perfected the killing machine."

As America moved west in search of gold and riches, escalating the genocide perpetrated against indigenous peoples, technology emerged that would again transform the political, social and commercial landscape. Although serving only one term, John Quincy Adams embraced infrastructure development that facilitated rapid industrial and commercial development. Technologies given birth during the Adams administration continue reverberating today. Consider computer technology as an extension of Morse Code.

INDICTING AMERICA

Transportation Revolutions

Harnessing of steam for generating power unleashed a wide range of technological development and equipment applications in 19th Century America. Railroads and steamboats developed so people could move across the country in a fraction of the time that it took them by horse and buggy.

The Industrial Revolution changed the trajectory of the Human Experience, once again. Not only had humans found a means for controlling access to food sources, now they were on the cusp of having machines do work for them. Infrastructure surged as a key for government action. The Army Corps of Engineers developed plans for roads, bridges, canals and more in facilitating a landscape suitable for industry.

McPherson says "Private companies, states, even the national government financed the construction of all-weather macadamized roads. More important, New York state pioneered the canal era by building the Erie Canal from Albany to Buffalo, linking New York City to the Northwest by water and setting off a frenzy of construction that produced 3,700 miles of canals by 1850."[125]

"During those same years, steamboats made Robert Fulton's dream come true by churning their way along every navigable river from Bangor to St. Joseph. The romance and economic importance of steamboats were eclipsed in both respects by the iron horse in the 1850s. The 9,000 miles of rail in the United States by 1850 led the world, but paled in comparison with the 21,000 additional miles laid during the next decade, which gave to the United States in 1860 a larger rail network than in the rest of the world combined."

"Adams celebrated the benefits," says Howe, "of improved transportation and communication and undertook to marshal the resources of the federal government to further them. The time had come to implement the projects planned by the General Survey enacted under Monroe, and the Army Corps of Engineers should be expanded to aid in the process. One of the president's favorite Scottish philosophers, Adam Smith, had declared that where private enterprise needed help, government should supply economic infrastructure and public education; this would be especially important in the early stages of economic development. Adams agreed."[126]

Transportation meant that inland lands could be developed and products shipped from inland cities to ports for shipping overseas. Urban centers within the interior of the continent emerged, just as shipping ports had in cities developed along the coast. A direct product of the railroad was a location in central north Georgia; a location first called Terminus, in 1837. Milepost Zero marks the spot in modern day Atlanta representing the starting point for rail service into inner lands of the continent. Terminus was later renamed Atlanta to symbolize the city's reaching to the Atlantic. This technology heralded emergence of an entirely new form of commerce.

By the outbreak of the Civil War, the modern American economy was taking shape. Mass production unleashed a consumer revolution leading to mass consumption, new more efficient means of agriculture was emerging requiring infusions of capital. [127]

Everything was changing, something like the impact of Artificial Intelligence in contemporary times. McPherson: "And even when more complex machine tools replaced some artisans, they expanded other categories of highly skilled workers— machinists, tool-and-die makers, millwrights, civil and mechanical engineers— whose numbers doubled during the 1850s. The transportation and communications revolutions created whole new occupations, some of them skilled and well paid— steamboat pilots, railroad men, telegraphers."[128]

Communications and Morse Code

Just as high-speed transportation altered the landscape, so too did the development of long-range communications. Morse code and the telegraph ushered in an industry that would forever change human existence. Messages, instantly transmitted along wires, revolutionized communications.

McPherson: "…the telegraph vastly increased the influence of newspapers, the country's principal medium of communication. The price of a single issue dropped from six cents in 1830 to one or two cents by 1850. Circulation increased twice as fast as population. The "latest news" became hours rather than days old. Fast trains carried weekly editions of metropolitan newspapers (like Horace Greeley's New York Tribune) to farmers a thousand miles away, where they shaped political sentiments. In 1848 several major newspapers pooled resources to form the Associated Press for the handling of telegraphic dispatches. [129]

The communications revolution also altered politics and political debate. "More than any other discussion," says Howe, "the debate over the future of human slavery in an empire dedicated to liberty threatened to tear the country apart. The communications revolution gave a new urgency to social criticism and to the slavery controversy in particular. No longer could slaveholders afford to shrug off the commentary of outsiders."[130]

Market Economy

Advances in transportation and communications provided the basic infrastructure for a truly global economy and marketplace. Instant communications and speedy transportation of products, expanded the marketplace. In the past, goods traded in the local market, but now goods traded internationally and were shipped using modern steam technology faster than what was previously imaginable.

Jockeying for political power in service of protection of slavery compelled southern slave masters to secede from the union. This, however, worked against the grain of the opportunities made possible by an expanded marketplace.

Although segregating itself from the non-slave states was compelling for the slave states, there were still many benefits of remaining a part of a central core. A central government was essential for implementing the infrastructure for these advances in technology, thereby creating a dilemma for those wishing for autonomy, while also desiring the economic benefits that could come from technology. The market economy demanded that products be transported and traded quickly and efficiently. Advances in transportation and communication required businesses in a competitive marketplace to embrace change or be run over by others. Simply creating an infrastructure for telecommunications required a strong central government with a capacity for implementing a network strategy.

While technology altered the landscape, most Americans were involved in agriculture, often at the level of family farmers. Finding contentment in working the land and remaining independent had an appeal, but it was out of synchronization with the technology revolutionizing commerce. The choice was to embrace technology and change or remain anchored in the past and be swept away by technology that could massively outproduce.

"The philosopher of republicanism, Thomas Jefferson," says McPherson, "had defined the essence of liberty as independence, which required the ownership of productive property. A man dependent on others for a living could never be truly free, nor could a dependent class constitute the basis of a republican government. Women, children, and slaves were dependent; that defined them out of the polity of republican freemen."

"Wage laborers were also dependent; that was why Jefferson feared the development of industrial capitalism with its need for wage laborers. Jefferson envisaged an ideal America of farmers and artisan producers who owned their means of production and depended on no man for a living. But the American economy did not develop that way," said McPherson.

Jefferson's view of industrial capitalism reflects his position in life. He was doing well, although he spent more than he took in. But he had control and when he needed more income, he could push his slaves harder. Indeed, he made considerable income by making nails. The young slaves who made them did so without shoes to wear in winter. Jefferson had wealth, power and control. He wanted to keep it that way.

But the economic system was in flux. New technologies meant several separate services needed to converge and that meant the paradigm of the small family farm had to change. Those who resisted required changes would inevitably be run over by change.

Artisans and craftsmen who marketed their skills for an hourly rate, adapted their skills to the mechanical industrial world, taking employment for an hourly rate. There was little choice. The machinery and tools required for operating and maintaining the machinery was too expensive for an individual craftsman to afford. A new economy emerged.

McPherson adds: The employee became dependent on the "boss" not only for wages but also for the means of production— machines that the worker himself could no longer hope to own. The emergence of industrial capitalism from 1815 to 1860 thus began to forge a new

INDIAN REMOVAL/GENOCIDE

system of class relations between capitalists who owned the means of production and workers who owned only their labor power.

This new relationship between employee and employee became known as wage slavery or free labor slavery. Defenders of slavery argued they were kinder than free labor capitalist because they, at least, fed their slaves, whereas the capitalist paid what they wanted, even if it failed to meet a livable wage.

"Capitalism was incompatible with republicanism," according to McPherson, "they insisted. Dependence on wages robbed a man of his independence and therefore of his liberty. Wage labor was no better than slave labor— hence "wage slavery." The boss was like a slaveowner. He determined the hours of toil, the pace of work, the division of labor, the level of wages; he could hire and fire at will."

This new economic system, it was argued, "created monopolies, concentrations of power that endangered liberty. They had also fostered a growing inequality of wealth (defined as ownership of real and personal property). In the largest American cities by the 1840s, the wealthiest 5 percent of the population owned about 70 percent of the taxable property, while the poorest half owned almost nothing," according to McPherson.

The cotton economy still dominated through the 19th century, however. "Cotton from the American South," says McPherson, "grown mostly by slave labor furnished three-fourths of the world's supply. Southern staples provided three-fifths of all American exports, earning foreign exchange that played an important part in American economic growth." [131]

The split between the north and the south was painfully evident, as the slave south continued its dependence upon cotton, as the north embraced the broader market economy; all of it leading to today's red state and blue states.

165

INDICTING AMERICA

Says Foner: "Their trip exemplified how the market revolution of the early nineteenth century was simultaneously consolidating the national economy and heightening the division between slave and free societies. In the North, the building of canals and the advent of steamboats and, later, railroads set in motion economic changes that created an integrated economy of commercial farms and growing urban and industrial centers. In the South, the market revolution, coupled with the military defeat and subsequent removal of the Native American population, made possible the westward expansion of the slave system and the rise of the great Cotton Kingdom of the Gulf states. Southern society reproduced itself as it moved westward, remaining slave-based and almost entirely agricultural, even as the North witnessed the emergence of a diversified, modernizing economy."[132]

The nation-state of the United States of America officially starts with adoption of the Constitution, but that is not when it began. It begins with the invasion of Europeans, led by Columbus and fueled by the Doctrine of Discovery; all on a quest for using brute force in taking natural resources, enslaving indigenous peoples, and creating wealth and power. If law and justice are to mean anything, this behavior, this moral bankruptcy, this cruelty is worthy of condemnation and punishment. Instead, it serves as the heart and soul of America. Wipe away all the spin, all the contrived tales of exceptionalism, all the utter nonsense of racial superiority, and look at the naked truth.

While this new nation-state perpetrated genocide, it also turned its attention to foreign lands. The emerging economy involved production of raw material, cotton, for feeding England's industrial machinery, using high speed logistics moving product to coasts for shipping to market. Shipping needed ports for resupply. For the new nation-state, shipping could go east, or it could go west. When leaders of the slavocracy looked toward the sunset, Japan appeared tantalizing. But Japan

INDIAN REMOVAL/GENOCIDE

was an isolationist state. It had limited relations with the Dutch, but it wanted even less with the rest of the world. That was unacceptable for the slavocracy.

And so, in July, 1853, America dispatched Commodore Perry and his black gunboats to "open up" Japan. Open up. That means do as we wish or our gun boats will kill you. The Japanese were terrified and they succumbed to their fear. Nearly 100 years later, that fear transformed into hate as they retaliated at Pearl Harbor.

America is charged with genocide.

Cotton Seeds of Worldwide War

WHILE TEACHING A CLASS ON American history, a student said to me "I wish we could look at other events around the world at the same time period." I stared at him for a few moments and said "huh, that's a good point." And so, I attempted to do so in future classes, while connecting it to the broad view and to the events in America.

While Jefferson enjoyed the status quo, his European friends were still itching for more. The New World "discovered" by Columbus provided an example for other nation-states when they joined the industrial revolution, seeking new resources for exploitation in service of greed. First, they had the Empire examples that flourished over thousands of years in the wake of agriculture. The formula was fairly simple: establish wealth resources, create a protective edifice, build it bigger and better than any adversaries, and then attack adversaries in stealing their wealth, enslaving their people, declaring dominion over the invaded lands, and do so under the disguise of a "defensive" war.

Secondly, they had the New World example. After invading a land, establish dominion so other invaders don't claim the same spot; elbow and muscle each other out of the way; while continuing to expand and arm the protective edifice. In the New World, England aggressively populated it "colonies" and staked its claim, eventually pushing aside, France, Spain, Russia and any other suitors, including the indigenous peoples. Those pushed aside by England would not let that happen again, if given the chance.

The Industrial Revolution provided that chance. Although America remained enmeshed in a slavocracy, other countries were moving away from a slave-based economy, led by England who outlawed the international slave trade. When Africa dried up as a source for slaves, it still retained a European trading infrastructure that could be applied for other business transactions. [133]

Slavery did not end easily as the entrepreneurs who benefited from slavery sought out new ways to deploy the business infrastructure that had been established during the Atlantic Slave Trade. As the embers of slavery diminished, the aristocrats provided funding for missionary explorations of Africa in search of resources for new enterprise opportunities. Exploration of Africa came at a time when European power structures were in flux. Technology continued reshaping political and social institutions. Monarchies were challenged by colonists, industrialists and new wealth creating technologies such as railroads, steam ships and mass communications. [134]

The 18th Century American Revolution was a harbinger of events to unfold, causing apprehension for the monarchs of Russia, France, and Great Britain. Those who attained power from birth based on imperialists empires created by their ancestors were wary of new challenges to their thrones. Great Britain may have been the first to abdicate power in the American colonies, but it surely would not be the last.

The American Revolution was an exertion of power by business interests against the power of the King. It gave birth to a new experiment in government based on rule by the governed (primarily land barons and aristocrats in the beginning). The American experiment, however, also provided an avenue for entrepreneurial initiative, supported and facilitated by government, leading to technological advancements reshaping the landscape. Steamships, canals, Morse code, and railroads provided opportunities for industrialization and markets that were heretofore unimaginable.

In transitioning from the Slave Trade and funding missionaries for reconnaissance, British aristocrats made deals with African tribal leaders allowing access by the European colonists who had previously been restricted from entering the continent. The decline of the slave trade, however, made tribal leaders pliable to new sources of income that could come from colonial settlements. Moreover, the depletion of men resulting from slave trading severely reduced the Continent's ability for resisting invasion. Although weapons had been provided to tribal leaders during the slave trade period, technological advances provided the colonists with superior fire power that dwarfed the combat readiness of the Africans.

Scramble for Africa

British aristocrats believed there were treasures to be found in Africa, but Africa remained a mystery well into the 19th Century. The aristocrats provided funding for David Livingstone's exploration of Africa. He spent over 20 years exploring Africa and was presumed dead. But then one day he was discovered by a journalist who went searching for Dr. Livingstone. Henry Morton Stanley found the elusive doctor in November, 1871, shortly before Livingston died in 1873.

Stanley continued the work of Livingstone and worked with the illicit slave trader Hamed bin Muhammad, better known as Tippu Tip, in search of the source of the Congo River. In the process he traversed the resource rich Congo. He attempted to get Britain to claim the Congo for the crown, but failed. Stanley was then approached by King Leopold II of Belgium who was very much interested in the Congo. [135]

King Leopold sponsored a conference of European powers under the agenda of ending the illegal slave traffic, but his real goal was to lay the ground work for Belgium's conquest of African resources. He created the International African Association which he used to disguise his real agenda. Belgium gained a footing in the Congo and opened the door for European colonization for African resources.[136]

Britain and France established large footprints in Africa as the industrial appetite for resources grew in the 19th Century. Germany was late in entering the African colonial competition, because Germany had its own resources. But as its industrial engine heated up, the need for more resources compelled Germany to seek external suppliers, too.

As the Scramble for Africa took shape, there was an increasing sense that conflict was inevitable. The Niger and Congo rivers were key conduits for moving materials in Africa. The Portuguese decided to initiate a conference of the European powers to discuss neutrality for the rivers and they asked Germany's Premier Otto Von Bismarck to host the conference in Berlin. The Berlin Conference of 1884-85 was designed to establish ground rules for African colonization and to agree upon the neutrality of the Niger and Congo rivers. The United States was invited but did not attend.

Before the Berlin Conference 80% of Africa was independent. Just twenty years later, 90% of Africa was colonized. Europe had taken control of Africa, led by the British and the French. When Germany entered the Scramble for Africa, it represented a threat to Britain and France. German industry was robust even before it entered the colonial environment. In the 1870s, German industrial production outpaced France and by 1900 it was greater than Britain, even though Germany did not have an equal colonial footprint or equal access to markets. Germany entered the colonial fray at the urging of German industrialists who wanted access to new markets and resources.

"Between 1881 and 1898 (the year of British victory over the Mahdi movement in Sudan)," Jürgen Osterhammel tells us in *The Transformation of the World: A Global History of the Nineteenth Century (America in the World)*, "nearly the whole of Africa was partitioned among the various colonial powers: France, Britain, Belgium (with King Leopold II rather than the Belgian state as "owner" of a colony), Germany, and Portugal (a few old settlements on the coasts of Angola and Mozambique). In a final phase Morocco became a French possession (1912), and the Libyan desert, scarcely governable but viewed with new interest in Istanbul, came under Italian control (1911–12).25 Only Ethiopia and Liberia (founded by former American slaves) remained independent. This "Scramble for Africa," as it was known, though often chaotic, opportunistic, and unplanned in its finer details, should be seen as a single process. Such an occupation of a vast continent within just a few years was without parallel in world history."

"Between 1895 and 1905, a similar scramble developed in China," according to Osterhammel, "although not all the imperial powers had their eyes on territorial acquisition. Some—especially Britain, France, and Belgium—were more interested in railroad or mining concessions and in staking out informal spheres of commercial influence. The United States proclaimed an "open door" principle for all countries in the Chinese market. At that time only Japan, Russia, and Germany appropriated quasi-colonial territories of any significance on the periphery of China: Taiwan (Formosa), southern Manchuria, and Qingdao with its hinterland on the Shandong peninsula. But the Chinese state remained in place, and the great majority of Chinese never became colonial subjects. The consequences of the "mini scramble" in China were thus much less grave than those of the "maxi scramble" in Africa."

"In Southeast Asia, however, the British established themselves in Burma and Malaya, while the French took control in Indochina (Vietnam, Laos, and Cambodia)," according to Osterhammel. "Between 1898 and 1902 the United States conquered the Philippines, first from Spain, then from the Filipino independence movement. In 1900, Siam was the only nominally independent (if weak and therefore cautious) country in this politically and culturally diverse part of the world. The same justifications were given everywhere for European (or American) conquests in Asia and Africa between 1881 and 1912: a "might is right" ideology, mostly suffused with racism; the supposed incapacity of native peoples to govern themselves in an orderly manner; and an (often preventive) protection of national interests in the contest with rival European powers."[137]

"We usually think of capitalism, at least the globalized, mass-production type that we recognize today," says Beckert, "as emerging around 1780 with the Industrial Revolution. But war capitalism, which began to develop in the sixteenth century, came long before machines and factories. War capitalism flourished not in the factory but in the field; it was not mechanized but land- and labor-intensive, resting on the violent expropriation of land and labor in Africa and the Americas. From these expropriations came great wealth and new knowledge, and these in turn strengthened European institutions and states— all crucial preconditions for Europe's extraordinary economic development by the nineteenth century and beyond. Many historians have called this the age of "merchant" or "mercantile" capitalism, but "war capitalism" better expresses its rawness and violence as well as its intimate connection to European imperial expansion."

He adds: "Latter-day capitalism rests upon the rule of law and powerful institutions backed by the state, but capitalism's early phase, although ultimately requiring state power to create world-spanning empires, was frequently based on the unrestrained actions of private individuals— the domination of masters over slaves and of frontier capitalists over indigenous inhabitants. The cumulative result of this highly aggressive, outwardly oriented capitalism was that Europeans came to dominate the centuries-old worlds of cotton, merge them into a single empire centered in Manchester, and invent the global economy we take for granted today."[138]

Asia and Africa had a long history of transforming cotton into textiles. A network of cottage industry enterprises produced clothing and other cotton-based products. Industrialization streamlined production far outstripping the capacity of home-based crafts-people. England had a purchasing power outstripping small buyers by way of the East India Company and soon took control over raw material supplies for feeding industrial production operations in Manchester. England used her muscle pushing small producers out of the way, later returning to Asia and Africa for marketing its finished products in the same locations where it obtained raw materials. This marked the opening of the British Empire.

Meeting demand for cotton and finished products represented an opportunity for enormous wealth. England would take all the cotton it could get from suppliers and it would embark upon colonial adventures taking lands and enslaving people inhabiting those lands for extraction of needed natural resources. In addition, England would create an empire in which it would sell its finished products in the colonial lands.

"The British Empire," says Osterhammel, "became the first in history to span the entire globe, while other empires ambitiously measured themselves by its model."[139]

Informed by lessons learned in the New World era, the rich and powerful seized upon opportunities for domination; staking out control of people and lands by way of colonialism; and engaging in competition with other world powers for taking as much as possible for themselves.

"Modernity came of age in Britain's Industrial Revolution," says Karen Armstrong, "which began in the later eighteenth century, though its social effects would not be truly felt until the early nineteenth. It started with the invention of the steam engine, which provided more energy than the country's entire workforce put together, so the economy grew at an unprecedented rate. It was not long before Germany, France, Japan, and the United States followed Britain's lead, and all these industrialized countries were forever transformed."

"Industrialized countries were soon compelled," she adds, "to seek new markets and resources abroad and would therefore, as the German philosopher Georg Wilhelm Hegel (1770– 1831) had predicted, be pushed toward colonialism. In these new empires, the economic relationship between the imperial power and the subject peoples became just as one-sided as it had been in the agrarian empires. The new colonial power did not help its colonies to industrialize but simply appropriated an "undeveloped" country to extract raw materials that could feed the European industrial process. In return the colony received cheap manufactured goods from the West that ruined local businesses."[140]

Colonialism was the mechanism for achieving the objectives of obtaining natural resources and obtaining labor on the cheap. Invasion of the New World by Columbus provided an example and a template for invasion of Africa and Asia. Staking out and defending colonial claims would be a priority and they would be wary of anyone elbowing them out of the way. The friction it generated became the root cause for the World at War: World Wars I and II.

INDICTING AMERICA

World Wars I and II are not separate and discrete events; they are one event. The root of it all—the insatiable greed, arrogance and power mania underpinning the worldview of European leaders—was not confronted at the end of the fighting in these war and has not been confronted since. Until it is, world leaders will continue to be informed by the accepted tenets of the World Wars and will continue to keep the world on the brink of another equally depraved battle, rather than paving a way to peace and harmony.

Cotton, however, was a key for the early period of the Industrial Revolution. "But because of the centrality of cotton," says Beckert, "its story is also the story of the making and remaking of global capitalism and with it of the modern world. Foregrounding a global scale of analysis, we will learn how, in a remarkably brief period, enterprising entrepreneurs and powerful statesmen in Europe recast the world's most significant manufacturing industry by combining imperial expansion and slave labor with new machines and wage workers."

"Why was it that the part of the world that had the least to do with cotton— Europe— created and came to dominate the empire of cotton?" asks Beckert. "Any reasonable observer in, say, 1700, would have expected the world's cotton production to remain centered in India, or perhaps in China. And indeed, until 1780 these countries produced vastly more raw cotton and cotton textiles than Europe and North America. But then things changed. European capitalists and states, with startling swiftness, moved to the center of the cotton industry. They used their new position to ignite an Industrial Revolution. China and India, along with many other parts of the world, became ever more subservient to the Europe-centered empire of cotton. These Europeans then used their dynamic cotton industry as a platform to create other industries; indeed, cotton became the launching pad for the broader Industrial Revolution."[141]

COTTON SEEDS OF WORLDWIDE WAR

The New World enterprise that began in 1492 transitioned into the Scramble for Africa, with subplots playing out in other parts of the globe. This new enterprise, the Scramble for Africa, was driven by the Industrial Revolution. Indeed, it was this insatiable thirst for wealth and power that provided the root cause for the World Wars of the 20th century; a period in which over 100 million humans would be killed in warfare.

Trading companies and the British Navy played a significant role in subjugating their burgeoning Empire. Under the reign of Queen Victoria, England led the Industrial Revolution. Egypt, India and China were key targets.

China was particularly vulnerable because its power was scattered between warlords. The East India Company, chartered by England as a monopolistic trading company, acted as the tip of the spear for English colonialism. The company traded for spices in China, but expanded into other resources as the Industrial Revolution took shape. China sold tea to England, but England didn't have much to offer China. England then took opium from India and sold it to China, sparking a drug epidemic. China attempted to stop the drug trade and England attacked. What became known as the First Opium War tested China's sovereignty and independence. The Second Opium War occurred in 1859.

"In India," Armstrong writes, "British traders ransacked the assets of Bengal so ruthlessly during the late eighteenth century that this period is regularly described as "the plundering of Bengal." The region was pushed into a chronically dependent role, and instead of growing their own food, villagers were forced to cultivate jute and indigo for the world market."[142]

"India was descending into anarchy," according to Arthur Herman in *Gandhi & Churchill: The Epic Rivalry that Destroyed an Empire and*

Forged Our Age. "In order to protect its interests against both local marauders and the French, the East India Company had created its own army, with regiments of native soldiers (or sepoys) and cavalrymen (or sowars) serving under British officers and using modern muskets and European-style discipline and training.16 Recruited largely from north India and the Hindu and Muslim villages between Bihar and Agra, these British-trained sepoys were far superior to troops any native ruler could field. So, with a few hundred of them and some supporting European troops, Clive was able to take Arcot, hold it against all comers, and then form an alliance with a local Maratha chieftain to begin driving the French out of southern India—and to make himself a fortune."[143]

The protective edifice developed by the East India Company served the interest of England who assumed control and deployed for removal of the French.

"This combination of industrialized technology and empire," says Armstrong, "was creating a global form of systemic violence, driven not by religion but by the wholly secular values of the market. The West was so far ahead that it was virtually impossible for the subject peoples to catch up. Increasingly the world would be divided between the West and the Rest, and this systemic political and economic inequality was sustained by military force. By the mid-nineteenth century, Britain controlled most of the India."[144]

The British Empire was all about dominating foreign lands, enslaving foreign peoples to the needs of the Empire, and taking resources for feeding industry. It also meant marketing finished products to foreign subjects.

And just as England flexed its colonial powers, America was not about to be left behind. The cotton market meant the U.S. needed access to foreign ports for logistical purposes in moving its product. It looked to the Pacific where Japan represented a substantial port potential.

The United States embarked upon Imperial enterprises, just as England and other European powers did in response to the unfolding Industrial Revolution, mass production and the need for markets. Seeking a logistical network for trade, Commodore Perry was dispatched to Japan demanding that Japan, an isolationist country, change its ways and "Open-Up."

The Industrial Revolution diverted America's path for ending slavery. The cotton enterprise required raw materials and markets. Colonization provided a source for raw materials and for distribution markets. To be sure, the insatiable drive for wealth and power provided the foundation for the Civil War; the same drive for power and wealth that provided the foundation for the World Wars.

Alliances

The Berlin Conference aimed at setting some rules for carving up Africa, but it only turned the heat down to simmer for a while. Britain and France were wary of Germany's intentions and, drawing upon past experience, sought alliances to fend off possible aggression. These alliances, however, set a stage for minor diplomatic brushfires to quickly escalate into a worldwide conflagration.

Germany formed an alliance with Austria-Hungary, 1879, with Italy in 1882 (Italy switched sides in 1915), and the Ottoman Empire, 1915. Russia allied with France, 1894, which connected Britain, 1907, and Belgium, 1839. Russia also had relations with Serbia. This meant that a relatively minor incident in one country could draw all of the other countries into a major, if not worldwide conflict.

The Balkans, a widely diversified intersection of culture, languages and religions, and a place where these same diversities erupted into widespread violence over hundreds of years, provided the stage for the opening act of Worldwide warfare, 1914, as Serbian resentments against Austria-Hungary resulted in the assassination of the heir to the Austrian Crown, Archduke Ferdinand. This event might have been contained to the Balkans, but the Alliances set in motion a series of fallen dominos resulting in war between the Triple Alliance of Austria-Hungary, Germany and the Ottoman Empire; and the Triple Entente of Russia, France and Britain. This ended a period of peace that existed for over 40 years.

Who Won the Civil War?

WITH ONE BULLET, LINCOLN'S assassin, John Wilkes Booth, determined the outcome of the Civil War. As Sun Tzu, author of *The Art of War*, argues, a combatant can win every battle yet still lose the war. [145]

Sun Tzu teaches that warfare is merely a tool for a political solution. As the Vietnam War exemplified, a country can win every battle, but lose the war. Top academic scholars, experts on the Civil War and Reconstruction, articulate how rebel leaders were reconstituted and put back into power after surrendering to the Union. But those same academic scholars resist, in some cases resent, the idea that the Confederacy won the Civil War.

When John Wilkes Booth assassinated President Lincoln, opening a path for Andrew Johnson to take control of the Oval Office, slavery, the central cause for the war, was certain to survive, thereby assuring victory for the Confederates. Yes, slavery had to be rebranded, but reinstituting slavery only required cosmetic changes. Chattel slavery was outlawed, but peonage was firmly entrenched. New laws were adopted in the south requiring black people to sign work contracts placing them under control of slave masters. And, if that didn't corral them back into slavery, the criminal justice system was lurking in the background, poised to arrest and convict former slaves, thereby rendering them slaves once again by way of a prisoner leasing system.

Booth's bullet ushered Andrew Johnson into the White House. Raised as a dirt poor white, Johnson clearly represented the culture of white slaves; a culture deeply ingrained with concepts of black inferiority. Johnson was determined to keep blacks in their place. Without a roadmap from Lincoln, Johnson assumed his duties focusing on his objective of reforming the union, while keeping blacks in their place.

Recognizing that slavery did not end with the Civil War and accepting that southern slave masters were redeemed and placed back in power is extremely difficult for Americans. The American story, communicated in primary and secondary schools, religious institutions, popular culture, family and friends, suggested that yes slavery was wrong, but America corrected it's wrong in the Civil War, when slavery ended and black people were freed. This is fictitious, contrived to present America as the land of the free and home of the brave.

Yes, slavery was outlawed, in theory at least, but black people were not equals in American Society. Republicans (Democrats in today's political landscape) had other ideas for the future. They wanted real emancipation, providing equal rights, including voting rights. But, Lincoln's successor, Andrew Johnson had his own ideas.

At first Johnson was averse to placating plantation owners, rich slave masters who looked down on him and his fellow poor white slave offspring, but as conflict with Republicans intensified, he used pardons for slave masters as a weapon against the Republicans, paving the way for returning slave masters to power and black people to a rebranded form of slavery, known as Jim Crow.

WHO WON THE CIVIL WAR?

In his campaigns for political office, Lincoln clearly signaled his views on slavery. He opposed slavery on moral grounds, but he did not see black people as simply people. He believed they were not equal to whites, but he viewed brutality inflicted upon slaves as immoral. He accepted the notion that black people needed the paternal support of white people. Still, he represented a threat to the institution of slavery, even though he only advocated for restricting expanding slavery into new states. His ascendancy to the White House was unacceptable to the south, motivating one southern (red) state after another to secede from the United States.

Colonists expanded west before the Louisiana Purchase, but in the years preceding the Civil War, expansion ramped up as plantation operators moved aggressively into the Mississippi River Delta. Expansion, however, led to conflicts over slavery with concerns over shifting the balance of political power between slave and free states. Mexico's restrictions on slavery was a key cause of the Mexican war, because Americans settling in Texas for growing cotton demanded enslaved people perform the work.

Victory in the Mexican War resulted in the U.S. taking large chunks of land to the west. Taking additional western lands was a positive in feeding the American Leviathan, but would these lands be slave or free states.

Despite intellectual gymnastics to redefine the heart of the war, the Civil War was about slavery, slavery, slavery. There are arguments that the war was about economics. No kidding, the economics of getting wealthy and powerful by way of slave sweat and blood. No, no, it is argued, the war was about State's Rights. Yes, the right of slave masters to control a state and maintain their human exploitation enterprise. The war was about "freedom and liberty" argues others. Yes, the freedom and liberty to deprive other humans of freedom and liberty thereby serving interests of the wealthy and powerful. This is the meaning of a disingenuous argument; it is argument for the sake of argument.

The rebel states, however, provide the evidence for the true cause of the war in their declarations for secession. Each seceding state in the south issued declarations stating their reasons for secession, stipulating that the threat to slavery apparent with the election of Lincoln compelled them to secede. In the post war, however, it is argued that they seceded over states' rights and economic principles, directly contradicting the historic documentation. The actual declarations, however, are insufficient for altering views of those refusing to admit the real cause of the war and for admitting that 700,000 people were killed in warfare in defense of slavery; admitting as much would be the equivalent of renouncing American Exceptionalism.

"Race," says Foner, "long one of many forms of legal and social inequality among colonial Americans, now emerged as a justification for the existence of slavery in a land of liberty. How else could the condition of blacks be explained other than by innate inferiority?"[146]

Lincoln is revered as the man leading America in addressing its original sin of slavery, but it cannot be avoided that he failed in creating an apparatus and an infrastructure for winning the peace. With one bullet, John Wilkes Booth stole victory from defeat. Respected historians reject this assertion, but their research articulates the many ways in which slavery was merely rebranded, commonly referred to as "Slavery by another name."

In his first inaugural address, Lincoln confronted secession by southern states stipulating that he was not a threat to slavery; he merely wanted to restrict expansion of slavery in accordance with his understanding that it was an accepted precept that slavery was incompatible with the ideals underpinning the American experiment in government based upon human liberty. [147]

The Constitution stipulated that Congress could not pass laws ending slavery before 1808. In 1807 an act was passed prohibiting participation in the international slave trade. This provision in the Constitution has been viewed as an expression by the founders that slavery was incompatible with liberty and it needed to end. This view of ending slavery is clearly expressed by Lincoln.

> Section 9 – Provision as to migration or importation of certain persons. Habeas Corpus, Bills of attainder, etc. Taxes, how apportioned. No export duty. No commercial preference. Money, how drawn from Treasury, etc. No titular nobility. Officers not to receive presents, etc.

> 1. The migration or importation of such persons as any of the states now existing shall think proper to admit, shall not be prohibited by the Congress prior to the year 1808, but a tax or duty may be imposed on such importations, not exceeding 10 dollars for each person.

The slave autocracy adopted political attitudes affiliated with the Articles of Confederation, a loose coalition of independent states. They wanted benefits of a strong state without giving up independence, leaving them with power to do as they pleased. In 1787, leaders of the revolution recognized the bankruptcy of that concept. Its weakness became the driving force for adoption of the U.S. Constitution calling for a strong federal government. The issue of federal power vs. states' rights, however, remained ambiguous creating an identity crisis still haunting the United States today.

The Louisiana Purchase upended that tacit agreement. The Industrial Revolution was underway; England needed raw materials for feeding its emerging textile industry. The Louisiana Territory, with its rich fertile soil, was a prime location for cotton production, beckoning slave masters craving more wealth and more power.

America stumbled into Civil War, even though it seemed inevitable based upon debates at the Constitutional Convention, less than 100 years before. Two mutually exclusive worldviews clashed over the idea that God made black people for slavery and the idea that slavery was an abomination. The Constitutional Convention was littered with debate over slavery. This conflict continues raging today as America remains separated by red and blue states; the Confederacy clearly represented by red states and abolitionists represented by blue. It remains notable that contemporary America sits on the edge of another Civil War with a former President, who is clearly aligned with bigotry, encouraging a Civil War behind thinly veiled threats.

What was Lincoln's objective in the Civil War? Was there a political and military strategy for achieving the objective? How does the war objective fit into the overall Master Plan for the country's future? At no point did Lincoln or the Confederates have an answer for any of these questions. Indeed, Lincoln merely reacted to events on an ad-hoc basis with a limited objective of restoring the union.

The northern objective drifted from the outset of the fighting, beginning with merely reuniting the union; then, shifting to emancipation. Lincoln did not have a blueprint for the war or the postwar. The political environment of the United States was upended with the Louisiana Purchase at the beginning of the century, because it changed everything. Coinciding with the burgeoning cotton market, the Louisiana Purchase was monumental.

As the war dragged on, Lincoln moved in the direction of abolishing slavery. The Emancipation Proclamation may be viewed as punishment for the Confederate States and as a means for creating a source of black troops for fighting the war. Emancipation aimed at depriving the South of free labor for producing its war making apparatus. More importantly, emancipation represented a significant shift from Lincoln's position at his first inaugural.

His second inaugural anticipates an end to the war and signals a soft landing for the Confederate States. This sets a stage for an internal conflict within Union leadership between those wanting a harsh approach at the end of the war and those who simply want the country reunited. Most importantly, during the war years, Lincoln failed in forming a consensus for objectives and a strategy for achievement of those objectives, beyond merely winning the war and reuniting the union. [148]

Defeated in battle, the confederates wondered what punishments awaited them. At best Lincoln offered a soft landing for the them. A mere 10% of a recalcitrant state's population was required for re-admittance to the Union, if they would pledge loyalty. The end of the war presented an opportunity for America to reset itself, transform the Constitution from protection of property to protection for humans, including life, liberty and pursuit of happiness. Rejoining the Union should have, but did not, require a demonstration of contriteness, a period of no political power, and something much more substantial than 10% of the population pledging loyalty.

Republicans were outraged, demanding a more aggressive approach. Lincoln argued for bringing the Union together again and putting the war in the rearview mirror. Instead, the war continues today.

How does a nation-state recover from a monumental event such as a Civil War? A wide range of political, social and economic issues await the outcome of warfare requiring a mature, thoughtful and sober set of objectives with a clear strategy for achieving them. To be sure, an ad-hoc approach, dealing with issues individually, absent an underlying strategy, is a recipe for disaster. Indeed, it may transform winning the war into losing the peace.

"Nearly two and a half centuries had passed," says Foner, "since twenty black men and women were landed in Virginia from a Dutch ship. From this tiny seed had grown the poisoned fruit of plantation slavery, which, in profound and contradictory ways, shaped the course of American development. Even as slavery mocked the ideals of a nation supposedly dedicated to liberty and equality, slave labor played an indispensable part in its rapid growth, expanding westward with the young republic, producing the cotton that fueled the early industrial revolution."[149]

The Civil War played out before a backdrop of genocidal assault upon the Native peoples. Louisiana needed slaves and it needed the Native inhabitants removed.

"The Louisiana Purchase," says Beckert, "represented dire consequences for the indigenous peoples inhabiting those lands, because plantation masters needed the natives removed. The full might on the newly formed country was brought to bear against the natives, including Indian Wars and the Indian Removal Act."[150]

"With the Indians removed and a slave system firmly in place, southern plantation masters were poised for obtaining great wealth and power. To be sure their power reverberates today."

"Europeans invented the world anew by embarking upon plantation agriculture on a massive scale. Once Europeans became involved in production, they fastened their economic fortunes to slavery. These three moves— imperial expansion, expropriation, and slavery— became central to the forging of a new global economic order and eventually the emergence of capitalism."

The cotton plantation south gave birth to a new and improved economic system that we know today as Capitalism. Assets, used as collateral for securing loans, were used for investments in income producing assets, such as slaves and plantations.

While the young nation remained conflicted about slavery, the assault upon indigenous peoples commenced. Western expansion that started in 1804, continued during the Civil War, and did not miss a step into the 20th century. To be sure, encroachment upon Native Americans, bullying them from lands, culture and sources of livelihood, pushed these Siberian people deeper into corners of the southwest and into Mexico. Ironically in the 21st century these people, brutalized by the white Europeans, who invaded the Americas, returned to their native lands in North America and were labeled as illegal immigrants who were rapists and drug dealers.

"Between 1846 and 1870," writes Madley, "California's Native American population plunged from perhaps 150,000 to 30,000. By 1880, census takers recorded just 16,277 California Indians. Diseases, dislocation, and starvation were important causes of these many deaths. However, abduction, de jure and de facto unfree labor, mass death in forced confinement on reservations, homicides, battles, and massacres also took thousands of lives and hindered reproduction."[151]

As Americans killed each other and Native peoples, England embarked upon building its empire. The British East India Company was much more than a commercial enterprise; it was also a mercenary force invading foreign lands, subjugating foreign governments, peoples and lands. English history touts this in terms of honor and glory; those confronting reality recognize it as an international crime.

England's invasion of India, China and Africa was a crime including rape, murder and enslavement. In the 20th century England protested the horrors inflicted by Nazi Germany, but it cannot avoid being named in the same indictments, because England established the precedent for Germany. America is also implicated in the case

INDICTING AMERICA

against the Nazis. To be sure, the Nazi template for invading lands and killing the inhabitants is taken from a page of Andrew Jackson's Indian Removal. Enslavement of the Jews and forced labor duplicates America's Jim Crow laws. Indeed, Nazi lawyers used America's Jim Crow for crafting the Nuremberg Laws.

"On June 5, 1934," says James Whitman in *Hitler's American Model: The United States and the Making of Nazi Race Law*, "about a year and a half after Adolf Hitler became Chancellor of the Reich, the leading lawyers of Nazi Germany gathered at a meeting to plan what would become the Nuremberg Laws, the notorious anti-Jewish legislation of the Nazi race regime."[152]

…the meeting involved detailed and lengthy discussions of the law of the United States.

…It is particularly startling to discover that the most radical Nazis present were the most ardent champions of the lessons that American approaches held for Germany.

…Indeed in Mein Kampf Hitler praised America as nothing less than "the one state" that had made progress toward the creation of a healthy racist order of the kind the Nuremberg Laws were intended to establish."

Yes, America's Jim Crow laws from all of it's 48 states, provided the template the Nuremberg Laws established by Germany's Nazis. America was praised by the Nazis, who shared their fervent belief in White Supremacy.

"W. E. B. DU BOIS," writes Ibram Kendi in *Stamped from the Beginning: The Definitive History of Racist Ideas in America*, "knew he was "entering the eye of one of the deadliest political storms in modern times" when his train rolled into Berlin on June 30, 1936. The new Atlanta University professor was on a research trip after being pushed out of the NAACP for advocating Black empowerment instead of integration and assimilation. It did not take long for Du Bois to write home that the Jew was the Negro in Germany's second year of Adolf Hitler's chancellorship."[153]

Racial segregation laws were only a part of the American-Nazi relationship. Eugenics also provided inspiration. According to Whitman, "During the interwar period the United States was not just a global leader in assembly-line manufacturing and Hollywood popular culture. It was also a global leader in "scientific" eugenics, led by figures like the historian Lothrop Stoddard and the lawyer Madison Grant, author of the 1916 racist best-seller The Passing of the Great Race; or, The Racial Basis of European History. These were men who promoted the sterilization of the mentally defective and the exclusion of immigrants who were supposedly genetically inferior."[154]

Germany's aggressive invasion of foreign lands and claiming those lands for Germany were also inspired by America's Manifest Destiny exemplified by America's stealing of Native American lands. "It is here, says Whitman, "that some of the most unsettling evidence has been assembled, as historians have shown that Nazi expansion eastward was accompanied by invocations of the American conquest of the West, with its accompanying wars on Native Americans."[155]

"Indeed, as early as 1928 Hitler was speechifying admiringly about the way Americans had "gunned down the millions of Redskins to a few hundred thousand, and now keep the modest remnant under observation in a cage";30 and during the years of genocide in the early 1940s Nazi leaders made repeated reference to the American conquest of the West when speaking of their own murderous conquests to their east.31"[156]

The myth of America as the stalwart for freedom and justice remains implanted in American minds. The reality is that America inspired Hitler's Nazis. It seems that if Americans truly embrace the ideas of freedom and justice and recognize that it is a myth, they may find the means for demanding that the myth become reality. Failing to do so may create vulnerability to a Hitler type political leader seizing the reins of power.

America is charged with creating a template for worldwide crimes against humanity and genocide.

Post-Civil War

TRANSFORMING A SLAVE SOCIETY INTO something else is formidable under any circumstance, but attempting to do so without a clear vision, an articulated objective and a detailed strategy for achieving it is a certain recipe for failure. Fierce resistance boiled in rebel hearts filled with beliefs of divine inspiration. Four years of hard fighting embittered the defeated who returned to a landscape littered with the residue of war. Freeing people from the bonds of enslavement and setting them on a path for self-sufficiency presented additional challenges on a monumental scale. Success required visionaries, thoughtful strategists, and organizational leadership capable of managing multiple inflammatory tasks simultaneously.

Lincoln merely reacted to events with a piecemeal approach for confronting daunting issues. Indeed, it wasn't until shortly before the war ended, that Lincoln sent Secretary of War Edward Stanton to Savannah, Georgia where he would join General Sherman to meet with local leaders of enslaved people for a discussion about how to manage freedom after the war.

"Secretary of War Edwin McMasters Stanton" says Kendi, "arrived in Savannah after the New Year and urged General Sherman to meet with local Blacks over their future. Meeting with twenty leaders, mostly Baptist and Methodist ministers, on January 12, 1865, General Sherman received a crash course on their definitions of slavery and freedom. Slavery meant "receiving by irresistible power the work of another man, and not by his consent," said the group's spokesman, Garrison Frazier (The Liberator editor's name was everywhere).[157]

…Frazier shared their preference "to live by ourselves." There was "a prejudice against us in the South that will take years to get over."

Reverend Frazier said the new government should give black people their rights, protect their rights, provide them with land for self-sufficiency, until they can earn enough to buy the land, and then just leave them alone. Beginning this process in January, 1865 is a clear indication that Lincoln and his administration were not prepared for the enormous task before them.

"On April 9," says Foner, "Grant accepted Lee's surrender at Appomattox. Amid this cavalcade of historic events, Reconstruction emerged as the central problem confronting the nation but, as James G. Blaine later remarked, Lincoln did not turn to peacetime with a "fixed plan" of Reconstruction. The President had approved the lenient policies of General Banks in Louisiana and the far more prescriptive acts of Andrew Johnson in Tennessee, all in an attempt to quicken Union victory and secure the abolition of slavery, rather than to fashion a blueprint for the postwar South. Nor had wartime Reconstruction been particularly successful. Union governments had been created within the Confederacy in Virginia, Tennessee, Arkansas, and Louisiana, but none had attracted truly broad support and none had been recognized by Congress." [158]

Obtaining a surrender does not mean the war is over; it simply means one Army is defeated for the moment. Lincoln's approach for winning the peace was to be kind to the rebels. It seems he wanted a return to normalcy so desperately, to put this ugly Civil War in the rear-view mirror, to return to the United States of America, that he simply could not accept that the vanquished in war would not, and perhaps could not, set aside the passions of the battle field, that ultimately emerged as the "Lost Cause."

Consider Lincoln's last speech. He had offered a soft landing for Louisiana, only requiring ten percent of the population to sign a loyalty oath for re-entry to the United States. Republicans were incensed over it. Rebels deserved punishment and should not be integrated into American society until they changed; socially, politically, and culturally. Anything less would snatch defeat from victory.

Lincoln's rebuttal is captured in his last speech. Lincoln wanted a return to normal, as if that was possible. Once a Rubicon is crossed, there's no turning back. The betrayed spouse cannot go back to normal as if nothing happened, even if the betraying party is genuinely contrite and a reconciliation is achieved. They may stay together but it will never be as it was before the betrayal.

The war took a heavy toll on Lincoln. The human sacrifice was more than he could bare. Keep focused on the good and rejoice in reconstitution of the Union, he believed. If Louisiana is the first to adopt a new constitution and has agreed to the amendment for freeing enslaved people, then the Union should welcome Louisiana with open arms and not dwell on the past. He desperately wanted it to be all over. The passions of war, however, mixed with the fear and hatred of black people would not simply dissipate. Indeed, the festering wound of defeat would metastasize into guerilla warfare (KKK), massive slaughter of black people across the south, lynchings, and disdain for northerners. Lincoln's tepid response provided the foundation for America's racial animus, a cancer that manifested Donald Trump and a period of political distress in the 21st century that threatens the end of the American Republic.[159]

INDICTING AMERICA

Foner: "The New York Times concluded that Lincoln had judged the time not yet ripe for "the statement of a settled reconstruction policy." Four days later, the President was assassinated by the actor John Wilkes Booth."[160]

When the Civil War ended, a handful of northern political leaders, the so-called "Radical Republicans" took up the cause of black people, only to be beaten back by recalcitrant southerners determined to redeem white supremacy. Some Republicans were gleeful about Lincoln's demise and thought his successor Andrew Johnson would work with them.

Andrew Johnson vs Radical Republicans

Lincoln's assassination altered what might have been. Andrew Johnson, a Tennessee Democrat, supported slavery, but opposed secession. Lincoln added him as his Vice-Presidential running mate in 1864 as a symbol of his willingness to offer the south a soft peace. He may as well have added Jefferson Davis to his ticket. Soon Johnson was on a path for confrontation with the Republicans.

Johnson held southern plantation owners in contempt, but his fight with Radical Republicans eventually drove him to favor the planters. When Johnson assumed the Presidency, he implemented a strategy that seemed consistent with Lincoln's objectives. Johnson issued an amnesty for the southerners, except for the large plantation owners. Johnson's disdain for blacks, however, held sway.

"Throughout the entirety of his political career," writes Gordon-Reed, "Andrew Johnson did everything he could to make sure blacks would never become equal citizens in the United States of America. Tragically, he was able to bring the full force and prestige of the American presidency to the effort."[161]

POST-CIVIL WAR

The Republican Party, the party of Lincoln which is today's Democratic Party, was split at the end of the war. The so-called Radical Republicans wanted to punish the south and to ensure that slaves were freed and enfranchised. This pitted the Radical Republicans against President Johnson.

"Johnson believed," says Gordon-Reed, "his job as president was to make sure that things went back to the way they were— except for slavery— circa 1789 when the original Constitution went into effect." The property protecting constitution was to remain intact.[162]

Johnson set forth ground rules for southern state governments. They had to abolish slavery, renounce secession and pay their war debts. Johnson wanted to reconcile with white southerners; again, the objective was not to reconcile injustice done to black people; it was to reconcile with the white south. Indeed, Johnson was clearly aligned with the off spring of indentured slaves, particularly poor white southerners who were threatened by the concept of free blacks. At first Johnson was hostile to the planter caste, but he later established a mechanism by which they could be granted amnesty and returned to political and social power.

The Radical Republicans struck back with Reconstruction Acts, which Johnson vetoed and Congress overrode. These acts addressed civil rights and voting rights. The recalcitrant south—the Barbadians and the off spring of indentured white slaves—put enforcement of these laws to the test. Harnessing dominant whites required a determination by the victorious north. Just how committed were the Civil War victors in their support of black people?

"Reconstruction was directed by Andrew Johnson, the Tennessee tailor who became vice president in March 1865, then succeeded Lincoln after his assassination a month later" writes C. Lane in *The Day Freedom Died: The Colfax Massacre, the Supreme Court, and the*

Betrayal of Reconstruction. "Johnson had ceded control of Southern state legislatures to former Confederates, who in turn enacted Black Codes that all but re-enslaved the freedmen. The codes contradicted the Thirteenth Amendment, which abolished slavery when ratified in December 1865, and Johnson faced growing resistance from a "Radical" Republican Congress— culminating in the Reconstruction Act adopted on March 2, 1867, over Johnson's veto."[163]

Freedman's Bureau

Congress established the U.S. Bureau of Refugees, Freedmen, and Abandoned Lands in 1865. This was a key mechanism in transitioning the south. It was abandoned in 1872 signaling the end of reconstruction.

"Throughout its existence, the Bureau regarded poor relief as a temptation to idleness" says Foner in *A Short History of Reconstruction.* Blacks declared Virginia Bureau head Orlando Brown, must "feel the spur of necessity, if it be needed to make them self-reliant, industrious and provident." Clearly, this position reflected not only attitudes toward blacks, but also a more general Northern belief in the dangers of encouraging dependency among the lower classes.[164]

Within a year of the war's end, the south had adopted laws against vagrancy that boxed the formerly enslaved into a corner. It mirrored the Enclosure Acts, in a way, where displaced common land farmers could sell themselves into indentured servitude and help in populating England's colonies, or they could try to survive on their own, get involved in crime and get shipped to a colony anyway. The southern legal machinations forced free blacks to sign a labor contract returning them to slave status, but without the slave designation, or be arrested for vagrancy and return to their former slave status by way of prison leasing.

"The definitive announcement of Johnson's plan of Reconstruction came in two proclamations issued on May 29, 1865," says Foner. "The first conferred amnesty and pardon, including restoration of all property rights except for slaves, upon former Confederates who pledged loyalty to the Union and support for emancipation." [165]

It was as if nothing had happened during the war years. Although Lincoln did not create a plan for reconstruction, he did sign into law the legislation creating the Freedman's Bureau. It did have potential for ushering in a new American landscape.

> The signature program of Reconstruction, the Bureau of Refugees, Freedmen, and Abandoned Lands, was the closest this country came in the 1800s to such a transformation in consciousness. Just before his assassination in 1865, Abraham Lincoln signed the bill establishing the bureau as a branch of the War Department. With thousands of agents across the South and hundreds of offices, the agency distributed basic necessities, including food, medicine, and clothing. It also founded thousands of schools, colleges, and hospitals, resettled refugees (white and black), administered confiscated properties, passed and enforced ad hoc laws, regulated labor relations and minimum wages, and levied taxes. It was, in potential and practice, the antithesis to Jacksonianism, an instrument of potentially awesome power, the "most extraordinary and far-reaching institution of social uplift that America has ever attempted," wrote W.E.B. Du Bois in the early 20th century.

But the triumphant backlash to the bureau and to Reconstruction more broadly empowered a new, postbellum generation of race hustlers. Chief among them was Lincoln's successor Andrew Johnson, who updated all the old Jacksonian tropes to intensify demonization of the federal bureaucracy, associating all social problems—corruption, dependency, poverty, unemployment, and crime—with black skin. He sharpened the Jacksonian opposition of free men fighting federal "enslavement," describing the Freedmen's Bureau as an "agency to keep the negro in idleness" and create a culture of dependency through the "lavish issuance of rations."

"There's One Heresy That Sets Bernie Apart From All Other Dem Contenders to Unseat Trump: And it's not simply that he calls himself a socialist," Grandin, G. **The Nation**, July 29, 2019[166]

Black Codes and Jim Crow

The Black Codes developed by white supremacists during reconstruction were state laws designed to re-establish slavery in the south. They were designed to box black people into an illusion of freedom, while still being enslaved. Black people were required to enter a contract with their formers masters that essentially maintained the status quo. If they did not enter into a contract, they were deemed vagrants subject to arrest, whereby they could be leased out by the state to the former master.

Black codes prohibited blacks from engaging in business enterprises, racial intermarriage, and property ownership. The Congressional Reconstruction Acts, along with the 14th Amendment, outlawed the black codes, but Supreme Court decisions (Slaughterhouse cases, 1873) restrained the federal government from interference with state laws controlling black people.

Subsequent southern state legislation re-introduced the black codes in what became known as "Jim Crow" laws. Jim Crow refers

POST-CIVIL WAR

to a blackface performance in a minstrel show and has been applied to state laws that re-enslaved black people after northern whites succumbed to the recalcitrant south and ended Reconstruction.

"Convict leasing," explains Bryan Stevenson in *Just Mercy: A Story of Justice and Redemption* "was introduced at the end of the nineteenth century to criminalize former slaves and convict them of nonsensical offenses so that freed men, women, and children could be "leased" to businesses and effectively forced back into slave labor. Private industries throughout the country made millions of dollars with free convict labor, while thousands of African Americans died in horrific work conditions. The practice of re-enslavement was so widespread in some states that it was characterized in a Pulitzer Prize– winning book by Douglas Blackmon as *Slavery by Another Name*. But the practice is not well known to most Americans."[167]

The Black Codes and Jim Crow had their genesis on Barbados where sugar plantation operators adopted Slave Codes considered the most draconian and severely depraved legal constructs for ruling over human beings. The Barbados Slave Codes provided the DNA for southern plantation owners; the Black Codes they created; the Jim Crow laws they used to continue slavery for another 100 years; and the stain that will forever scar the soul of America.

Stevenson: "Jim Crow," is the legalized racial segregation and suppression of basic rights that defined the American apartheid era. It is more recent and is recognized in our national consciousness, but it is still not well understood. It seems to me that we've been quick to celebrate the achievements of the Civil Rights Movement and slow to recognize the damage done in that era. We have been unwilling to commit to a process of truth and reconciliation in which people are allowed to give voice to the difficulties created by racial segregation, racial subordination, and marginalization.[168]

Contemporary political arguments based on slavery ending in 1865 are disingenuous, at best, if not completely ignorant of reality. Post-Civil War America reconciled with southern white plantation owners leaving black people in a society of Slavery by Another Name. These "Jim Crow" laws provided a template for Nazi Germany. Indeed, when Nazi lawyers introduced the Nuremberg Laws, they presented America's Jim Crow as precedent setting.

PTSD and Religion of the Lost Cause

At the end of the war, Confederate soldiers returned home defeated in battle. Demoralization was palpable. There was a malaise desperately needing some means for accepting the unacceptable. Southern Protestant preachers stepped in to provide answers. Drawing upon Old Testament resources, they preached that the rebel soldiers fought the good fight in service of God and a desire to fulfill the vision called for in the Bible. Blacks were designed for slavery, they argued, and it said so in the Bible. Moreover, the rebel soldiers sacrificed in a cause for bringing the Kingdom of God to earth just as the Bible proscribes.

Describing the defeated Confederate troops as demoralized does not capture the profound emotional distress stemming from the war. Today, their mental state would be diagnosed as Post Traumatic Stress Disorder (PTSD). A sense of betrayal, alienation, and psychic scars etched on their brains. Confederate troops experienced deep emotional distress resulting in volcanic eruptions of violence against those viewed as the "others," better described as scapegoats, representing the power apparatus that initiated the war and failed to win it.

The symptoms can range in severity from mild to devastating, and not everyone will have all of the symptoms at the same time.

POST-CIVIL WAR

Symptoms include hypervigilance in anticipation of a lethal threat; triggering of combat skills; a pervasive sense of betrayal and lack of social trust; ruminations about war experiences; isolation and thoughts of suicide; substance abuse; and sense of meaninglessness.

"Such unhealed PTSD," says J. Shay in *Achilles in Vietnam: Combat Trauma and the Undoing of Character*, "can devastate life and incapacitate its victims from participation in the domestic, economic, and political life of the nation. The painful paradox is that fighting for one's country can render one unfit to be its citizen."[169]

Troops refused acceptance of an outcome that was unacceptable. Some resorted to drug and alcohol abuse. Others looked to religion. In contrast to healing, the characteristics of PTSD were inflamed, fueled by preachers in the pulpit.

Confederate troops and Southerners were determined to redeem the south during the decade following the war. The concept of the "Lost Cause" emerged and history was manipulated to paint the south as righteous. Indeed, the racism of slavery was defined as ordained by God.

The pro-slavery argument leaned more heavily on the sanction of the Bible than on anything else, writes C.R Wilson in *Baptized in blood: The religion of the lost cause, 1865-1920*, "Ministers cited biblical examples of the coexistence of Christianity and slavery, quoted Old Testament approvals of slavery, and interpreted a passage from Genesis to mean that blacks were descendants of the sinner Ham and destined to be forever bondsmen."[170]

"In 1862 the Episcopal Bishop Stephen Elliott observed, "All nations which come into existence at this late period of the world must be born amid the storm of revolution and must win their way to a place in history through the baptism of blood." [171]

Racial hatred and domination were approved by God, as was believed by southern redeemers, and served as an underpinning of the brutality against black people in post-Civil war America.

INDICTING AMERICA

Ideas of racial hatred, contempt and disdain for the "others," and rationalization of brutality inflicted upon the "others" is a product of cultural messages communicated by family, school, the arts, friends, and the community at large, including religion.

Is it for religious institutions to stipulate morality for community guidance in creating a culture? Or, are institutions of faith handcuffed by the community's culture and somehow required to follow the culture's wishes.

"The cross and the lynching tree are separated by nearly 2,000 years," according to James Cone in *The Cross and the Lynching Tree*. "One is the universal symbol of Christian faith; the other is the quintessential symbol of black oppression in America. Though both are symbols of death, one represents a message of hope and salvation, while the other signifies the negation of that message by white supremacy."

"Until we can see the cross and the lynching tree together, until we can identify Christ with a "recrucified" black body hanging from a lynching tree, there can be no genuine understanding of Christian identity in America, and no deliverance from the brutal legacy of slavery and white supremacy."[172]

Lincoln's Hope for Louisiana Eclipsed by White Supremacy

It began as a fraternal organization, something like the Veterans of Foreign Wars (VFW), but angry PTSD Confederates who joined the Klu Klux Klan, promptly created something far more ominous than the VFW; they created a terrorist organization.

General James Longstreet, a key member of Lee's command, represents the profound distress of the Post War period. A loyal

POST-CIVIL WAR

Confederate General, he embodies the conflict of accepting the unacceptable and working for reunification of the country. His efforts in restoring Peace resulted in his death.

Confederate response to Post War Reconstruction was immediate. Massacres, lynching, brutalization of black people spread through the Confederacy.

Foner: "In some areas, violence against blacks reached staggering proportions in the immediate aftermath of the war. "I saw white men whipping colored men just the same as they did before the war," testified ex-slave Henry Adams, who claimed that "over two thousand colored people" were murdered in 1865 in the area around Shreveport, Louisiana.

…In Texas, Bureau records listed the "reasons" for some of the 1,000 murders of blacks by whites between 1865 and 1868: One victim "did not remove his hat"; another "wouldn't give up his whiskey flask"; a white man "wanted to thin out the niggers a little"; another wanted "to see a d— d nigger kick." Gender offered no protection— one black woman was beaten by her employer for "using insolent language," another for refusing to "call him master," a third "for crying because he whipped my mother."[173]

A race riot in Memphis left 50 black people dead in 1866, while in New Orleans, black people were murdered in the streets. Louisiana, the state Lincoln believed would represent positive results from his soft-landing approach, became a cauldron of southern recalcitrance.

In July of 1866, blacks met for political organizing. It ended in a massacre.

"On the morning of July 30," writes Charles Lane in *The Day Freedom Died: The Colfax Massacre, the Supreme Court, and the Betrayal of Reconstruction*, "city policemen, the vast majority of whom were ex-Confederate soldiers, mobbed the gun shops of New Orleans, buying up pistols. Along with like-minded white civilians, they gathered around the convention site: the Mechanics' Institute on Baronne Street. As a parade of Negro Republicans led by colored Union army veterans approached the fortresslike building, black marchers and white onlookers exchanged a few pistol shots."

… When it was over, thirty-eight people were dead, all but four of them people of color; and 184 lay wounded."[174]

Foner: "On the appointed day, July 30, only twenty-five delegates assembled, soon joined by a procession of some 200 black supporters, mostly former soldiers. Fighting broke out in the streets, police converged on the area, and the scene quickly degenerated into what Gen. Philip H. Sheridan later called "an absolute massacre." By the time federal troops arrived, thirty-four blacks and three white Radicals had been killed, and well over 100 persons injured. Even more than the Memphis riot, the events in New Orleans discredited Presidential Reconstruction. Many Northerners agreed with Gen. Joseph Holt that Johnson's leniency had unleashed "the barbarism of the rebellion in its renaissance." [175]

"As militia commander," says Lane, "he appointed James A. Longstreet, a former general in Robert E. Lee's Army of Northern Virginia, who had moved to Louisiana and registered Republican."[176]

"Warmouth knew that sending armed negroes after Delos White's killer could inflame the white population. The U.S. marshals were part of the Custom House apparatus, and, by this point, any cooperation with the Custom House was distasteful to the governor. But given the gravity of the crime and the threat to order it represented, the governor had little choice but to lend the marshals Ward's company. In October 1871, Warmoth had his militia chief, James Longstreet, send Ward about ninety Enfield rifles—surplus weapons that had been supplied to Louisiana by the War Department. But Longstreet

POST-CIVIL WAR

attached orders telling Ward that he was to keep them stored unless he had specific permission to take them out.

Warmoth ordered Longstreet to rein in Ward. The militia commander sent an officer to Colfax in early December, apparently to get Ward to demobilize quietly. When Ward refused, Longstreet issued a "special order" on December 11, 1871, claiming the governor never authorized Ward's campaign and that Ward had "armed and paraded his company in violation of the laws of the state and the orders governing the State Militia."

Just a few years later, 1872, came Colfax which provided a preview of January 6, 2020. Colfax, Louisiana represents a direct rebuke of Lincoln's peace. Colfax became the eye of the storm for murder. Whites attacked blacks in what has been termed a Massacre.

William Kellogg won the race for Governor, but his opponent, John McEnery refused acceptance of the outcome. Colfax Courthouse was the seat of power for Grant Parrish. Black supporters of Kellogg went to the courthouse to prevent insurrectionists supporting McEnery from taking it over.

"Between the reports of Negro mischief and Manning's soothing words, Kellogg decided not to send troops, state or federal, to Colfax," says Lane. "A large force would be unduly provocative at this stage, he told himself. He ordered a single officer, the militia commander General James A. Longstreet, to go to Grant Parish to investigate. Kellogg told General William H. Emory, commander of the U.S. Army's Department of the Gulf, based at the Jackson Barracks near New Orleans, that he would like a federal officer to accompany Longstreet. But when Emory demurred, saying that he feared the presence of a federal officer might undercut Longstreet's authority, Kellogg shrugged and went along. An editorial in the Republican summed up his thinking. "The opinion was entertained yesterday that the excitement would die away and the parties quietly disperse and resume their ordinary avocations before a force sent from the city could arrive at Colfax," it explained."[177]

"When the one-hour battle was over, the White League had lost twenty-one dead and nineteen wounded; Kellogg's side counted eleven dead and sixty wounded, among them James Longstreet, the militia commander, who had been thrown from his horse and hurt his right arm. "[178]

Nicholas Lemann writes in *Redemption: The Last Battle of the Civil War* "…a day later, on Tuesday, April 14—a boatload of "Metropolitan Police" dispatched by the Republicans in New Orleans—the town was littered with unburied bodies. Wild dogs and buzzards were picking at the flesh of the corpses. James Longstreet, the Confederate general best known for having unsuccessfully advised General Lee not to attempt a frontal attack on the Union Army at Gettysburg, was now, to the bitter consternation of his unapologetic former comrades, a Republican supporter of President Grant, and commander of the Metropolitan Police in New Orleans. He dispatched a colonel named T. W. DeKlyne to lead the force to Colfax. This was DeKlyne's first impression of Colfax after the battle:

> "About one-third of a mile below the courthouse we came upon a party of colored men and women carrying away a wounded colored man upon a sled. At a little distance in the field were the dead bodies of two colored men. About two hundred yards nearer the courthouse were three dead bodies of colored men, and from that point to the courthouse and its vicinity the ground was thickly strewn with dead." [179]

Southern Gentlemen, the men who were too good to work and had others to do work for them, were never going to give up slavery.

Rationalizations and justifications, no matter how absurd, provided a smoke screen disguising the tarnished and cancerous soul of America's elite.

At one point, Thomas Jefferson wanted an end to slavery. He believed it might happen in the future. "It would arrive," writes Wiencek, "when white people experienced "a revolution in public opinion," as he wrote to yet another correspondent who brought up emancipation. But in an 1805 letter to an intimate, his private secretary, William Burwell, he wrote, "I have long since given up the expectation of any early provision for the extinguishment of slavery among us." The governments of all the Southern states were in the hands of slaveholders whose sense of justice and morality was defined not by the soaring language of the Revolution but by their pocketbooks. Among this class, Jefferson said to Burwell, "interest is morality." As a senator from Georgia declared: "You cannot prevent slavery—neither laws moral or human can do it. Men will be governed by their interest, not the law."[180]

The slave masters and the business infrastructure that grew from slavery lived to fight another day. They were weakened by the Civil war and its aftermath, but they were not done expressing their anger, resentments and hatred. They continued their fight for power, complete and total power. They would not be governed by laws; they would govern by their interests. It has taken many years, but their efforts culminated in the Donald Trump presidency of 2016.

Praeger University, an imitation university, markets American history videos for kids. They suggest black people recognize that slavery, brutal though it may be, was necessary so the great American nation could be great.[181]

Alan Taylor suggests slavery did not have to be inhuman:

"Kingsley rejected the American obsession with white supremacy, for he trusted and freed Black people who helped him prosper. Kingsley promoted his "patriarchal or co-operative" version of slavery as less brutal to slaves and less dangerous for masters. Kingsley claimed that his slaves "love me like a father," but of course many were his children."[182]

…A free thinker, Kingsley dismissed key notions cherished by most white Americans. He derided their racist stereotypes of Blacks and insistence that all whites were superior; their naïve belief that mass colonization could remove millions of Blacks from America to Africa; and the democratic cult of public opinion as just and wise.

…Applying African and Spanish concepts to his practice of mastery, Kingsley deployed the task system, in which a laborer could stop working after completing that day's assignment. This contrasted with the despised gang system of American plantations, where an overseer compelled slaves to labor long days under close and painful supervision. Kingsley's slaves also enjoyed Saturday afternoons and all of Sunday as their own. In that time, they could fish and hunt, tend gardens, and make crafts for sale. With the proceeds, they could buy their freedom, which Kingsley set at half the market price. As he expected, these incentives encouraged his slaves to work harder with less friction.

America is charged with enslavement, murder, theft of labor, rape, kidnapping and sabotage of government.

Imperialism

AMERICA'S DIVIDE BETWEEN SLAVERY AND abolition fueled passions erupting into a Civil War. That divide, so evident today, seemed to be resolved with the surrender at Appomattox, but it was not. Slave Masters and the political apparatus sustaining them were given a reprieve. Winning the Civil War, it appeared, put to rest the conflict between those supporting government for the Common Good and those demanding a government for Individual Gain. This ideology, underpinning selfishness, given a reprieve by Andrew Johnson, however, survived the war.

This force for selfishness demanded that laws did not apply to them, but law did apply to anyone who threatened them. They abhorred the concept of equal justice under the law. Following precedence established with Protestant Supremacy in Barbados, they fought back against laws restrained them, using the courts and legal machinations, along with bribery, extortion, fraud, even murder. This truculent force did not acquiesce. The Barbadians, imported into South Carolina by England's Lords Proprietor, established this force demanding government in service of anything and everything that benefitted them. From the inception of the United States and long before the Civil War, they have been in conflict with those believing in America as a force for the Common Good. This is at the heart of the divide. It remains obfuscated by bright shiny objects that distract, confuse and manipulate. Even those wanting Common Good can be manipulated into supporting initiatives for sabotaging the Common Good.

Resurrecting the individual gain forces at the close of the Civil War placed the country on a self-destructive path. It didn't happen immediately; it would take some time. They orchestrated a strategy for neutering constitutional amendments emancipating enslaved people, permitting them to vote, and protecting their rights by due process of law. The 13th amendment outlawed slavery for all except prisoners. That was easy. Make former slaves into prisoners and create a prison leasing system returning them to plantations. The 14th amendment providing equal protection was narrowed to federal laws, not state laws, by way of a convoluted ruling in the Slaughterhouse cases in which the petitioner turned the amendments against themselves. The 15th amendment prohibited denying voting privileges based on race. Another easy one: simply deny voting rights for black people for a reason other than skin color.

Jim Crow laws reconstituted slavery and the slave masters were back in business. Still, they wanted more. The industrial revolution was expanding and they wanted more of it. The concepts for stealing Indian lands and seizing control of resources for the industrial machine could be applied to foreign lands under the auspices of the U.S. government.

The forces of greed refined their skills at corruption, as they applied the technique for taking resources for personal enrichment by invading, sabotaging and subjugating foreign lands and peoples. Imperialism, in service of greed, sprouted from the blood-soaked lands of the Civil War.

The system for accumulating wealth, as noted in the discussion about the Triangle Trade, reigns Supreme. Whatever it takes for system preservation must be done. Moral constraints be damned. Scholars debate the difference between Colonialism and Imperialism. Within this context, the difference is irrelevant. One nation asserting its muscle in dominating another, albeit for resources, slaves, shipping ports, markets or anything else is simply wrong and a crime. The system, noted in the chapter, **Industrial Revolution, Cotton, Capitalism and Road to Civil War**, required nothing less.

As the drums were beating for Civil War, America exerted its aggressive instincts, first attacking Indians and taking their lands; then in the Mexican War, a war based upon a fraudulent predicate—fooling no one—a clear exercise of power; and expanding onto lands not contiguous to the continent, such Puerto Rico, Cuba, Japan, the Philippines and Hawaii.

Cotton provided a path to wealth and power. Yes, the market fluctuated, some good years, some bad, but that is true for any commodity. Logistics were critical. Growing cotton, harvesting it and quickly moving it to manufacturers was critical.

Railroads and a network of canals linked the inner continental lands to the coasts along with interconnecting shipping lanes such as the Mississippi. Long voyages required refueling stations with advanced port operations. Cotton slave masters depended upon the might of the central government in paving the way for international cooperation.

"The peculiar combination," says Beckert, "of expropriated lands, slave labor, and the domination of a state that gave enormous latitude to slave owners over their labor was fabulously profitable for those positioned to embrace it: As early as 1807 a Mississippi cotton plantation was said to return 22.5 percent annually on its investment."[183]

England established the standard for 19th century imperialism, invading and colonizing foreign lands; taking resources for feeding industrial machinery and returning with finished products for sale to the colonized. Perhaps it was no different from the Spanish invasion of the New World. America demanded its spot in the imperialist contest.

From the earliest days of Civilization, aggression for expanding control over people, land and resources afforded the wealthy and the powerful a mechanism for ever greater wealth and power. Indeed, the history of the civilized world exposes naked aggression, the essence of Imperialism, rationalized and justified as some noble enterprise.

As America looked ahead considering its logistical network, it not only looked to the east for shipping to Manchester, it also looked to the west. Japan, Hawaii and the Philippines appeared as inviting shipping ports.

Japan

As America scanned the globe assessing possible shipping ports, attention became focused upon Japan. Before the Scramble for Africa and before the Civil War, the United States entered the imperial enterprise in 1853 by way of an expedition led by Commodore Matthew Perry. America demanded that Japan open ports for trade. The Japanese resisted relations with peoples outside its borders for over 200 years, but Perry argued they would have to change; because the civilized world had determined that it do so.

American bullying of Japan, however, would be long forgotten by December 7, 1941. On that day the Japanese vented resentments that had been brewing since July 14, 1853, when Commodore Perry appeared with his black ships, intimidated the Japanese, and set in motion the humiliating period in which Japan would attempt to become westernized, using Germany as its role model.

When Commodore Matthew ("Old Matt") Calbraith Perry sailed into Edo Bay on July 8, 1853, "writes Ian Buruma in *Inventing Japan: 1853-1964* , "with four heavily armed ships, on a mission to open up Japanese ports to American ships, he could be forgiven for thinking the Japanese were an ignorant people. Japan had been cut off from most other countries for roughly two hundred years."

…"It was one of the most extraordinary confrontations in modern history," says Buruma. "There was Perry with his four "black ships of evil," thundering an ominous salute at the Japanese coast by firing his cannon. And there were the Japanese, lined up on the shore, armed with swords and old-fashioned muskets. Commodore Perry insisted on dealing only with the highest representatives of the Japanese government, without really knowing who they were."[184]

"Japan's emergence as a modern nation was stunning to behold: swifter, more audacious, more successful, and ultimately more crazed, murderous, and self-destructive than anyone had imagined possible," says John Dower in *Embracing defeat: Japan in the wake of World War II*. "In retrospect, it seemed almost an illusion—a ninety-three-year dream become nightmare that began and ended with American warships. In 1853, a modest fleet of four vessels, two of them coal-burning "black ships," had arrived to force the country open. In 1945, a huge, glistening armada came back to close it."[185]

"By the time Perry arrived," writes George Feifer in *Breaking open Japan: Commodore Perry, Lord Abe, and American Imperialism in 1853*, "Japan had been at peace for two and a half centuries, longer than a similar respite enjoyed by any other major nation. Peace helped to dull the memory of the old bloodshed, and a growing sense of security

INDICTING AMERICA

nourished confidence that foreigners wouldn't invade because they perceived the country was too strong." [186]

The Japanese succumbed to Commodore Perry agreeing to the "Unfair Treaties" as they became known which "opened up" Japan. The impact upon Japan was monumental impacting every facet of its society.

The United States of America was a by-product of the European invasion of the Americas. The U.S. as an aggressive invader taking land from others and declaring it for itself was an integral component of the country before separation from England. Indeed, it was England's resistance to opening the west and risking wars with so-called Native Americans that contributed to the rift with the British Parliament.

Invasion of the New World informed and prepared late 19th century European leaders as they engaged in the Scramble for Africa. This time each country would stake out its claim, embrace ruthless brutality, and crush any and all opposition. They would not stumble and flail about as they did in the New World; this time they would apply lessons from the past.

Manifest Destiny, the American doctrine for removing Indians and taking their lands, represents America's Imperialism, starting with invasions of lands within the continent, but later expanded to foreign lands. This rationalization for stealing lands and removing indigenous people inspired a veteran of the First World War: Adolph Hitler.

"It is here that some of the most unsettling evidence has been assembled, says Whitman, "as historians have shown that Nazi expansion eastward was accompanied by invocations of the American conquest of the West, with its accompanying wars on Native Americans.[187]

After the Civil War, imperialism blossomed. Consider the following:

IMPERIALISM

Hawaii

"In 1993, one hundred years after the American-backed revolution that brought down Hawaii's monarchy, this movement achieved a remarkable success," says Kinzer in *Overthrow: America's Century of Regime Change from Hawaii to Iraq*. "Its leaders persuaded the United States Senate and the House of Representatives to pass a resolution declaring that Congress "apologizes to Native Hawaiians on behalf of the people of the United States for the overthrow of the Hawaiian Kingdom on January 17, 1893," and for the subsequent "deprivation of the rights of Native Hawaiians to self-determination.""[188]

"History remembers," adds Kinzer in *John Foster Dulles, Allen Dulles, and Their Secret World War*, "John Watson Foster's brief term as secretary of state for a singular accomplishment. In 1893 he helped direct the overthrow of the Hawaiian monarchy. President Harrison had discreetly encouraged white settlers in Hawaii to rebel against Queen Liliuokalani, and when they did, Secretary of State Foster endorsed the landing of American troops at Honolulu to support them. The settlers proclaimed themselves Hawaii's new government, the United States quickly recognized their regime, and the monarchy was no more."[189]

Philippines

After the Spanish American War, 1898, the Philippines was assigned to America. Filipinos' rebelled and fighting broke out. America prevailed in that fight making the Philippines an American colony. Most Americans remained unaware of it. Americans know little about their colonies. During World War II, American troops were surprised to find Filipinos were, indeed, American citizens.

Daniel Immerwahr in *How to Hide an Empire* recounts this story: "The Second World War in the Philippines rarely appears in history textbooks. But it should. It was by far the most destructive event ever to take place on U.S. soil.

Oscar Villadolid, a boy at the time, remembers a familiar scene from the aftermath of Manila's "liberation." A GI came down his street handing out cigarettes and Hershey bars. Speaking slowly, he asked Villadolid's name. When Villadolid replied easily in English, the soldier was startled. "How'd ya learn American?" he asked.

Villadolid explained that when the United States colonized the Philippines, it had instituted English in the schools. This only compounded the GI's confusion. "He did not even know that America had a colony here in the Philippines!" Villadolid marveled.

Take a moment to let that sink in. This was a soldier who had taken a long journey across the Pacific. He'd been briefed on his mission, shown maps, told where to go and whom to shoot. Yet at no point had it dawned on him that he was preparing to save a U.S. colony and that the people he would encounter there were, just like him, U.S. nationals.

He thought he was invading a foreign country."[190]

Cuba

Kinzer: "In 1898 the United States definitively embraced what Senator Henry Cabot Lodge called "the large policy." Historians have given it various names: expansionism, imperialism, neocolonialism. Whatever it is called, it represents the will of Americans to extend their global reach.[191]

…The Republic of Cuba came into existence on May 20, 1902. Its early years were marked by sporadic uprisings and attacks on American property. After a protest against electoral fraud in 1906,

American troops landed and placed the country under direct military rule. They stayed for three years.

"In fact, the McKinley administration wanted more than that," according to Immerwahr. "It wanted to ensure that U.S. property claims were protected (a serious concern, given that the Cuban revolutionaries had torched sugar plantations), and it wanted the right to intervene if Cuban politics started looking wobbly. Using the threat of continued military occupation as leverage, Wood got the Cuban legislature to agree to both demands— not only agree to them but write them into law. For more than thirty years the Cuban constitution contained an astonishing clause granting the United States the right to invade Cuba (which it did, four times)."[192]

"The longer the Philippine War groaned on," Immerwahr adds, "the better the Cuban path looked to would-be imperialists. Though nominally independent, Cuba was easily absorbed into the U.S. sphere of influence. North Americans owned its sugar fields, its mines, its tobacco industry, its banks, and much of its land. Young Cubans learned English and played baseball."[193]

"After Franklin Roosevelt became president of the United States in 1933," says Kinzer, "he decided that the Machado dictatorship had become an embarrassment and encouraged the Cuban army to rebel. It did so, and out of the ensuing turmoil emerged a sergeant named Fulgencio Batista. By the mid-1930s he was master of Cuba, and he shaped its fate for most of the next quarter century."[194]

…the United States had not crushed Cuba's drive to independence in the early twentieth century, if it had not supported a series of repressive dictators there, and if it had not stood by while the 1952 election was canceled, a figure like Castro would almost certainly not have emerged. His regime is the quintessential result of a "regime change" operation gone wrong, one that comes back to haunt the country that sponsored it."[195]

Guatemala

The indigenous people of Guatemala arrived in that land at the end of a journey that began in Africa; migrated across Iran and Kazakhstan; into Russia and the tundra of Siberia; across the Chukchi Sea to Alaska; following herds into the Great Plains and south to Mexico; and finally, into Central America.

The fertile lands also beckoned corporate agriculturalists. United Fruit laid claim to vast areas of land, but only planted on a portion of the land. The Guatemala government offered to purchase the land for redistribution to Guatemalans living there so they could address poverty. United Fruit did not like that and used the U.S. government to overthrow the Guatemala government.

"The land reform bill," according to David Talbot in *The Devil's Chessboard: Allen Dulles, the CIA, and the Rise of America's Secret Government,* "that the new president hammered out and then ushered through the legislature two years later was relatively moderate—Arbenz's government only expropriated acreage from United Fruit's huge holdings that was not under cultivation, and it offered the multinational corporation fair compensation for the seized land. But by Guatemala's retrogressive standards, Arbenz's land redistribution measures were breathtakingly bold."[196]

"Before the CIA," says Kinzer, "deposed the government of Guatemala in 1954, for example, United Fruit was not free to operate as it wished in that country; afterward it was."

"On December 9, 1953," Tim Winer says in *Legacy of ashes: the history of the CIA,* "Allen Dulles formally approved Operation Success and authorized a $3 million budget. He appointed Al Haney as field commander and named Tracy Barnes as its chief of political warfare. "[197]

"In 1954 the CIA had successfully used radio to spread fake news during a coup it helped stage to overthrow Guatemala's democratically elected but left-leaning government," says Immerwahr. "With its transmitter on Swan Island, it could run an even more secure and sophisticated operation, this time directed at Fidel Castro's socialist regime in Cuba."[198]

"Late on September 9, 1954," says Talbot, "as midnight approached, Jacobo Arbenz, the recently deposed president of Guatemala, was escorted into the Guatemala City airport with a small entourage, including his wife, Maria Vilanova, and two of their children. Arbenz was beloved among his dirt-poor country's peasants and workers for his land and labor reforms, but he was reviled by Guatemala's aristocracy. As he prepared to leave his homeland, Arbenz was showered with abuse by a smartly dressed crowd of several hundred ill-wishers. "Assassin! Thief!"[199]

"Few private companies have ever been as closely interwoven with the United States government as United Fruit was during the mid-1950s," says Kinzer. "Dulles had, for decades, been one of its principal legal counselors. His brother, Allen, the CIA director, had also done legal work for the company and owned a substantial block of its stock."[200]

United Fruit contracted with Edward Bernays, Sigmund Freud's nephew and the father of Public Relations. Bernays was an expert in propaganda, the mass communications technique for manipulating the mass public into believing the unbelievable.

Kinzer says, "American hearts and minds had already been won. Thanks largely to a brilliantly executed propaganda campaign paid for by United Fruit and directed by the legendary opinion-maker Edward Bernays, press coverage of Arbenz in the United States was overwhelmingly negative. When a New York Times reporter in Guatemala, Sydney

Gruson, began filing stories about the benefits of land reform, Allen quietly protested, and the Times's publisher, Arthur Hays Sulzberger, obligingly had Gruson recalled."

"The new man was Edward Bernays, a nephew of Sigmund Freud and the dominant figure in his young profession. Bernays was one of the first masters of modern mass psychology. He liked to describe himself as the "father of public relations," and no one disagreed. His specialty was what he called "the conscious and intelligent manipulation of the organized habits and opinions of the masses." He proposed to Zemurray that United Fruit launch a campaign to blacken the image of Guatemala's government. That, he argued, could decisively weaken it and perhaps set off events that would trigger its collapse."

"Propaganda," says Bernays, "becomes vicious and reprehensive only when its authors consciously and deliberately disseminate what they know to be lies, or when they aim at effects which they know to be prejudicial to the common good."

"His next effort is to analyze his public. He studies the groups which must be reached, and the leaders through whom he may approach these groups. Social groups, economic groups, geographical groups, age groups, doctrinal groups, language groups, cultural groups, all these represent his divisions through which, on behalf of his client, he may talk to the public.

The Bernays playbook informed Movement Conservative, an offspring of the Slave Masters, in forming a long-term strategy for dismantling the American government. Indeed, Americans who once loved their country turned to an autocratic bigot in 2016 for leadership.

"Men are rarely aware," says Bernays, "of the real reasons which motivate their actions. A man may believe that he buys a motor car because, after careful study of the technical features of all makes on the market, he has concluded that this is the best. He is almost certainly fooling himself. He bought it, perhaps, because a friend whose financial acumen he respects bought one last week; or because his neighbors believed he was not able to afford a car of that class; or because its colors are those of his college fraternity."

"A thing may be desired not for its intrinsic worth or usefulness, but because he has unconsciously come to see in it a symbol of something else, the desire for which he is ashamed to admit to himself. A man buying a car may think he wants it for purposes of locomotion, whereas the fact may be that he would really prefer not to be burdened with it, and would rather walk for the sake of his health. He may really want it because it is a symbol of social position, evidence of his success in business, or a means of pleasing his wife."

This concept, focusing on emotions, is at the heart of today's Culture War. Political activist "Viguerie was also well aware that abortion, busing, pornography, gun rights, and crime were exactly the kinds of morally charged and dramatic issues that were capable of galvanizing public support, according to Phillips-Fein. "To imagine that the New Right has a fixation on these issues misses the mark," Viguerie wrote. "The New Right is looking for issues that people care about, and social issues, at least for the present, fit the bill."

"Never before had an American corporation waged a propaganda campaign in the United States aimed at undermining the president of a foreign country. Zemurray was reluctant to make United Fruit the first. Then, in the spring of 1951, Bernays sent him a message with alarming news. The reformist leader of faraway Iran, Mohammad Mossadegh, had just done the unthinkable by nationalizing the Anglo-Iranian Oil Company. "Guatemala might follow suit," Bernays wrote in his note."[201]

"To ensure political and financial "stability," says Immerwahr, "U.S. troops entered Cuba (four times), Nicaragua (three times), Honduras (seven times), the Dominican Republic (four times),

Guatemala, Panama (six times), Costa Rica, Mexico (three times), and Haiti (twice) between 1903 and 1934. The United States helped to put down revolts, replaced governments when necessary, and offered battleships-in-the-harbor "advice" to others. But the only territory it annexed in that period was the U.S. Virgin Islands, peacefully purchased from Denmark in 1917."[202]

Nicaragua

In 1909, President Howard Taft authorized the sabotage of the Nicaraguan government. Acting behind a pretense of security and democratic principles, Taft authorized deposing José Santos Zelaya from power. Zelaya wanted foreign powers to leave Nicaragua to itself. This represented a threat to U.S. business interests.[203]

"During the last decades of the nineteenth century," says Kinzer, "the ideals of social and political reform swept across Central America. Visionary leaders, inspired by European philosophers and nation builders, sought to wipe away the feudal systems that had frozen their countries into immobility. One of them, President José Santos Zelaya of Nicaragua, took his nationalist principles so seriously that the United States felt compelled to overthrow him."

"Zelaya was six weeks short of his fortieth birthday when he was sworn in as president of Nicaragua. He proclaimed a revolutionary program and set out to shake his country from its long slumber. He built roads, ports, railways, government buildings, and more than 140 schools; paved the streets of Managua, lined them with street lamps, and imported the country's first automobile; legalized civil marriage and divorce; and even founded the nation's first baseball league, which included a team called "Youth" and another called "The Insurgency."

IMPERIALISM

He encouraged business, especially the nascent coffee industry. In foreign affairs, he promoted a union of the five small Central American countries and fervently embraced the grand project that had thrust Nicaragua onto the world stage: the inter oceanic canal."[204]

The canal across Nicaragua, however, conflicted with the wishes of French engineers who wanted to build the canal in Panama. To make sure they got what they wanted they hired Sullivan and Cromwell, a law firm with deep connection with the Dulles Brothers. [205]

In later years during the Reagon administration, disgruntled Nicaraguans rebelled. They came to power in 1979, formed an alliance with Cuba and established its stance against American imperialism.

"The CIA island," says Immerwahr, "was in fact a central node in the vast and distinctly not-legal plot to overthrow the Nicaraguan government. That plot in its fullness incorporated arms dealers, drug traffickers, Middle Eastern governments, religious organizations, Cuban exiles, retired generals, and Rambo-style soldiers of fortune. Had such a multifarious scheme appeared in one of Fleming's novels, it might have strained his readers' patience. It is a victory for the forces of concision that today we know it simply by two words, albeit incongruous ones: the Iran-Contra affair."[206]

Let's not forget the American colonies:

What is more, a lot of people have lived in that other part. Here's the census count for the inhabited territories in 1940, the year before Pearl Harbor:

Territory	Years held	1940 pop.
Philippines	1899– 1946	16,356,000
Puerto Rico	1899– present	1,869,255
Hawai'I	1898– 1959 (state after)	423,330

INDICTING AMERICA

Territory	Years held	1940 pop.
Alaska	1867– 1959 (state after)	72,524
Panama Canal Zone	1904– 1979	51,827
U.S. Virgin Islands	1917– present	24,889
Guam	1899– present	22,290
American Samoa	1900– present	12,908
	Total in Territories	18,833,023

Immerwahr, Daniel. **How to Hide an Empire** (pp. 10-11). Farrar, Straus and Giroux. Kindle Edition.

Blowback

Americans have short memories, but victims of crime do not. For many, vengeance is the sole reason for carrying on.

"After two and a half centuries of relative tranquility under the Tokugawa shogunate," says Eri Hotta in *Japan 1941: Countdown to Infamy*, "Japan was forced to shake itself out of a self-imposed isolation that had limited the country's contact with the outside world. China's weakness in the mid-nineteenth century meant that it could no longer be a buffer— Japan had to face the Western powers on its own. Equally worrying was that, immediately to the north of Japan and China, czarist Russia appeared eager to extend its already overextended empire. Completely new to the great-power game, Japan had to learn its rules quickly. That it was able to do so owed a great deal to a group of remarkably talented young visionaries who gave birth to modern Japan. By the early twentieth century, Japan, amazingly for an Asian power, had attained a certain standing in the elite club of Western imperialists, though it never felt entirely at home in such company. Theodore Roosevelt's reported comment, meant as a compliment, that the Japanese were an "honorary white race" explains why."[207]

"After the first Opium War," according to Rana Mitter in *Forgotten Ally: China's World War II, 1937–1945*, "it was Japan's turn to confront the West, this time led by the United States. In 1853 Commodore Matthew Perry sailed into Tokyo Harbor, requesting that Japan abandon its centuries of near-isolation and open itself to a wider range of trading partners. Perry's demand was politely issued, but it was backed up by the force of gunboats. The next decade and a half saw a major crisis in Japan as the shoguns, the Tokugawa family who acted as regents on behalf of the emperor, found they had no solutions to offer to ward off the foreigners. One scion of the family, Tokugawa Nariaki, advocated all-out war. "If we put our trust in war the whole country's morale will be increased," he claimed, "and even if we sustain a defeat we will in the end defeat the foreigner."[208]

"In 1922, General Utsonomiya Tarô," Mitter adds, "had lain on his deathbed and pointed to a world map, declaring, "That must all become Japan's!," indicating territory that stretched from Siberia to New Zealand. Yet in making such declarations, Japanese imperialists felt that they were merely learning from their Western counterparts. "Haven't you ever heard of Perry?" asked General Ishiwara Kanji of an American prosecutor at the Tokyo war crimes trials in 1946, referring to the US commodore, Matthew C. Perry, who had forced Japan open in 1858. Japan "took your country as its teacher and set about learning how to be aggressive. You might say we became your disciples."[209]

In June, 2024, Chiquita Brands International was found liable for funding drug cartels in Columbia that provided muscle for their banana operations there. National Security Archives provided documentation for the case.

While Imperial Invasions were underway, new technological developments emerged. Converging with Imperial impulses, technology, particularly in communications, provided a critical mechanism for delivering propaganda, mass manipulation tools for mass populations. The modern era is enveloped with bold and outright lies; reality and truth be damned. Slave Masters and their progeny are sustained by a sophisticated cadre of mass communication and social psychology experts dedicated for creating spin (outright lies with just a hint of truth) in service of the Power Elite, the Slave Masters.

Osterhammel explains development of the foundational infrastructure:

"...**telegraph** came into use in 1844. The first durable underwater cable was laid across the English Channel in 1851, and a permanent transatlantic link was established in 1866. By 1862 the worldwide terrestrial telegraph network was 150,000 miles in length; by 1876 India and all the settler colonies of the British Empire were linked to the home country and one another; and by 1885 Europe could be reached from nearly all large cities by underwater cable. The telegraph network was much too cumbersome, overloaded, and expensive to be described as a "Victorian Internet"— it absorbed 15 percent of the Times'expenditure for 1898— but the basic model was there for a historically unprecedented world wide web."

Julius Reuter from Kassel, Germany, opened his office in London in 1851— the same year that transmission time across the Channel was shortened to a couple of hours. Two other Jewish entrepreneurs had already founded news agencies or "telegraph offices": Charles Havas in Paris and Bernhard Wolff in Berlin. The Associated Press came into being in the United States in 1848.

...**magazines.** The special characteristics of the newspaper were: (1) publication at regular intervals; (2) production by an editorial team; (3) division into separate departments and fields; (4) reporting that went outside the regional and social horizon of its readers; (5) a rise in topicality, which in Germany meant that the proportion of news less than a day old rose from 11 percent in 1856 to 95 percent in 1906; (6) increasingly industrial production, based on the latest technology, which required considerable capital investment for a mass circulation press; and (7) a fluctuating market that depended on daily decisions by customers at the newsstand, except in the case of subscribers."

Geography was a globally sighted but locally rooted science. As economic geography it accompanied the industrialization process in America and North America; as colonial geography it consorted with the West's land-grabbing expansion. An even more important organ of self-observation was the newly emerging social sciences.

Sociology, whose founding fathers were Auguste Comte in France and Herbert Spencer in Britain, thought of itself mainly as a theoretical discipline.

In 1915, when Émile Durkheim, Max Weber, and Georg Simmel were still flourishing, the first sociological account of Chinese society by Chinese authors appeared in print; and in the same year, the subject started to be taught by Chinese lecturers at a few universities. Chinese sociologists subsequently developed numerous analyses of contemporary society, with an increasingly Marxist orientation. "[210]

America is charged with invading sovereign nations in violation of International Law, assassination, corruption of foreign governments, and sabotage of foreign governments.

World Wars

VIEWED THROUGH A CONTEMPORARY LENS, outcome of the World Wars seemed inevitable. Viewed through a lens of 1940, it was viewed with uncertainty. Indeed, fear permeated the globe as all felt threatened by the blood of war. The blood of World War Part One had barely dried as the drums were beating for Part Two.

Invasion, occupation and colonization of Africa converged with England's invasion and subjugation of China and India, along with Japanese aggression aimed at making Asia for Asians, setting the stage for intense antagonisms. These were not new antagonisms; they were animosities brewing for many centuries.

The French Revolution at the end of the 18th century developed into Napoleonic Wars that raged across the globe. As it came to conclusion, European powers joined at the Congress of Vienna in 1814 determined to quiet the passions for warfare by establishing a lasting peace. They succeeded for the most part and peace lasted for about a century, until the Industrial Revolution fueled the drive for new sources of wealth and power derived from industrial machines fed with natural resources obtained from around the globe. They didn't obtain the natural resources by way of fair-trade practices;

they did so by way of invasion and brute force, euphemistically labeled colonialism. [211]

England "colonized" lands in China, India, the Middle East and Africa. France staked its claims in Africa and Southeast Asia. Belgium pursued its fortunes in the Congo, followed by Germany, the Dutch and other European powers staking claims on the African continent and Asia. America laid claim to the Philippines, Guam, The Virgin Islands, Samoa, Puerto Rico and the Aleutian Islands.

The New World enterprise that began in 1492 transitioned into the Scramble for Africa, with subplots playing out in other parts of the globe. Indeed, it was this never-ending thirst for wealth and power that provided the root cause for the World Wars of the 20th century; a period in which over 100 million humans would be killed in warfare.[212]

Wars are viewed as independent discreet events, but they never are; indeed, they are all connected. World Wars I and II were preceded by Japanese aggression in Manchuria, an aggressive behavior provoked by the Commodore Perry episode. Japan also engaged in battles with the Russians over Korea. Korea experienced being "opened up" by the French and more "unfair treaties." England flexed its muscles numerous times in India and China in maintaining colonial control. These conflicts erupted while the Scramble for Africa was underway, including the brute force inflicted upon Africans by Cecil Rhoades, King Leopold and others. [213]

The First World War began long before the events typically associated with the start of the war, such as the killing of the Archduke Ferdinand. That was but a spark. Once again, lacking a vision with an objective and a strategy for achieving it, the world powers merely reacted to events based on alliances that were tenuous at best. The First War ended with an armistice, which means it didn't really end.

Germany was punished and that fueled anger that erupted again about 20 years later.

When did the Second World War begin? It is debatable. Traditionally history has focused upon the European War, but contemporary historians suggest attention should more appropriately consider Asia.

"What began on July 7, 1937," says Mitter, "as an unplanned local conflict between Chinese and Japanese troops near Beijing, known as the "Marco Polo Bridge Incident," escalated into an all-out war between the two great nations of East Asia; it would not end until August 1945."[214]

Ferocious fighting exploded between Japan and China. Commodore Perry's humiliation of Japan manifested a deep provocation for fighting back and demonstrating that Japan was not a weakling or cowering nation. The powerless wanted power; the bullied wanted to punch back; grievances born by insult needed redress. Perhaps China was a surrogate for America, but the rage exhibited by Japan has been overshadowed by attention on Europe. China, under the leadership of Chiang Kai-shek, achieved the unachievable: it held off the Japanese onslaught.

He appealed to India's Prime Minister Jawaharlal Nehru to join the fight against the Axis Powers (Germany, Japan and Italy), even though both India and China were targets of England's colonial adventures. Chiang Kai-shek argued the English were monsters, but the Axis powers were much, much worse.

"In my farewell statement," he wrote," says Mitter, "I completely supported the liberation of India. The British may not understand this, but I deeply believe it may be of advantage to Britain." He noted that Nehru had complained of the contradictions in Chiang's attitude to India, supporting independence but also requesting that it throw its lot in with the British war effort; Chiang had replied that all politics was confusing, and if it were clearer then it would be "philosophy, not politics."[215]

For China the death toll topped 14 million people.

Mitter: "The toll that the war inflicted on China is still being calculated, but conservative estimates number the dead at 14 million at least (the British Empire and United States each lost over 400,000 during the Second World War, and Russia more than 20 million). The number of Chinese refugees may have reached more than 80 million. The greater part of China's hard-won modernization was destroyed, including most of the rail network, sealed highways, and industrial plants created in the first decades of the twentieth century: 30 percent of the infrastructure in the rich Pearl River delta near Canton, 52 percent in Shanghai, and a staggering 80 percent in the capital, Nanjing.9 The war would undo two empires in China (the British and the Japanese) and help to create two more (the American and the Soviet). The narrative of the war is the story of a people in torment: from the Nanjing Massacre (widely known as the Rape of Nanking, December 1937–January 1938), when Japanese troops murdered and looted in the captured Chinese capital, to the blasting of dikes on the Yellow River in June 1938, which bought time for the Chinese Army but at a terrible price for hundreds of thousands of compatriots."[216]

"For decades, our understanding of that global conflict has failed to give a proper account of the role of China. If China was considered at all, it was as a minor player, a bit-part actor in a war where the United States, Soviet Union, and Britain played much more significant roles. Yet China was the first country to face the onslaught of the Axis Powers in 1937, two years before Britain and France, and four years before the United States."[217]

"Nor has the outside world ever fully understood the ghastly price that China paid to maintain its resistance against Japan for eight long years, from 1937 to 1945. Some 14 million deaths, massive refugee flight, and the destruction of the country's embryonic modernization were the costs of the war."[218]

The industrial revolution was but another milestone in the story of excess, wealth, power and greed. Following the pattern of the New World Invasion, European powers invaded China, India and Africa; soon spreading to every corner of the globe. Wars have been rationalized as Just Wars for the purpose of emotionally energizing internal populations for support while demonizing the adversary as less than human. But all of that is nothing more than spin, pure manipulation for obfuscating true motivations of excess, wealth, power and greed.

Woodrow Wilson and Franklin Roosevelt understood colonialism as the primary source of the World Wars. Both, FDR and Wilson, attempted and failed in confronting colonialism. FDR was on a path against his allies, England and France, for ending colonialism, but he died before he concluded his objective and was replaced by Harry Truman who was insulated from FDR's thoughts.

"Therefore all colonies should be given their independence," says Frederick Logevall in *Embers of War: The Fall of an Empire and the Making of America's Vietnam*. "The president's son Elliott records FDR as saying, some months after U.S. entry into the war: "Don't think for a moment, Elliott, that Americans would be dying in the Pacific tonight, if it hadn't been for the shortsighted greed of the French and the British and the Dutch. Shall we allow them to do it all, all over again [after the war]?" Although the reliability of Elliott's direct quotation may be questioned, there is little doubt he captured his father's basic conviction."[219]

America was never more united than at the end of World War II, the Great War. Americans basked in victory; they didn't seek war, but when war came knocking at their door, they had the courage, bravery and wherewithal for victory. It was a shared sacrifice; everyone did their part. That was just one of the attributes making America special, egalitarianism, no special caste or class, just common people working together, doing their fair share in fighting the Nazis. This worldview of what America is all about—standing for freedom and justice, willing to do for a cause greater than themselves—made Americans proud to be Americans. Indeed, it seemed to validate the mythical story of American history.

At the end of the war, polls indicated close to 80% of Americans loved their country. Today, it is estimated at less than 20%. Something happened between then and now: the Slave Masters and their progeny.

In the post war, America was all about the Common Good. Labor unions were favored, returning war veterans honored, and the visceral sense of shared sacrifice by all Americans honored. For the first time America felt like a united United States. If the aristocrats were to resume their ruling position of power, they needed a strategy for undoing the country's sense of unity, driving wedges between Americans and reversing the gains of the New Deal.

For the Slaveocracy the task of regaining political ascendency was daunting, but they were determined. They needed a plan, a strategy for upending the New Deal and Americans love affair with America. Drawing upon the playbook of Bacon's Rebellion in 1667, driving wedges between Americans was a key. Over years they would test assorted wedges issues and settle on those that worked best. Abortion, gun rights, gay marriage, segregation, family values, religious freedom and more emerged as effective tools for dividing Americans. The techniques for public persuasion that Bernays termed Public Relations represented the sword and shield for their battle.

Power elites focused on their power, control and wealth enhancing enterprises. At the turn of the 20th century countervailing forces advocating for Common Good threatened the power elite. World War II represented a clear danger to them and the economic systems favoring them. Forces for change were a direct threat, prompting the power elite to fight back. And fight back they did, but they did so covertly, away from public scrutiny, because the patriotic America of the mid-20th century would never support them. Instead, they hid their agenda, their goals and objectives. Using the latest and most sophisticated techniques for Public Relations (propaganda), they reframed issues so their self-interested initiatives were defined as efforts for Freedom and Liberty strategically disguising their real agenda.

Nazism threatened America's core so FDR orchestrated a sense of desperation and a sense of shared cause in joining together in fighting Hitler and his Nazis. It was one for all and all for one, even if elitists refused cooperation. In meeting the challenge for producing war machinery, FDR seized the means of production placing America's manufacturing in service of the war effort. Government owned, Government operated manufacturing terrified the elite. Even during the war, they mounted public relations campaigns promoting their interests and diminishing government's role.

But government control of manufacturing was critical for the war effort. America produced the weaponry for the Allied forces and it won the war: Cooperation in a share task for the Common Good. Before World War Part Two erupted, FDR asked government, industry and academia to examine the assets essential for fighting another war. They concluded that rubber was vital. Between the first and second war, auto and aircraft technology boomed. The military was now dependent upon these forms of transportation and they were dependent upon rubber. But they cautioned that the world's supply of rubber was largely controlled by adversaries. If new sources for rubber were not found, America would surely lose another worldwide war.

Without access to rubber, the American military was impotent. Indeed, in preparation for war, the War Production Board (WPB) warned that without rubber, the military machinery would be useless. The WPB, a government agency, seized control directing industry and academia to take on the problem. How to create rubber, when access to raw materials is cut off? It was the key for America's ability to fight the war. Those working collaboratively under a government funded and controlled project won the Second World War.

"Between 1860 and 1920: says Immerwahr, "world rubber consumption grew nearly two-hundred-fold. In the auto-mad United States, rubber thirst was unshakable. By the eve of the Second World War, the country consumed some 70 percent of the world's supply, bought mostly from Europe's Asian colonies. If war came, the United States would need still more. A Sherman tank used half a ton of rubber, a heavy bomber used a full ton, and a battleship used more than twenty thousand rubber parts, totaling eighty tons. As the president of the tire manufacturer B. F. Goodrich warned, without rubber the United States "could offer only 1860 defenses against 1942 attacks." [220]

"Without rubber— it wasn't a hypothetical scenario. On December 7/ 8, 1941," says Immerwahr, "Japan, worried about its own access to rubber and other critical raw materials, expanded its war beyond China and moved on to the resource-rich lands of Southeast Asia. Within months, it conquered the European colonies that accounted for 97 percent of the U.S. rubber supply. The United States and its allies were virtually cut off."

It is hard to convey how dire a threat this was. "If a survey were made to determine the most frequently asked question in America today, it would probably turn out to be: 'When are we going to get rubber— and how much?'" wrote secretary of the interior in mid-1942. "We must get rubber— lots of it— and get it rather quickly, or our whole manner of living will be sadly awry."

Immerwahr: "Difference two: the U.S. program worked. There was no "eureka" moment when the secret to rubber synthesis was revealed. It was the result of a thousand little discoveries made by a small army of well-funded industrial chemists. Those scientists remembered it as a golden age, when men who had formerly labored as rivals in different companies could collaborate with a shared sense of purpose. "I don't think I have ever seen as congenial a group of people work together," said one. "[221]

"The industrial achievements were as impressive as the scientific ones. By the end of the war, the government had built fifty-one synthetic rubber plants (compared with Germany's three)," according to Immerwahr, "operating at the collective cost of $ 2 million a day. Just one such plant, which might employ 1,250 workers, made enough rubber to replace a rubber plantation that had twenty-four million trees and a workforce of at least 90,000. In mid-1944 the supply of rubber met the government's requirements. By 1945, it overshot them. At that point, the plants, not even operating at capacity, were pumping out eight hundred thousand tons a year. That was one-third more than the amount that in 1942 had seemed as if it would require "a miracle."

"One of the biggest mobilization projects of 1942– 43 was the creation of a huge new GOCO synthetic rubber industry," says Mark Wilson in *Destructive Creation: American Business and the Winning of World War II (American Business, Politics, and Society)*. "After Japan moved quickly after Pearl Harbor to dominate Southeast Asia, it controlled about 95 percent of the world's natural rubber supply. Suddenly, the Allies faced the real prospect of running out of rubber. This was an ugly problem that exposed some corporations' early unwillingness to relinquish patent rights, as well as poor decisions in 1940– 41 by Jesse Jones and President Roosevelt. Of all major American war industries (outside the atomic bomb project), rubber was the one that required the most extreme expansion of prewar capacities. By war's end, the United States was making nearly three hundred times as much synthetic rubber as it had done in 1940. "[222]

"The big synthetic rubber expansion of 1942- 43 was handled almost entirely by the GOCO method. In the opening weeks of 1942, the DPC financed the construction of eleven Buna-S synthetic rubber plants, each at least three times bigger than the four 10,000-ton plants that Jones and Roosevelt had authorized in 1941. The DPC would end up spending $ 700 million on the synthetic rubber program, which included three dozen facilities."

Industry, academia and government then worked together in tackling this problem. They developed synthetic rubber, another technological solution and one that would play a critical role in American commerce post war.

"The second account tells a far more critical story about American business leaders," says Wilson. "Indeed, it claims that big industrial corporations exploited the war emergency, to regain political power and reap economic gains. This story emphasizes the activities of corporate executives who went to Washington to run the war economy, in special civilian mobilization agencies such as the Office of Production Management and its successor, the War Production Board. Using their new foothold, so the story goes, the big corporations allied themselves with a conservative military establishment to thwart smaller firms, New Dealers, consumers, workers, and other citizens. According to this account, big business enjoyed huge wartime profits, thanks to an abundance of no-risk, cost-plus military contracts, which evidently prefigured the Cold War–era "military-industrial complex."[223]

"Government control and investment in industry during the war spearheaded Hitler's defeat. It also provided an infrastructure for a thriving industrial based after the war giving birth to America as the world's industrial giant. At the end of the war, America accounted for 50% of the world's manufacturing."

Industrialists did not rejoice in the success of the effort led by America, they were threatened. If the American government asserted some form of government manufacturing after the war, they would not be competitive. In contemporary times, universal healthcare is strenuously opposed by the industry, as it argues that it cannot compete with government.

"J. Howard Pew, the Sun Oil Company president," says Wilson, "explained to his fellow industrialists in early 1941. "All the citizenry is watching. With a vigorous public relations program, competitive enterprise can dramatize its strength more successfully today than its enemies have ever been able to dramatize its occasional temporary mistakes." [224]

Industry considered ideas of communism and socialism as enemies, including the U.S. government and all those ideas about patriotism and love of country.

"For Pew and many of his fellow business leaders," says Wilson, "the stakes in this public-relations struggle seemed sky-high. Success would mean convincing Americans that victory in World War II should be attributed to the accomplishments of private enterprise. Failing to do so might result in challenges to the private sector that could go well beyond those that had emerged during the Great War and the New Deal. "Whether the free enterprise system prevails in America after the war," explained the public-relations department of the Automotive Council for War Production (ACWP) in early 1942, "may depend on the extent to which the American people associate this system with industry's wartime record."

The National Association of Manufacturers (NAM) jumped into the forefront of the Public Relations campaign.

Wilson: "At the NAM's large "Congress of American Industry" conference, in New York in December 1941, several business leaders used their speeches to demand that the war not be used as an opportunity to encroach further upon private enterprise. If the United States were to abandon its tradition of competitive capitalism "and supinely rely on government control and operation," declared J. Howard Pew of Sun Oil, "then Hitlerism wins even though Hitler himself be defeated." Fuller, the outgoing NAM president, suggested that using seizures as a technique for achieving stability in industrial relations was akin to Hitler shooting hostages in France."[225]

Decades following the war Americans strutted their pride in the World War II culture of "one for all and all for us." Shared sacrifice, egalitarianism, northerners and southerners, even white troops and black troops, Americans defeated forces of evil. But while that illusion sunk in, powerful forces operating away from the public eye planned and strategized ways for subversions.

Aristocrats, the people of wealth and power, use their power for dominance. Unrestrained by morality, a segment of this population uses their resources for dominance of the political system and the people making rules and regulations, so the game is crafted in service of the elite, not the common good.

Their initiatives know no boundaries. They are not racist, but they use racism as a tool for achieving their goals. They are not homophobic, but they use it as a tool. They are not ideological, but they use that as a tool, too. They care only about their personal wealth and power and they will do anything, anything serving their riches, including murder, fraud, enslavement, poisoning of the air and water, selling toxic products, sponsoring wars resulting in massive death and destruction, anything serving their wishes.

In the past they were known as Kings and Queens; today they are hedge fund managers, oil barons, financiers, and corporate executives. They are the power elite, but they do not wear crowns, they do not hold political office, and they do not advertise themselves. They do, however, control political people using them in gaming the system. They shun the spotlight preferring secrecy and stealth for accomplishing their goals. They disdain democracies because the electorate is too unpredictable, but they are very skillful in controlling and manipulating democratic processes.

Consider how the National Association of Manufacturer's (NAM) spun the Great Depression of 1929.

"But NAM spent millions to convince the American people of the truth of the Tripod of Freedom, and to persuade Americans that the villain in the story of the Great Depression was not "Big Business," but "Big Government," writes Naomi Oreskes in *The Big Myth: How American Business Taught Us to Loathe Government and Love the Free Market*. "They spread this myth to weaken Americans' confidence in government institutions that reined in abusive business practices and protected ordinary citizens.[226]

Another technique for influencing worldview involves use of a prestigious individual for validation of the idea put forth, even if it means snipping out key words from the prestigious author, thereby misrepresenting the ideas of the prestigious person.

"Chicago economist George Stigler would become a leading voice against government regulation and win a Nobel Memorial Prize in Economic Sciences for this work; he would also produce an edited version of Adam Smith's Wealth of Nations that expunged nearly all of Smith's caveats about free market doctrine, including his extensive discussion of the need for bank regulation, for adequate wages for workers, and for taxation for public goods such as roads and bridges."[227]

Creating a myth and giving it credibility required carefully crafted long-term strategies.

When electricity became available for wide distribution, there was a debate about industry ownership. Should it be operated by government or should it be subject to the whims of corporate titans.

The National Electric Light Association had a long-term vision, investing in techniques for influencing the worldview of children.

"Pleased with the results of their experts-for-hire campaign," says Oreskes, "NELA executives moved on to their second phase: rewriting American textbooks and, in effect, American history. The goal was to foster not just a positive view of the American electricity industry, but a positive view of capitalism and a negative view of government engagement in economic affairs."[228]

"NELA rated 105 textbooks as good, fair, bad, or very bad.112 The bad books were labeled biased and socialistic; they needed to be replaced with more "objective" works."

Efforts at manipulating America's worldview, however, required operating covertly so the broad population did not become aware of their manipulation.

"Realizing that pressuring academics and publishers might be considered inappropriate, NELA urged its members to regard the program as "confidential," hoping "through quiet and diplomatic measures to have some of these inimical textbooks discarded" or at least revised."[229]

The National Association of Manufacturers (NAM) expanded initiatives for covertly influencing American's worldview.

"They would do so not merely by fighting specific New Deal initiatives, but by framing the lessons people drew from the Depression experience. Like NELA and the American Liberty League before them, they intended to change how their countrymen thought about capitalism and its role in America."[230]

NAM produced Uncle Abner.

INDICTING AMERICA

"Curmudgeonly Uncle Abner was the antithesis of an adorable little girl, but his message was the same: industrialists were benevolent, they knew what they were doing, and government should leave them the heck alone.[231]

"Uncle Abner Says was printed with only the signature of the cartoonist who drew them and no indication that NAM authored the captions, let alone that NAM had developed the series and supplied it free of charge.

"And in 1944, NAM produced its own textbook, The American Individual Enterprise System, written by its "economic principles commission." Intended as a "Bible" of the free-enterprise system, the textbook was distributed free of charge to twenty-four thousand school libraries."[232]

The progeny of Slave Masters had their work cut out for them. Americans' love of their country and their government had to be severed, if they were to hold control again. Fear and hatred of black people, once again, would provide them with a tool for driving wedges between America and Americans and, once again, this is clearly evident in the phenomenon of Donald Trump.

Communism Incited by the Capitalists

When the U.S. had its most significant influence at the end of World War II, Truman waffled on anti-colonialism and focused on anti-communism. To be sure, those nations under colonial rule turned to communist super powers for support, because there was no place else to go. Capitalist greed was the root cause of the wars, so they needed something different, even if they had but a vague understanding of the different economic systems of Communism or Socialism.

FDR turned a cold shoulder to Churchill at Yalta and engaged with Stalin, signaling his resolve in ending colonialism. He set a direction for the end of the war in opposition to returning colonized lands to their European overlords. Indeed, American military officials were confused by conflicting messages when Harry Truman supported the French in Vietnam.

When Truman was thrust into the Presidency, he was not prepared for implementing FDR's direction, because he was not in FDR's inner circle. Isolating Truman could be the most selfish act of FDR's legacy. FDR refused to accept the inevitability of his death, as if he somehow would be around to oversee rebuilding of the world. Truman assumed the Presidency and merely reacted to events. Once again ad-hoc management prevailed without a long-term vision, objective and strategy. Soon, Truman was faced with a decision for opening the door for nuclear warfare; the unthinkable became real. It should be noted that development of the atomic bomb is another example of cooperative collaboration between academia, industry and government.

Truman's ignorance of the relationship between FDR, Stalin and Churchill and of FDR's view of colonialism left him vulnerable to manipulation by forces determined for reinstitution of the greed infrastructure. The public relations campaign conducted by the titans of greed began long before the war ended using sophisticated and effective means for public manipulation.

The titans of industry were afraid of Hitler and Nazi Germany, but they also shared with them a visceral fear of Communism. Communism threatened their domination of political and social power.

Anti-communism was not new. As World War I neared conclusion, combatants were exhausted. Those fighting the war clearly understood the insanity of warfare, killing each other for the benefit of the elite. Russians walked off the battle field. Few had weapons and those with weapons had even fewer bullets. Germany put the exiled Lenin on a train and shipped him back to Russia where he could foment a revolution thereby taking Russia out of the war. It worked.

The Communist Lenin succeeded in kicking out the Russian monarchy but just what kind of Communist was he? Remember Communism is a product of the Common-ists, the people kicked off Common Lands by the greedy. The underlying ideas are founded in hunter-gatherer societies, each according to need and ability, suitable for small egalitarian communities. In the modern day with expanded populations and its need for industrial mass food production, the hunter-gatherer model is ridiculously absurd. At first Lenin attempted a Communist structure, but the realities of a nation destroyed by war; human suffering and starvation; cities ruined in ruble; a desperate need for food, shelter and medical care; quickly compelled a pragmatism causing Lenin to modify his approach; Lenin's New Economic Policy based on free market economics. [233]

When World War I ended, the other combatants also flirted with Communism. They, too, wanted an end to the brutality in service of wealthy elites. England, France and Germany teetered on the edge of revolutionary change. Political leaders managed to hold off those demanding change, but only for the short term. These forces would not be held back at the end of the next war.

German industrialists—the wealthy, greedy elite—were obsessed with anti-communism. Fritz Thyssen, Helmach Schacht, and others determined to fight communists or anyone else who might threaten their excess producing wealth and power enterprises provided essential funding for the Nazis, the ultimate anti-Communist protective edifice, mega force; the monster unleashed by the wealthy and powerful for their protection. Hitler has become the face of the Nazis and the sin of World War II, but Hitler was merely an employee of Germany's industrialist and financiers. Karma has a way of playing itself out, however, as Thyssen and Schacht both wound up in concentration camps.[234]

By the end of World War II, Stalin was far from a hunter-gatherer village chief, the model for a Communist society; he was a military commander applying autocratic rule for rebuilding a country that had been in the eye of the storm. Stalin cared nothing for ideology; he was a military commander in the mold of Grant, Curtis LeMay, and Patton; smash mouth brute strength; accepting death as collateral damage; while remaining riveted upon the mission, building power plants, roads, bridges, mass produced housing, no frills, no consumer products, just bare necessity shelter, food and infrastructure. For a country gutted by war, it was a remedy for survival, bare survival perhaps, but survival nonetheless with no armies coming across the Urals.

Post World War II Communists should have been poised for control of Europe as those exhausted by war demanded change. But something else emerged, the Social Democrats, a non-ideological force pragmatically confronting the same issues Stalin confronted, recovering from war. Western Europe turned away from warfare, adopting significant social systems for a more secure and thriving society with a more equal distribution of resources.

First, they seized upon the fear of another war. Although Nazism (extreme right wing) was the antithesis of Communism (leftist), the power elite managed to equate them as one and the same. The slave masters raised the Red Scare after the World War I and the Russian Revolution, but they elevated it to ever greater heights with the Second Red Scare at the end of World War II.

"The Second Red Scare stunted the development of the American welfare state," says Landon Storrs in *The Second Red Scare and the Unmaking of the New Deal Left (Politics and Society in Modern America)*.

"In the 1940s and 1950s, conservatives in and out of government used concerns about Soviet espionage to remove from public service many officials who advocated regulatory and redistributive policies intended to strengthen democracy. The crusade against "Communists in government" had even more casualties than we thought. In addition to its well-known violation of civil liberties and destruction of careers, the Second Red Scare curbed the social democratic potential of the New Deal through its impact on policymakers who sought to mitigate the antidemocratic tendencies of unregulated capitalism."[235]

FDR's New Deal drew the best and brightest into government. They played an important role in winning the war and ending the Great Depression. With victory against Hitler, they were poised to lead America to ever greater heights. Conservative slave masters would fight them.

"During the crises of the Great Depression and Second World War," Storrs adds, "service in the dynamic Roosevelt administration offered the luster and cachet— although not the financial rewards— that in other eras would be found on Wall Street or in Silicon Valley, and the federal government hired some of the nation's most brilliant and ambitious talent. That high-powered group included some people who were inspired by the opportunity to forge policies they believed would prevent future depressions and wars by reducing inequalities— of class, race, and even gender— within the United States and abroad. Although a few of them were or had been members of the Communist Party, most never were. They did not dominate the policymaking arena, but their increasing influence provoked a powerful reaction from American conservatives. That reaction included exploiting Americans' fear of Soviet espionage to ensnare left-leaning officials in investigations that either marginalized them or forced them toward the political center."[236]

Fear of another war preyed heavily on America's mind. Using public relations techniques and without any supporting evidence, the power elite exploited their fears with communists equated to Nazis.

"The federal employee loyalty program," says Storrs, "was a crucial instrument of the Red scare that gripped the nation after the Second World War, climaxing in the ascendance of Senator Joseph R. McCarthy (R-Wis.)."[237]

The public relations campaign against Communism, however, was very effective giving birth to the Cold War in which super powers pointed life destroying neutron bombs at each other for protection of the wealthy and powerful. Truman absorbed the anti-Communist rhetoric and set America on another path to warfare in Korea and Vietnam.

Days after the bombing of Hiroshima and Nagasaki, John J. McCloy and Dean Rusk met at the War Department and decided Korea's future. Without consultation with the Russians or the Koreans, they decided the country be divided at thirty-eighth parallel with Russia overseeing the North and the United States asserting control over the South. The Russians had plenty of their own problems and did not want responsibility for Korea.

Korea had also been isolated from the world before the colonial assault upon Asia. They, too, were forced to accept "unfair treaties" and they were constantly abused by foreign forces seeking hegemony over Korea. China asserted control, so did Russia and then the Japanese. By the end of World War II, Koreans wanted independence. Post war dictates by the victors would not permit independence. The Russians slipped away from the assignment opening a path for China's re-assertion of influence over North Korea, while America stationed over 20,000 troops in the south.

As the Cold War took shape, North Korea was labeled Communist, while the South represented Democracy. Soon Korea was merely a platform for a proxy fight between Communist Chinese and Imperialist America. When the Chinese asserted themselves in Korea, Truman decided the U.S. must stand against Communist aggression. Vietnam was viewed through the Cold War lens compelling Truman to support France's fight for reestablishing its colonial rule in Vietnam. Truman supported returning French colonial rule; a rule that was at the heart of the World's bloodiest warfare. A popular song at the time asked plaintively "when will they ever learn, when will they ever learn."

As the U.S. attempted development of a coherent foreign policy, domestic issues began boiling over, specifically on issues of race.

America is charged with fraud by using the manipulative tools of "public relations."

Race, Fear and Hate

THEN, ALONG CAME THE BROWN v Board of Education case that desegregated public schools. Nothing makes salient racial fear more than the response to school desegregation. Seating black kids in a classroom with white kids terrified White skinned Americans. America's pride in itself and its government was rocked by this court decision.

"What's wrong with the country?" was a frequent refrain. Desegregation disrupted the norm. No longer could white Americans find solace in the notion that black people liked the way things were. No, they did not and all of America needed a painful awakening. Even in contemporary times, 2024, America's bigots express their contempt and disdain for anyone able and human enough to confront that "awakening," bigots refer to "them" as "woke."

This event converged with elitist schemes for seizing power. Racist whites could not and would not accept the unacceptable. The University of Virginia became a focal point for resistance to the court's decision. They organized as conservatives, but their true goal was dismantlement of government.

"Brown so energized this ragtag collection of outraged radicals of the right," says MacLean, "that some were no longer happy calling themselves "libertarian." The name had no passion and fire; with its seven Latinate syllables, it could never become a household word. Some wanted to call themselves what they were: "radicals" of the right. Others understandably feared that any name with the word "radical" in it might turn off the wealthy men of affairs who would be needed to fund the cause, and so opted for "conservative" as interchangeable with "libertarian." Yet while "conservative" might help in attracting powerful allies, that name understated the demolition-minded nature of their vision."[238]

The frenzy struck a chord at the University of Virginia. MacLean writes: "As 1956 drew to a close, Colgate Whitehead Darden Jr., the president of the University of Virginia, feared for the future of his beloved state. The previous year, the U.S. Supreme Court had issued its second Brown v. Board of Education ruling, calling for the dismantling of segregation in public schools with "all deliberate speed." In Virginia, outraged state officials responded with legislation to force the closure of any school that planned to comply. Some extremists called for ending public education entirely. Darden, who earlier in his career had been the governor, could barely stand to contemplate the damage such a rash move would inflict. Even the name of this plan, "massive resistance," made his gentlemanly Virginia sound like Mississippi."[239]

"On his desk was a proposal, written by the man he had recently appointed chair of the economics department at UVA. Thirty-seven-year-old James McGill Buchanan liked to call himself a Tennessee country boy. But Darden knew better. No less a figure than Milton Friedman had extolled Buchanan's potential. As Darden reviewed the document, he might have wondered if the newly hired economist had read his mind. For without mentioning the crisis at hand, Buchanan's proposal put in writing what Darden was thinking: Virginia needed to find a better way to deal with the incursion on states' rights represented by Brown."[240]

RACE, FEAR AND HATE

Buchanan became the chief economic theorist behind the far-right movement. He wanted democracy in chains so government could not intrude on the creativity of the "job creators," the millionaires and billionaires who make it all work. Government should only do what wealthy property owners allow it to do; no restraints, no regulations, bifurcated laws with one for the powerful and the other for "them." It sounds like a page taken from the Barbadian Protestant Supremacy playbook. If courts made a decision integrating white and black students, then the courts needed correction.

This cauldron had been brewing for 500 years, maybe longer. White dominance held black people down, while dictating a narrative of America as freedom loving. The World Wars exposed the lie that black people liked the paternal white supremacy system. Blacks who volunteered for service returned home expecting a new found respect. Instead, they found a lynching tree. White America was determined to keep them in their place.

Lynchings had several purposes. Lynching terrorized everyone. It revealed the raw brutality of the community, demonstrating that anyone opposing those with power could be met with a rope and a tree. It also made everyone in the community come out and show their support. Failing to show up exposed the absentee as someone who might not hold the proper attitude about white supremacy. This could have very serious consequences. So, they packed a picnic lunch and brough the whole family to watch the lynching. This may seem macabre, but protecting your family and yourself from the wretchedness emanating from wretchedness was essential.

When black troops returned from World War Part 1, they expected a modicum of respect for their endurance. Some proudly wore their uniforms and, of those, many were attacked and lynched. There are far too many examples across the nation to recount all. The story of one

World War II black veteran makes salient the point. The Slavocracy south did not wait for him to actually arrive at his home. On the bus ride home, Sgt. Woodward was attacked, he was beaten and blinded by police.

"On February 12, 1946, Sergeant Isaac Woodard, a decorated African American soldier," writes Richard Gergel in *Unexampled Courage*, "was beaten and blinded in Batesburg, South Carolina, by the town's police chief on the day of his discharge from the U.S. Army and while still in uniform. The brutality and injustice of Woodard's treatment encapsulated the angst and outrage of the nation's 900,000 returning black veterans, who felt their service in defense of American liberty was not appreciated. Soon, protests and mass meetings in response to the Woodard incident were held in black communities across America. Civil rights leaders demanded federal action to hold the police officer accountable for Woodard's brutal treatment and to protect the rights of the nation's black citizens from racial violence." [241]

The assault of Sgt. Woodard set in motion a series of events, transforming the ideas of a U.S. District Judge, who dedicated himself in the fight against segregation, into an action plan for over turning Plessy v Fergusen, the Supreme Court ruling that established the separate but equal standard. Federal Judge Waties Waring joined the fight against racial hate.

"But whatever impression Waties Waring might have had about the merits of the Shull case before the trial commenced," says Gergel, "the moving testimony of Isaac Woodard as the opening witness made him realize there was much more to this case than he had appreciated. With Elizabeth observing in the courtroom, both Warings saw for the first time the ugly underbelly of southern racial practices. Unable to avert their eyes, they were forced to stare into the southern racial abyss, a view that would forever transform them both."[242]

Judge J. Watties Waring wanted a case for challenging Plessy v Ferguson, the landmark case establishing the doctrine of separate but equal. "Waring carefully reviewed his pending cases and eyed an NAACP case from the rural community of Summerton, South Carolina, Briggs v. Elliott, as a potential vehicle to raise a frontal challenge to Plessy," says Gergel. "Briggs was a rather straightforward Plessy case in which the plaintiffs alleged that white children in this predominantly rural school district were provided with school bus transportation and superior facilities and textbooks denied to black children."[243]

Thurgood Marshall led the NAACP effort in the fight for civil rights. Marshall proceeded with caution, but Judge Waring had another idea.

"When Marshall arrived at the courthouse," says Gergel, "he was advised by court personnel that Waring wished to see him in chambers. In a private closed-door meeting, Waring informed Marshall he had bigger plans for the Briggs case. He told Marshall, "I don't want to hear another separate but equal case. Bring me a frontal attack on segregation." Marshall resisted, telling him, "This is on our agenda but it's not tonight. We don't think this is the case. We don't think this is the time.""[244]

Waring and the NAACP wanted a more aggressive plan.

"Marshall, whipsawed by Judge Waring and the leadership of the NAACP to adopt a more aggressive (and risky) strategy than he was comfortable with, reluctantly agreed to Waring's plan, later telling colleagues that he felt he had no other choice. Waring then stated, "Very good. I'll sign an order, dismissing without prejudice, and I'll expect you to file a suit bringing that issue clearly before the Court." As the former NAACP general counsel and Sixth Circuit Court of Appeals Judge Nathaniel Jones later observed, "Waring's reasoning encouraged the NAACP legal team to shift its strategy from pushing for equalization of facilities to total elimination of segregation, root and branch."[245]

Marshall went on to win the Brown v Board of Education case that overturned Plessy. When he did, white supremacists refused acceptance of the unacceptable and the University of Virginia became their center of operations. A new race war driven by the Brown decision was engaged. The slave masters would not let go of the reins of power. They would overthrow governments, kill Presidents, game the electoral system, and control public debate. They would not give up at the end of the Civil War and they would not give up after Brown. To be sure, they will not give up today.

Just consider this: JFK appeared open to civil rights legislation for black people, reducing antagonisms with communism and leading a progressive agenda. He was murdered in 1963 at a spot that was the precisely perfect spot for an ambush along a motorcade route; a spot where the motorcade car would turn into the kill zone so the assassins could not be viewed on approach; a spot where killers had easy access by rail and bus; a spot where major roads intersected for easy access by car for delivery and removal of weapons; a spot that even provided a railroad overpass for shooters to comfortably get into position. Moreover, JFK was allegedly killed by a former Marine with a Top-Secret clearance who defected to the Soviet Union and then returned home without going to prison. The alleged assassin is then killed by a mob thug inside the Dallas Police Headquarters. Please.

The Public Relations Industrial Complex employed by those of excess, wealth, power and greed worked overtime labeling anyone who questioned the official version of the JFK assassination as a "conspiracy nut." Assassinations of JFK, Malcolm X, Robert Kennedy,

Martin Luther King and others, including Oswald, were a product of sophisticated operations, not a "lone gunman." Believing otherwise is, indeed, nuts.

Almost 50 years after the New Deal, America's aristocrats, patrons of Buchanan and Friedman, seized power in the form of Ronald Reagan, campaigning that government is not the solution to problem, government is the problem. Reagan became the spokesperson for attacks on the American government. It began with cutting taxes.

"The details of the plan devised by four right-wing Reagan advisors—economist Milton Friedman, Martin Anderson, a lawyer named Anthony Kennedy, and Chief of Staff Edwin Meese—were confusing," writes Rick Perlstein in *The Invisible Bridge: The Fall of Nixon and the Rise of Reagan*. "The aim was to put a ceiling on state taxes and spending. But it seemed to bestow most of its favors on those who were already well-off—and what sort of political sense did a giveaway to the rich make for Ronald Reagan? sneered the Los Angeles Times in a May 16 article about allegations that state employees were gathering signatures while on the job."[246]

The campaign against government began before World War II but became increasingly sophisticated as American manufacturers feared Government Owned and Government Operated manufacturing would outshine private industry. Those of wealth and power orchestrated a long-term strategy to restrain government so government could not restrain greed. Racial animus became the tool of choice for those advancing interest of wealth, power and greed.

Reagan understood white resentment against the civil rights movement. Philadelphia, Mississippi earned notoriety as the location where civil rights workers were murdered. Reagan honored this place of death by kicking off his 1980 Presidential campaign there sending a clear signal that he was the white candidate.

"When Ronald Reagan campaigned in Mississippi at the Neshoba County Fair in 1980, I was quick to defend him against charges of race-baiting," writes Republican campaign strategist Stuart Stevens in *It Was All a Lie*. "Yes, Neshoba County had the horrible legacy of three civil rights workers murdered and buried in a dam in 1964, but I had grown up going to the Neshoba County Fair hearing politicians speak. It was a ritual of passage, like town halls and house parties in New Hampshire. That a future president would speak there was to be celebrated, not criticized."

"But I was wrong. Reagan did not give an explicitly racist speech, but the totality of the place and what he said—and didn't say—was a direct racist appeal to white Mississippi voters."[247]

The Republican Party was Lincoln's at the time of the Civil War and was aligned with emancipation, even though many in the union held deeply racist views. Still, Republicans were aligned with civil rights for black people. The Democrats, in contrast, were aligned with racial animus.

FDR signaled a shift as Democrats, at least tentatively, softened on racial issues. Two decades later, the Civil Rights Movement was firmly established and demanding change. The southern Democrats remained stalwart in resisting change, but then one of their own, Lyndon B. Johnson of Texas, took the reigns as President after the assassination of JFK, and Johnson embraced civil rights for people of color.

LBJ represented a tectonic shift in the political landscape. Democrats were now the party for Civil Rights. Over the ensuing years, southern Democrats changed party affiliation, rebranding Republicans into the party of racial animus.

In 1963 the political landscape rumbled with the anticipation of a gathering storm. Black people in America were demanding an end to slavery, a real end, and not just some empty words that provide inspiration, but failed to actually deliver on the promise. The American Civil War ended slavery in theory, but in reality, Jim Crow laws ruled the south. A hundred years after the Civil War, black Americans were still living in bondage.

As a big man, LBJ sought big challenges. He would take on risk, but in return he wanted adoration, power, and more power. Perhaps the Civil Rights cause truly touched the enigmatic Johnson. But perhaps he saw in the civil rights movement an opportunity for him to be the savior and earn a place in history of enormous monument. Did Johnson dedicate himself to Civil Rights because he truly believed in the cause, or did he do it because he believed it would bring him everlasting fame? For whatever his motivation may have been, Civil Rights were LBJ's signature issue; he was going to make right what should have been made right 100 years ago.

All of his skills and talents were directed to the Civil Rights cause, because it would seal his place in history. As black Americans continued to push for real and substantive change, the conflict with white America intensified. Across the nation, riots erupted, cities were set on fire, fear and hatred permeated the land, and tension was palpable.

Both houses of the U.S. Congress, the House and the Senate, were lost. They knew they needed to do something as the country was fracturing, but what, what should they do? In 1964 Congress passed the Civil Rights Act in response to the pleas for righteousness. But it was not enough. Black people were still blocked from the one thing that could give them equal footing: the right to vote. The racial crisis inched every closer to the boiling point. They looked to the President for leadership. On March 15, 1965, the day before a joint session of Congress, they asked Johnson to address them and provide some direction. That night Johnson prepared what many historians have judged as the greatest speech of his political career and certainly one of the most significant speeches in American history.

INDICTING AMERICA

On March 16, 1965, LBJ spoke before a joint session of Congress and made a compelling and articulate case for human rights. It echoed the sentiments in the Declaration of Independence, draped in human rights, not property rights. It was a shining moment for Lyndon Johnson. Clearly Civil Rights were Johnson's issue. He closed by quoting Dr. King "and we shall overcome."[248]

Richard Nixon recognized the shift in political brandings and crafted the "Southern Strategy." This strategy, designed for appeal to bigoted voters, was crafted so racist messages were disguised using techniques later described as "Dog Whistle Politics." Nixon squeaked into office, aided by the racist George Wallace who siphoned off a sizeable chunk of the Democratic vote. The strategy worked. It would later be refined by George H.W. Bush when he trailed his opponent Mchael Dukakis by 18 percent just before the election. Bush introduced the infamous Willie Horton advertisement, a vile racist political advertisement based on black people as killers and rapists. Bush won the election.

Echoing past racist, "dog whistle," campaigns, Donald Trump extolled how he would "Make America Great Again," while slinging racial antagonisms that aided his campaign. Russia supported his campaign using disinformation and inflammatory social media messages. Over half of Russia's messages aimed at racial animus, antagonizing both white and black voters. Abolitionists and Slave Masters continue dominance of the political landscape and racial animus continues infecting the American populace.

Brutalization of black people rages on. Emmitt Till, Tamir Rice, Trayvon Martin, George Floyd. This list is never ending.

In 1991, I was a member of a People-to-People Program (initiated by Dwight Eisenhower, 1956) delegation to the Soviet Union shortly before the Soviet disintegration. I met with young security analysts eager for information about the process for analyzing security. I suggested that it seemed Russia evaluated security on the basis of its muscle, specifically its nuclear arsenal. I presented a process for analysis and indicated that in reviewing vulnerability attention must consider history. Any security analyst considering America's vulnerability would quickly identify racial animus as the top vulnerability easily exploitable in turning Americans against Americans. To be sure, this was central for Slave Masters in driving a wedge between Americans and the America they loved at the end of the worldwide wars.

America is charged with the murder of black people motivated by the insidious disease of bigotry.

Vietnam

CONTEMPORARY WORLD AFFAIRS REQUIRE MATURE, capable and thoughtful leadership. Decisions have consequences demanding that leaders identify possible consequences associated with an array of decisions, so a decision does not create a more dire circumstance than the one under consideration. Time, extensive consultation and wisdom are essential. If they could just take one issue at a time. But they cannot, because world events have independent time tables for eruption. And there is never time for contemplation and consultation. Leaders must act quickly based on scant information, under constant pressure for action. Snap, ad-hoc decisions rule the day resulting in massive human catastrophes.

LBJ seemed acclimated for getting the racial issue right. He never had the time or resources to do so. As he ascended before a joint session of Congress advocating for the Voting Rights Act of 1965, Vietnam loomed large in the background. It was complicated and LBJ did not have time for a history lesson. What he wanted was simple. Draw up some plans (paraphrasing) to whip the hell out of em, then give em a bundle of money so they come away happy. Just keep South Vietnam free of communist rule. He wanted a Korea solution with communists in the north and democracy in the south. Note the choice between communist and democracy is convoluted, but that is how the conflict was understood at the time.

LBJ's wish would never happen and could never happen. For context consider the war in Vietnam began in 1858 when Napolean III invaded for colonization. On that September day, the Vietnamese could succumb to the invader or fight back. If they succumbed, they must accept all that comes with colonial invasion, including murder, rape, theft and enslavement, to name a few. If they fought back, it would be long and arduous, oceans of blood and horror. A determined few decided to fight. Their objective: Toss out foreign invaders, all of them.

By 1965, 80% of the Vietnamese countryside sided with those fighting back. French collaborators sat in power in Saigon, they were despised by the Vietnamese and would never be acceptable. LBJ was backing the wrong horse and no matter how much he whipped that horse, it could not win the race.

So, as he attempted to deal with racial animus, he also had to deal with a war; a war that would suck America into a quagmire, provoke international condemnation and protest, and fracture the united United States possibly beyond repair.

LBJ also had to confront profound and widespread poverty, technological developments reconfiguring the landscape, and a world still recovering from the ravages of worldwide wars. The sheer scale of issues on a President's desk is more, much, much more than one person can handle. In contemporary times there is a belief in what is known as the "Unitary" Presidency. This gives the president unilateral decision making free from consultation. Now, there is a useless idea, since the issues of the day demand thoughtful leadership and consultation. Of course, when the political landscape is such that one political party can simply refuse to participate and abhors collaboration—the antithesis of mature, capable and thoughtful, then perhaps a unitary idea is appropriate in some way, but it still fails in confronting what are daunting issues.

The Civil Rights Movement attracted young Americans, the so-called baby boom generation coming of age in the 1950s and 60s. In the Post World War, Americans conceived babies, a lot of babies. By the 1960s, half the population of American was under the age of 25. Their World War II parents were proud of America and passed along the values that made America great, such as freedom of speech, equal protection under the law regardless of color, freedom and opportunity for all. This message was reinforced in school, church and cultural centers.

When the Civil Rights Movement exposed pervasive racism and the existence of two societies, as a Presidential Commission defined it: one white and one black, separate and unequal, the baby boomers joined in political action. And as the war in Vietnam heated up, they expanded their view and joined opposition to a war they considered illegal and immoral.

LBJ wanted the Vietnam War to go away, he was busy with other pressing matters. Leaders overwhelmed with pressing matters want to lessen their load by making issues go away. But these issues come back and bite. Nixon was not involved with Watergate; he was involved with the cover-up which was another exercise in making an annoying problem disappear.

LBJ knew the war was not of significant American interest. When he came into office, he conferred with Senator Richard Russell, a solid deep south Democrat. Russell told him Vietnam wasn't worth it, there was nothing to gain. He thought the U.S. should pack up and leave. LBJ feared his political right wing would not stand for it and would attack him as weak on communists. So, the war continued and escalated as the pesky Vietnamese would not tolerate foreign invaders nor their collaborators. [249]

VIETNAM

United States involvement with Vietnam predated America's entry into World War II. In the battle against Japan, U.S. intelligence agents covertly worked with Vietnamese fighting Japanese. U.S. combat troops entered Vietnam in 1965. The predicate for invasion was an alleged "unprovoked" attack by Vietnamese on U.S. battleships in the Gulf of Tonkin. The attack was, indeed, provoked. Hubert Humphrey confirmed as much. LBJ was infuriated with Humphrey. "You can't go out telling people about war plans." It wasn't about war plans; it was about the U.S. Navy provoking a Vietnamese attack so they could gage the radar effectiveness of the Vietnamese. LBJ lied, lied, lied, when he said it was an unprovoked attack and he knew it. Subsequent American Presidents refined the art of lying.

Twenty years after the war was over, Robert McNamara, Secretary of Defense for both JFK and LBJ, met with his Vietnamese counterparts at a symposium at Brown University to review what happened and why.

"You mean you never read our history," said Nguyen Co Thach, former Vietnamese Foreign Minister, when meeting with former U.S. Secretary of Defense Robert McNamara in 1995. The meeting was a symposium at Brown University for the Americans and Vietnamese to reflect on the American War. The Foreign Minister was astonished that America killed 4 million Vietnamese based on the false premise that the Vietnamese were merely Chinese puppets.

McNamara said "we almost came to blows," because it was the first time he understood the fierce independence of the Vietnamese; an independence that compelled them to fight off Chinese domination for over 1000 years. That conference gave McNamara a new found respect for History.[250]

In studying the Vietnam War, there is only one date that matters, September 1, 1858. French forces landed on September 1; an invasion authorized by Napolean III. On that day, Vietnamese had a choice. They could accept an invading force and all that came with it: occupation, enslavement, exploitation, rape, murder, kidnapping; or they could fight. They chose to fight. Certainly not every Vietnamese supported or joined the fight. Few persisted, but over subsequent decades more and more Vietnamese joined and supported them.

This is important because all the Vietnam War events to follow began with the French invasion.

Once again America stumbled into war. FDR understood colonialism's toxicity; Truman did not. When Truman was elevated to the highest office, the issues before him were daunting and overwhelming. War with the Japanese continued with prospects for horrific bloodshed before reaching conclusion. A new weapon offered an alternative to continued ground operations, but it too offered horrific bloodshed. Corralling the Nazis, holding them accountable, and beginning a process for European recovery also crowded Truman's agenda.

The world was anything but stable. Clement Atlee replaced Churchill. Stalin, with ruthless resolve, asserted ever more autocratic rule, determined to defend Russia with protective borders. Europe and Asia were on life support. After years of struggling to hold China together while fighting off an intense Japanese assault, a tired and exhausted Chaing Kai Skek was losing to a Communist insurgency led by Mao. There was no time for reading history; the exigencies of the moment required decisions however ill-conceived and uninformed.

Vietnam was not a priority; it was a small country in Southeast Asia. The victors of World War II deferred action while addressing higher priorities. In the interim England was assigned oversight. It did not go well. American intelligence officers with deep ties to Vietnamese officials, who assisted the U.S. in its war with Japan, supported Communist leader Ho Chi Minh. Ho represented a threat to the French who wanted their Vietnamese colony returned to French rule. England wanted the

French restored in Vietnam, because they wanted their colonies restored. With FDR out of the picture, they had hopes for restoration of the British Empire. In the background American Industry and Financiers continued the Public Relations campaign for demonizing Communism and Socialism; it was extraordinarily successful. Corruption: that's ok; economic systems serving the Common Good and threatening American greed most certainly were not.

Fighting communism positioned the U.S. in support of colonial imperialism, a phenomenon made clearly evident in Vietnam. From the perspective of the Vietnamese, the Americans merely replaced the French as the Vietnamese fought for independence and freedom from the crushing slavery of colonialism. This central concept eluded the highest levels of the U.S. government throughout the war. Indeed, it wasn't until 20 years after the war concluded that McNamara, former Secretary of Defense at the height of the fighting, finally understood the essence of the war after meeting with his Vietnamese counterparts in 1995.

For LBJ being labelled soft on communism was totally unacceptable. He believed right wing Republicans would attack him and thwart his efforts on Civil Rights. It may be speculated that LBJ fought the war in Vietnam to hold off the right wing as he addressed civil rights in America. Such a decision, however, came with consequences. That young generation consumed information on Vietnam for which LBJ simply did not have the time. When they did, the war and civil rights blurred into one common issue. They took to the streets against the war, along with support for civil rights.

Martin Luther King Jr. was distraught about Vietnam. The protesting students made him see the war and civil rights intersected. King took a stance against the war. LBJ was crushed. He expended so much political capital on civil rights, how could King, a civil rights leader, turn on him like this. Meanwhile, the war effort deteriorated. America was not winning the war. How could it be? How could a world power fail in crushing this khat of a nation?

Then came Tet, the Vietnamese New Year of 1968. The Vietnamese orchestrated attacks across the south. It was stunning. The Americans turned back every attack, but the notion that the Vietnamese could orchestrate an attack as such was a shock to Americans. At the same time Marines were under siege at Khe Sahn where they were bombarded with up to 1300 rounds per day.

LBJ quit. He decided to resign at the end of his term. He did what the troops he led could not do. He walked away.

LBJ's exit left the Democrats in disarray just months before the 1968 convention in Chicago. His Vice President, Hubert Humphrey seemed the likely replacement. Demonstrations against the Vietnam War intensified from 1965 through 1968. The spirit of youth and the righteousness of opposing war mixed with the lessons from childhood about American freedom of speech, a government responding to the will of its people and the notion of an illegal and immoral war ignited the youth movement into a determination to end the war. They took that spirit to the convention.

Students demonstrating against the country during a time of war was incomprehensible to the Greatest Generation, the generation that fought and defeated Nazis in World War II. The issue split the nation between those opposed to the war and those dedicated to the American government supporting decisions to go to war. Once again, America was fractured.

At the same time, riots rooted in racial animus erupted across the country. Cities were burned down. Police and black people engaged in combat. As one commentator put it: "LBJ's Great Society had transformed into a sick society."

Richard Nixon appeared to have the answers. He crafted a campaign based on law and order, and he had a plan for extracting America from the Vietnam War that he called "Peace with Honor." He won the race against Humphrey narrowly as George Wallace took a share of the vote.

Not much changed under Nixon. Peace with Honor meant more bombing of the Vietnamese, expansion of the war into Laos and Cambodia, while distancing America from the Saigon regime. Nixon struck a deal with the North Vietnamese that included support for the Saigon government, a government certain to collapse without American troops. By 1975, South Vietnam was no longer.

Nixon

On domestic issues, Nixon did not want to undo LBJ's Great Society; he wanted to out do it. He proposed a guaranteed income, universal health care, the Occupational Health and Safety Administration, the Environmental Protection Agency and more. He initiated détente with Russia and China seeking to ease tensions of the Cold War. Nixon was popular, even though antiwar protesters continued demonstrations. He won re-election easily, but actions by campaign officials to sabotage the Democrats gave birth to the Watergate scandal.

Watergate remains inexplicable. There was little reason for the break-in at the Democratic National Committee (DNC) headquarters that would produce anything significant. The break-in also didn't make sense because it was led by a former FBI official who had vast experience with break-ins, perpetrated by Cuban CIA operatives, and uncovered by a security guard. The incongruency lies in the fact this episode was crafted and led by professional criminals, yet it was amateurish.

INDICTING AMERICA

Nixon tried to cover it all up and get rid of it, but an FBI official insider leaked damning information to the press, ultimately leading to an impeachment inquiry. Nixon resigned.

It must be noted that during the 1970s, the ultra-right wing, disguised as Conservatives, emerged from the shadows, actively seeking an end to American government. They had been working on it since before the end of World War II. Nixon's initiative, particularly détente with Russia and China was troubling for them, but they decided to cast their lot with the Republicans anyway, despite reservations.

The Vietnam War, known in Vietnam as the American War, was a dark chapter in American history. In every respect America lost and deserved to lose, because it was an intruder into a sovereign state. It was also propping up colonialism. The Pentagon Papers documents the flawed, if not incompetent decision-making placing America in the eye of that storm.

1979

America would make the same mistakes again, just shy of two decades later, when George H.W. Bush intervened in a conflict between Iraq and Kuwait, in a mission aimed at redeeming America's pride after the humiliating defeat in Vietnam. Once again decisions were reached in reaction to events, clouded by nationalistic emotions, and a desperate need for exhibiting toughness. The Gulf War, however, was but one domino in a row of dominoes that started before the H.W. Bush administration.

In 1979, in the midst of the Cold War, America's administration identified a conflict that could suck the Russians into a battle that would be the equivalent of the Vietnam quagmire, thereby giving the Russians their Vietnam. Over 40 years later, blood continued to spill, a result of decisions reached by Jimmy Carter in 1979.[251]

The year 1979 was a pivotal year. Carter authorized the CIA to sabotage the Afghanistan government where tribal leaders conflicted with a progressive government. Carter supported the tribal leaders in the hope that Russia would come to the aid of its friends in the Afghan government. Note at this time Osama bin Laden did not exist. Yes, he was alive, but he did not gain notoriety until years later stemming from his joining the fight against Russia. The Taliban also did not exist. They emerged from the embers of the Russia war.

In 1979, Carter supported his friend the Shah of Iran as a revolution dethroned the Shah. Carter allowed the Shah into America for medical treatment as the revolutionaries demanded the Shah be returned to Iran to face criminal charges. Carter refused. Revolutionaries attacked the U.S. Embassy taking the occupants as hostages. One year later neighboring Iraq engaged Iran in warfare over a border dispute, presumably as a proxy for America in an effort to repair frayed relations with America over Iraq's nationalization of oil fields claimed by western oil companies. [252]

Yes, it is difficult to keep track of the tenacles stemming from "giving the Russians their Vietnam. Arguably, the following stemmed from that decision and represents the consequences not considered. The Soviet Union collapsed; civil war erupted in Afghanistan giving rise to the Taliban and Bin Laden; Iran came under the rule of a sectarian government; Iraq's government collapsed unleashing pent-up animosity between Sunni, minority with power, and Shia, majority without power, and a new force known as the Islamic State raining violence, death and destruction across the Middle East; and the September 11, 2001 attack on America.

There is more to be listed, but the point is that decisions in 1979 continue infecting the world. Refugees, an inevitable product of warfare, flooded into Europe, sparking an epidemic of xenophobia that toppled governments, inspired terror attacks, and resuscitated right-wing Nazi type autocratic governments. Most Americans, however, fail in connecting these dots back to the Carter administration, including all of the subsequent occupants of the White House who merely responded to events of the moment—ad-hoc government—that refuses historical context so decisions are better informed. No, do not confront complications, just give simple answers that fail as solutions.

America is charged with crimes against humanity by unleashing warfare against International Law resulting in the death and injury of millions across the globe, including its own citizens sent to die in warfare.

2008 Crash

AS THE VIETNAM WAR CAME to a close, the progeny of the Slave Masters, operating covertly, seized opportunities for pressing their agenda. A student demonstration against the war at Kent State University in 1970 resulted in four students killed by National Guardsmen. This incident seemed to be a culmination of the state's assault upon free speech, one American characteristic treasured by the Greatest Generation and at the heart of protesting students.

Research by Madison Avenue Advertising and Marketing firms indicated that the demonstrators essentially surrendered. They had been beaten and arrested so many times they had to accept the police were more powerful than they were and the fight for justice just wasn't worth this futile effort. The research suggested they were turning inward, simply working to be a good person, but not demonstrating against not-so-good persons. The advertisers labelled them the "Me Generation." The idea that we are all in this together gave way to "it's all about me."[253]

As student movement forces receded, forces of greed accelerated. Some analysts mark the beginning in 1975 when banks refused to purchase New York City Municipal Bonds. This was a means for strangling government, an opening salvo in placing "Democracy in Chains," as Nancy MacLean suggests.

It may be argued their goal was for rolling back progress since the end of the Civil War. Indeed, the Supreme Court in 2023-24 turned the clock back more than 50 years over-ruling court precedent on abortion, civil rights, voting rights, gun laws, even the authority for executive agencies to do their tasks. Their overall long-term objective is aimed at reversing FDR's New Deal, Social Security, Medicare and Medicaid; imposing "small" government which translated into ending social programs; reinstitution of segregation based on color, sexual preference and religion; outlawing rights for LGBTQ people; and neutering government regulations.

The 2024 Trump campaign introduced Project 2025. According to Heather Cox Richardson, "…Russell Vought, the hard-right Christian nationalist who is drafting plans for a second Trump term. Vought was the director of the Office of Management and Budget from July 2020 to January 2021 during the Trump administration. In January 2021 he founded the Center for Renewing America, a pro-Trump think tank, and he was a key player in the construction of Project 2025, the plan to gut the nonpartisan federal government and replace it with a dominant president and a team of loyalists who will impose religious rule on the United States. [254]

"Vought advised the far right, calling for draconian cuts to government agencies, student loans, and housing, health care, and food assistance. He called for $2 trillion in cuts to Medicaid over ten years, more than $600 billion in cuts to the Affordable Care Act, more than $400 billion in cuts to food assistance, and so on."

…Vought argues that the United States is in a "post constitutional moment" that "pays only lip service to the old Constitution." He attributes that crisis to "the Left," which he says "quietly adopted a strategy of institutional change," by which he appears to mean the growth of the federal government to protect individual Americans."

Washington Post reporter Beth Journalist Reinhard points out that "Trump strategist Steve Bannon recently praised Vought and his colleagues as "madmen" who are going to destroy the U.S. government. "We're going to rip and shred the federal government apart, and if you don't like it, you can lump it," Bannon said. "

Accomplishing this was difficult, however, because the broad base of the population embraced the New Deal and loved their post-World War II image of themselves. And if that was not enough, post war years were prosperous.

This marks a stark departure from Ronald Reagan, a hero of the GOP. MacLean says, "True, the economist said approvingly, Reagan had fed "widespread public skepticism about government's capacities" and about "the purity of the motives of political agents," a crucial contribution to the cause. But the president had proved to be too much of a pragmatist, too deferential to public opinion and those concerned about the health of his party, and so he allowed "the rent-seekers" to continue to practice "exploitation through the political process." [255]

"These libertarians seemed to have determined that what was needed to achieve their ends was to stop being honest with the public. Instead of advocating for them frontally, they needed to engage in a kind of crab walk, even if it required advancing misleading claims in order to take terrain bit by bit, in a manner that cumulatively, yet quietly, could begin to radically alter the power relations of American society. The program on which they tested this new strategy was Social Security. "

World War II presented the gravest threat to the power elite. Unity was essential for defeating Nazis. The political elites, the progeny of slave masters, advocated for a stark departure from the unity inspired

INDICTING AMERICA

by FDR. Americans were seduced in support of the war in Europe in a united, "all for one; one for all" mentality in which "we are all in this together." War profiteering was anathema to World War II America and corporations responded accordingly. Profits were limited and employees were showered with benefits as they refined America's industrial machines that were supplying the Allies.

This new political force, operating covertly, promoting the ideology of markets. Based upon thoughts of novelist Ayn Rand, a product of the American Manufacture's public relations campaign against common good thinking, inspired a stable of economic theorists such as Alan Greenspan. Most importantly reverence for the market meant no government interference; no governments forcing integration; no governments restraining greed or corruption. Without government setting guardrails and rules for competition, the elite would be unshackled and unrestrained in stealing as much as they could steal; morality meant nothing. As Milton Friedman asserted, the only thing that matters is stockholder wealth. Stone cold racists disguised as Christian evangelicals jumped onboard. Common Good be damned. [256]

Free marketeers argued government involvement inevitably leads to state control along the lines of Nazi Germany. Government rules and regulations assaulted freedom making everyone a slave. Political Public Relations campaigns convinced ordinary people that government regulations ensuring safe drinking water threatened individual freedom.

"Much of what appears 'natural' today," says Judt, "dates from the 1980s: the obsession with wealth creation, the cult of privatization and the private sector, the growing disparities of rich and poor."[257]

Friedman's stockholder wealth doctrine elevated him as greed's most vocal spokesperson. Friedman and his acolytes contrived elaborate mathematically models supporting economic theories in support of unrestrained greed. And when their theories failed, the Federal

276

Reserve and the U.S. Treasury stood ready to bail them out. Poverty and hunger in America would be eviscerated, if the Fed applied its authority for "quantitative easing" to those who are poor and hungry. That authority, however, is only used for anemic banks drained of cash by failed economic theories and fraudulent actions.

"Shareholder theory asserts that shareholders advance capital to a company's managers, who are supposed to spend corporate funds only in ways that have been authorized by the shareholders," wrote H.J. Smith in *Sloan Management Review*. "As Milton Friedman wrote, "There is one and only one social responsibility of business — to use its resources and engage in activities designed to increase its profits so long as it ... engages in open and free competition, without deception or fraud." [258]

Friedman and the University of Chicago law faculty laid the ground work for transformation of American values from "one for all" to "one for all and all for us: the .1%." In essence freedom means the freedom for greed and exploitation.

Friedman more generally expressed this idea in his widely acclaimed *Free to Choose* (1980):

> "Economic freedom is an essential requisite for political freedom. By enabling people to cooperate with one another without coercion or central direction, it reduces the area over which political power is exercised. In addition, by dispersing power, the free market provides an offset to whatever concentration of political power may arise. The combination of economic and political power in the same hands is a sure recipe for tyranny."

This was a dramatic shift from "one for all, all for one" thinking. Profits soared. Corporate thinking about employee benefits, customer quality and community involvement transformed virtually overnight into providing the lowest cost product for the highest price possible. Wherein past priorities were rank ordered as customers, employees, community and profit; the new agenda attended to stockholders (profit) first and last.

Clearing the path for unrestrained greed requiring stacking the courts and obtaining legal rulings eviscerating the guardrails established by Teddy Roosevelt and his cousin Franklin. The forces of greed used the courts for changing laws against monopolies, price fixing and bribery.

"He fails to consider the revolution in monopoly law in the last 40 years," writes Zephyr Teachout. "Beginning in the 1970s, a group of activist lawyers associated with the University of Chicago persuaded courts to gut well-established principles designed to protect open markets and decentralized power, and to replace them with an ideology of efficiency that has contributed to our current crisis of monopoly capitalism and inequality. Winkler mentions the Chicago school in passing, but he doesn't address the post-1980 antitrust cases, a striking oversight because they fit neatly into his theory: Corporate monopolies gained rights by asserting that they benefited the rights of others (in this case, consumer)." [259]

"The free-market mantra meant not just stripping away old regulations but also doing nothing to address the new challenges of twenty - first - century markets, including those posed by derivatives," says Joseph Stiglitz in *Freefall: America, Free Markets, and the Sinking of the World Economy*. "And not only didn't the U.S. Treasury and the Federal Reserve propose regulations; they forcefully — sometimes almost brutally — resisted any initiatives to do so. In the 1990s, the head of the Commodity Futures Trading Commission, Brooksley Born, had called for such regulation — a concern that took on urgency after the New York Federal Reserve Bank engineered the 1998 bailout of Long - Term Capital Management, a hedge fund whose trillion - dollar - plus failure threatened to bring down the entire global financial market. But Secretary of Treasury Robert Rubin, his deputy, Larry Summers, and Alan Greenspan were adamant — and successful — in their opposition. 2 And just to ensure that regulators in the future don't come to their senses, those in financial markets lobbied hard, and successfully, for legislation to make sure that derivatives remained unregulated (the Commodity Futures Modernization Act of 2000.)[260]

Vilification of Brooksley Born was astonishing. She exposed the derivatives market as an unregulated enterprise threatening the world economy. Greenspan bullied her over lunch. He asked her if she thought fraud should be regulated. He felt it did not because the markets would handle it. [261]

Derke Thompson writing in the Atlantic about the decline in entrepreneurism says "This decline in dynamism has coincided with the rise of extraordinarily large and profitable firms that look discomfortingly like the monopolies and oligopolies of the 19th century. American strip malls and yellow pages used to brim with new small businesses. But today, in a lot where several mom-and-pop shops might once have opened, Walmart spawns another superstore. In almost every sector of the economy—including manufacturing, construction, retail, and the entire service sector—the big companies are getting bigger. The share of all businesses that are new firms, meanwhile, has fallen by 50 percent since 1978. According to the Roosevelt Institute, a liberal think tank dedicated to advancing the ideals of Franklin and Eleanor Roosevelt, "markets are now more concentrated and less competitive than at any point since the Gilded Age." [262]

Lobbyist emerged as a critical link to government and making the playing field conducive for-profit maximization. For this new agenda, the rules of business and government needed renovation. So as not to raise the ire of anti-monopolists, competition had to be limited to two competitors so a duopoly could be a path for dominance. Government agencies charged with enforcement of regulation of business needed budget cuts so they could not enforce rules and regulation. Moreover, the legal system needed modification so lawsuits were limited, if not prohibited, labor would be decimated and restrictions lifted on political bribery. In short, the courts needed stacking so laws would be interpreted in accordance with profit maximization. Regulations protecting consumers, the environment, worker safety and unionization needed new interpretations, if not elimination. Over many years, after manipulating the legal system, corruption contaminated the landscape. In 2024, it was revealed that a property developer and business office entrepreneur, with issues before the court, funneled millions of dollars to a Supreme Court Justice. Brazenly the Justice refused to recuse from cases.

It is within this landscape that Artificial Intelligence entered the American economy in the 21st Century. Jobs could be automated with no consideration for the people and communities crushed in its wake. Reducing competition to two competitors meant that consumers had no real choice, particularly as the two competitors bench marked themselves into exact copies of each other. Automated service systems providing horrible service were implemented because consumers had no choice but to adapt.

The assault on government for over 50 years defanged government rules that protected consumers, workers, the environment and the social structure which includes the safety net. Profits have soared and the wealthy have grown enormously wealthier, while America's middle class has contracted dramatically and the underclass expanded.

"An obscure item in Newt Gingrich's Contract with America," writes George Packer in *The Unwinding: An Inner History of the New*

America, "became the highlight of Connaughton's tenure in the White House. The Private Securities Litigation Reform Act of 1995 was drafted by Republicans to weaken the antifraud provisions of the Securities Exchange Act of 1934 and to make it harder for companies whose executives talked up their stock prices with misleading forecasts of performance to be sued."

"One of its authors was Christopher Cox, who would go on to preside over the gutting of the Securities and Exchange Commission in the administration of George W. Bush and whose performance during the financial crisis of 2008 was so passive that he would earn the contempt, once they needed him, of the very bankers who had profited from his negligent approach to regulation. By the time the bill got the full attention of the Clinton White House, in the early summer of 1995, it had passed the House of Representatives and was under consideration in the Senate."[263]

FDR's New Deal and the growth of the Executive branch aimed at a government for the Common Good. Fighting against it was the force for Individual Gain. This meant America's burgeoning Middle Class was under attack, but it didn't know it.

Assaulting the middle class resulted in guaranteed retirement plans replaced by risky stock portfolios, known as 401k plans; health plans with limits on coverage and costly copays, not to mention cancellation for a range of reasons, all favoring the elites; and job security replaced with pervasive job insecurity. The World War II workforce that saved America was imperiled.

"Today," says Y.N. Harari, "the richest 1 percent own half the world's wealth. Even more alarmingly, the richest one hundred people together own more than the poorest four billion."[264]

"The wider the spread between the wealthy few," says Judt, "and the impoverished many, the worse the social problems: a statement which appears to be true for rich and poor countries alike. What matters is not how affluent a country is but how unequal it is. Thus Sweden, or Finland, two of the world's wealthiest countries by per capita income or GDP, have a very narrow gap separating their richest from their poorest citizens—and they consistently lead the world in indices of measurable wellbeing."[265]

Wage stagflation meant accumulating debt to pay for everything the middle class could not afford. Jimmy Carter warned about America living beyond its means. He advocated for a conservative lifestyle. But then along came Ronald Reagan who told Americans they could have it all. Reagan showed them how by creating the largest amount of deficit spending known to government up till that time plunging the country deep into debt. And Reagan did this under the banner of Conservatism.

"In November 2002 O'Neill tried to warn Vice President Dick Cheney," says Adam Tooze in *Crashed*, "that the surging "budget deficits... posed a threat to the economy." Only for Cheney to cut him off with the following remark: "You know... Reagan proved deficits don't matter." The Republicans had won the congressional midterms; tax cuts were the Republican "due."[266]

As debt became the source of income, American commerce transformed from a manufacturing economy to a finance economy. Business shipped manufacturing to foreign shores where labor was cheap with few restrictions on operations; no need for protections against pollution, worker safety and all that stuff. Displaced American workers found new jobs making less money, but they supplemented it with debt.

With maximization of profit as its focus of attention, American business shipped jobs overseas where labor costs were a fraction of the costs in America. Moreover, overseas manufacturing operations faced few regulatory restrictions. Loss of well-paid manufacturing jobs, pushed America's middle-class into new lesser paying jobs. When middleclass Americans wanted to buy a new home or car, they borrowed. This meant that lending supplemented their income. Mortgages were structured using adjustable rates. This meant that in the early years of loan repayment, the borrower repaid on the basis of a low interest rate. As the adjustable rate increased, so to did the repayment amount, often beyond the borrower's ability to pay, resulting in a loan default.

The bank took control of the property through foreclosure, but the property is not liquid cash that can be used for paying the mortgage-backed bonds. Over many years of selling mortgage-backed securities, rated as AAA, but actually backed by a ton of mortgages sold to unqualified buyers, the banks had tons of defaulted properties that could not be sold for cash and used for payment to holders of the mortgage-backed securities. Investment banking teetered on the edge of default, just as their unqualified home buyers defaulted. Keep in mind these securities were traded on the unregulated derivatives market. It may be speculated that regulating the derivatives market may have included audits of the mortgaged backed securities, ensuring the underlying mortgages were given to qualified buyers. At least, regulation may have identified that the securities were not, indeed, AAA securities.

Banks inability for payment to securities holders, placed the industry on the brink of default. Some banks, however, purchased a form of insurance known as a Credit Default Swap. Insurance companies operating under state laws requiring cash reserves for meeting potential claims, entered the Credit Default Swap business, which is a derivative business because it is derived from the Mortgage-Backed Security market. No one regulated the derivative market, so the insurance companies did not have to maintain reserves, should the securities default. They could not use the reserves required by their state regulated business. So, they took on the additional risk in the Credit Default Swap, even though they didn't have the financial resources to do so. If the banks defaulted, they depended upon insurance to cover them, but if insurance defaulted, both the banking and insurance industries could be bankrupted.

American commerce was transformed, by the progeny of slave masters and bankers, into a financial Ponzi scheme. This replaced American manufacturing, a key player in defeating Nazis, providing decades of financial health for America and creating a solid middle-class living for the bulk of America. Government saved the financial system through bailouts and quantitative easing, but the middle class crashed, leaving millions desperately wounded financially and emotionally as they lost homes, jobs, families and self-respect in the process.

This catastrophic manipulation of commerce, driven by craven elites operating by stealth, shattered the love affair Americans had with America. It cultivated a political landscape ripe for a demagogue. Capitalizing on this contaminated landscape, Donald Trump stepped forth using bigoted appeals for channeling America's anger at minorities, foreign governments, and, perhaps most importantly, the American government.

It all came to a head in 2008.

Bill Clinton, Democratic President, 1993-2001, angered Democrats by softening positions on social safety nets, while also angering Republicans by stealing part of their constituency when he pandered to Wall Street bankers and financiers. One of his signature achievements for the barons of Wall Street was repeal of the Glass-Steagall Act of 1933, a post 1929 Wall Street crash piece of legislation separating commercial banking (savings and loans) and investment banking (stocks and bonds).

"The New Deal– era regulations," says Tooze, "that separated retail from investment banking had to fall. The Clinton Treasury, first under Rubin and then under Larry Summers, gave them what they needed. In 1999 the last remnants of 1930s banking regulations were swept aside."[267]

This opened a door for the financial industry in creating inventive ways for debt; ways in some circles known as fraud. Home loans (commercial banking) were securitized (investment banking) into bonds. The bonds were backed by home mortgages which were considered low risk because mortgage borrowers went through a qualification process ensuring the borrower's capacity to repay the loan.

These loans were popular prompting investment bankers to encourage mortgage bankers to write more mortgages. Now that both were intertwined under one roof, significant pressure was brought to bear for more mortgages for packaging into bonds. To meet the demands, borrower qualifications were lowered so more people qualified for loans, thereby producing more loans. The mortgages of these lesser qualified buyers were mixed in with quality borrowers so it appeared as if the bond was safe. As time went on more and more of the packaged mortgages were stacked with lower quality borrowers, but they were presented as containing high quality borrowers.

"The message that this communicated," according to Tooze, "down the food chain was simple: We want more mortgage debt to process, and the worse the quality, the better. By the magic of independent probabilities, the worse the quality of the debt that entered into the tranching and pooling process, the more dramatic the effect. Substantial portions of undocumented, low-rated, high-yield debt emerged as AAA. In any boom, irresponsible, near criminal or outright fraudulent behavior is to be expected. But the mortgage securitization mechanism systematically produced this race to the bottom in mortgage lending quality."[268]

A low qualified buyer could get into a house with a low interest rate mortgage that they could afford for the moment, but these were variable rate mortgages, meaning that the rate would go up periodically, sometimes to a level that the low qualified borrower could no longer afford. When that borrower defaulted, it meant that a mortgage packaged into a security would go bad. As long as there were but a few of these, there was no problem. But when there were more than a few, there were a lot, the securitized bond put the investor in jeopardy. In 2008 the panoply of mortgaged backed securities went bust, crippling the world-wide economy.

Tooze: "By 2006, 70 percent of new mortgages were subprime or other unconventional loans destined for securitization not by the GSE, but as private label MBS. In both 2005 and 2006, $1 trillion in unconventional mortgages were issued, compared with $100 billion in 2001.[269]

By 2005 at the latest it was clear that low-quality mortgage debt was a ticking bomb. Many of the subprime mortgages were on balloon rates that would rapidly increase after a period of two or three years. In 2007 the typical adjustable-rate mortgage in the United States favored by low-income borrowers was resetting from an annual rate of 7– 8 percent to 10– 10.5 percent. 65 As traders such as Greg Lippmann at Deutsche Bank realized, between August 2006 and August 2009, $ 738 billion in mortgages would experience "payment shock." 66 As the escalated interest payments hit, a wave of defaults was more or less inevitable."

It didn't blow up under Clinton. It waited until George W. Bush was nearing the end of his second term. It did not end well. America's banking system was on the verge of collapse, a collapse that would likely take down the world banking system with it.

"On the morning of September 20, the US Treasury secretary alerted Congress," writes Tooze, "to the fact that unless they acted fast, $ 5.5 trillion in wealth would disappear by two p.m. They might be facing the collapse of the world economy "within 24 hours." 75 In private session with congressional leadership, Bernanke, who is not given to overstatement, warned that unless they authorized immediate action, "we may not have an economy on Monday." [270]

Mortgages were just one aspect of consumer debt. The crash of 2008 exposed extensive debt driving the U.S. economy. Millions were put out of work, never to recover. Cities and towns were boarded up, closed and never to reopen. America was in deep trouble and the population was angry.

Free market economics was revealed as little more than a Ponzi scheme. The system was corrupt and gamed for the elite to grow in power and wealth, while the bulk of the population was left behind.

"Martin Wolf, the Financial Times's esteemed chief economic commentator, dubbed March 14, 2008, "the day the dream of global free-market capitalism died." 1 That was the day the Bear Stearns rescue was announced. It was only the beginning," according to Tooze.[271]

"The result is moral hazard," says Judt. "The popular cliché that the bloated banks which brought international finance to its knees in 2008 were 'too big to fail' is of course infinitely extendable. No government could permit its railway system simply to 'fail'. Privatized electric or gas utilities, or air traffic control networks, cannot be allowed to grind to a halt through mismanagement or financial incompetence. And, of course, their new managers and owners know this. [272]

Curiously, this point escaped the otherwise sharp eye of Friedrich Hayek. In his insistence that monopolistic industries (including railways and utilities) be left in private hands, he neglected to foresee the implications: since such vital national services would never be allowed to collapse, they could take risks, misspend or misappropriate resources at will, and always know that the government would pick up the tab."

Barack Obama came into office on a theme of "Change you can believe it." He managed to stop America's financial bleeding. The Federal Reserve Bank used monetary policy, which can be translated into printing money or expanding the money supply, to drag America off of life support. [273]

"Insofar as the first Obama term had been disappointing, this could be laid at the door of conservative opposition," says Tooze. "That was depressing but predictable. Modernity and the global capitalism that gave it so much of its dynamic are demanding pacesetters; foot-dragging from conservatives is only to be expected. But in the end history moves on. Even in Europe, pragmatic managerialism in the end prevailed over conservative dogma."[274]

"When the music in the private money markets stopped, the Fed took up the tune, providing a stopgap of liquidity that, all told, ran into trillions of dollars and was tailored to the needs of banks in the United States, Europe and Asia. It was historically unprecedented, spectacular in scale and almost entirely unheralded. It transformed what we imagine to be the relationship between financial systems and national currencies."[275]

"America's downward slide, the long-running trends toward inequality and oligarchy, the disaster of 2008, the lopsided recovery from it, were all symptoms of the profound corruption brought about by big government meddling and its capture by interest groups. Obama's crisis politics were simply the latest phase."[276]

Those of excess, wealth, power and greed became wealthier, were not held accountable for the fraud they perpetrated, and became ever wealthier.

For the middle-class status person who lost a job, sold off 401ks to save their home, but eventually defaulted on that, the world turned upside down. They came to a place much like the place where English yeoman farmers who farmed Common Lands in 15th century England found themselves just before they were enslaved in the indentured servitude system populating the colonies. They were angry, bitter, and resentful. Little wonder they gave us Donald Trump.

"Among the many symptoms of unease and crisis that have afflicted us in the wake of Donald Trump's victory is the extraordinary uncouth variety of postfactual politics that he personifies," says Tooze. "He doesn't tell the truth. He doesn't make sense. He doesn't speak coherently. Power appears to have become unmoored from the basic values of reason, logical consistency and factual evidence. What has caused this degeneration? One can cite a complex of factors. Certainly, unscrupulous political demagoguery, the debasement of popular culture and the self-enclosed world of cable TV and social media are part of the problem, as is Trump's personality."[277]

A man, who failed at everything he touched, but survived by way of corruption, tax evasion and money laundering, occupied the White House. When a pandemic hit America, it revealed his utter incompetence, and it revealed objectives of the elites who wanted a government for themselves and no one else.

"What no one reckoned with was the astonishing aggression and energy of the Far Right, which was not interested in reducing government so much as stopping it altogether," says Tooze.[278]

"Though a disaster was avoided, it is important not to normalize what had happened. The radical right wing of the Republican Party, xenophobic nationalists, many of them evangelical zealots, motivated by a worldview fashioned by the alt-right, or Pat Buchanan's extreme America-first nationalism, a group whose hard core accounted for 10 percent of the House of Representatives, had threatened to paralyze the most important nation-state in the global system. As Steve Bannon, the editor of the Breitbart news site, a cheerleader of the Tea Party and a rising star of the alt-right, gushed to a Daily Beast journalist in November 2013: "I'm a Leninist. Lenin wanted to destroy the state, and that's my goal too. I want to bring everything crashing down, and destroy all of today's establishment." What no one reckoned with was the astonishing aggression and energy of the Far Right, which was not interested in reducing government so much as stopping it altogether.[279]

By the year 2020, America arrived back to the debate over the Articles of Confederation, a loose coalition of independent states serving power elites, and the Constitution, a centralized federal government united for the Common Good.

We have entered an age of fear," says Judt. "Insecurity is once again an active ingredient of political life in Western democracies. Insecurity born of terrorism, of course; but also, and more insidiously, fear of the uncontrollable speed of change, fear of the loss of employment, fear of losing ground to others in an increasingly unequal distribution of resources, fear of losing control of the circumstances and routines of our daily life. And, perhaps above all, fear that it is not just we who can no longer shape our lives but that those in authority have also lost control, to forces beyond their reach."[280]

The Crash of 2008 was built on a house of card. Greenspan attributes it to a Flaw in his thinking.[281]

America is charged with fraud.

American Democracy on the Edge; Civil War; and New Constitution

TODAY THE UNITED STATES STANDS perilously close to the edge of civil war and dictatorship. The clarion call of World Wars I and II to Make the World Safe for Democracy has been silenced by the drums for Make America Great Again, as Americans line up and march for Autocracy and Dictatorship. If American Democracy, now teetering on life support, is to survive, Americans must recognize the broad scope of the issues before them. It did not start with Trump; the roots are much deeper.

At its inception, America was a slave nation. Its Slave Masters enjoyed wealth and prosperity. They held power and held on to it tightly, regardless of moral persuasions to right what was clearly wrong. The Civil War signaled an end to their reign of power, but they persisted and fought tirelessly in regaining the throne.

Andrew Johnson returned the slave masters to power. Although weakened, they created the ideas of the Lost Cause. They recruited religious institutions for support and they exploited the Post Traumatic Stress Disorders of Confederate veterans arguing that the fight was for a noble cause. That was what they wanted to hear and they would go on to invent the Klu Klux Klan.[282]

The fight for power would not come easily, but over the long term, they managed to form multiple coalitions advancing their view of government and its proper role. They have operated by stealth implementing sophisticated plans and techniques of social psychology. The Slave Masters reject democratic ideas for an elected government leading and organizing contemporary society. They want a government subservient to the Power Elite who issue decrees for implementation by government. Participatory democracy; a government serving the Common Good of the population; and an authority over the citizenry, regardless of status or ethnic designations, in which all are equal before the law; are anathema to the Slave Masters. Elections, rule of law, and compassion mean nothing to them.

Greed and the immorally based governmental and legal system serving it represents the goal of the slave masters. It is, indeed, a terminal cancer, if not identified and properly treated. Greed and domination drove the country's founding and development. Powerful slave masters rode the wave of the sugar and cotton economies, accumulating enormous amounts of wealth and its consequent power. The Civil War disrupted their rule, but they were undeterred and determined in regaining the throne. The Civil War presented an opportunity for confronting the disease, but the victors in war failed in recognizing the disease and understanding possible treatments.

At the end of the Civil War, America needed a new Constitution. The product of 1789 was written for slave owners; there was no way to amend such a document in transforming it into a constitution for free people. Although many remain confused about the difference between the Declaration of Independence and the Constitution, it is clear that ideas about life, liberty and the pursuit of happiness are completely absent from the Constitution. Indeed, the Constitution lays out an organization for government involving three branches with each assigned separate and distinctive tasks. It also establishes a reverence for property, not people. To be sure it is a property Constitution, not one "of, by and for the people." Enslaving humans as property was a central cause of the Civil War. When the war concluded, America needed a new Constitution, because it is not possible to amend a property Constitution and transform it into a people Constitution.

Nancy MacLean writes that John Calhoun, a South Carolina Slave Master advocated for state's rights, shifting control from the federal government to the states because the states were easier to manipulate. "Calhoun led a campaign in the early republic that, in the name of property and individual rights, took powers away from local authorities, on whom ordinary people had more influence, and shifted them to central state governments. Why? State government was the level that men like him could most easily control. In South Carolina, he implemented a new style of state government with centralized power that, the legal historian Laura Edwards explained, was "a radical departure from the past." Under his leadership, South Carolina became the one state in antebellum America furthest from the ideal of government of, by, and for the people."[283]

"For most of us today," she adds, "the story of this period is one of righting wrongs long overdue for correction. It's about basic fairness and equal treatment under the law. As important, what was happening in the South until that time illustrated the probability of absolute power to corrupt absolutely. When one set of rights— those of propertied whites— rarely, if ever, had to give way to any other rights, even when the inequity they inflicted on others (such as tar-paper-covered schools for black youths) far outweighed the damage they inflicted on those with property (slightly higher taxes), a system that started out with strong protections for property rights became, over time, a system where only property rights were protected. Indeed, only white property rights at that."[284]

MacLean exposes the forces unleashed after Brown v Board at the University of Virginia where economist James Buchanan formed ideas for ending American democracy. He wanted a constitution protecting the power elite beyond the 1789 version. "Buchanan wanted to see, somehow, a "generalized rewriting of the social contract." America needed "a new structure of checks and balances," well beyond that provided for in its founding Constitution, itself already a very pro-property-rights rulebook, as he well knew."[285]

Contemporary political combat, including Trumpism, centers on a battle between those desirous of a government serving the Common Good—a government of, by and for the people—against Power Elites representing a minority who do not want Democracy, but instead want an oligarchy in which Power Elites control government serving the needs of the wealthy and powerful.

"White nationalist Nick Fuentes," reports Heather Cox Richardson, "told his audience that the solution to the fact Republicans are in a minority and keep losing elections is to establish "a dictatorship." "We need to take control of the media or take control of the government and force the people to believe what we believe or force them to play by our rules." [286]

New slave masters, the barons of industry emerged in the 20th century, eventually joined forces with the slave masters. Industrialization expanded in northern factories providing power elites with prosperity. Abundance did not satiate their wealth and power genes; it merely fueled ever greater desires for more. The titans of business rejected ideas about a Common Good.

Free market enterprise theory became a mantra for the power elite. Novelist Ayn Rand, a fiction writer, became the center of attention as Kim Phillips-Fein notes in her *Invisible Hands: The Businessmen's Crusade Against the New Deal*, Rand believed American morality needed a makeover. "(Ayn) Rand thought that FEE should do more to take aim at the underlying moral system that, she was persuaded, supported collectivism—the idea that people should be devoted to an idea of the "common good," that they were obligated to aid the poor and those less fortunate, that "everybody is responsible for everybody's welfare." This moral code, more than mistaken ideas about economics, was, she believed, the real danger to capitalism."[287]

"But take a longer view— follow the story forward to the second decade of the twenty-first century— and a different picture emerges," says MacLean, "one that is both a testament to Buchanan's intellectual powers and, at the same time, the utterly chilling story of the ideological origins of the single most powerful and least understood threat to democracy today: the attempt by the billionaire-backed radical right to undo democratic governance.

…Koch contributed generously to turning those ideas into his personal operational strategy to, as the team saw it, save capitalism from democracy— permanently."[288]

Note that those, benefitting from an economic system, believe they benefit because of their esteemed skills and competence, not because of privilege. Rationalizations and justifications protect those benefitting from an inhuman system by suggesting that their success may be attributable to a special blessing from God.

Consider this description of Charles Koch by MacLean: "Perhaps this arch sense of his own achievement also helped explain the lack of charity (or what most would call compassion) for nearly everyone else—not just wage earners but also businessmen who did not see things as he did. He came to disdain those who ran publicly traded corporations. Such people mistakenly imagined that because they possessed elegant high-rise corner offices, they were his equals, especially the moderate managers who then played an important role in the Republican Party. By his lights, they were just hired hands, beholden to shareholders and lacking in appreciation of true liberty. No, the real heroes were men like himself, from the Midwest, the West, and the South, who had built their own businesses, kept them private, and were not inclined to compromise."[289]

The Power Elite created sophisticated mechanisms for rationalizing and justifying their privileges and the systemic apparatus exploiting other humans who exist in a less than human world. Intellectual gymnastics, economic and social structural barriers, and a corrupted political system are key tools for that small percentage of the population—the one percent—that dominate. For the Power Elite, the notion of liberty and freedom meant the freedom to enslave others humans and the liberty to defraud anyone and everyone. They like to call it Libertarianism, but may more accurately be labeled Anarchism.

"The wider the spread between the wealthy few and the impoverished many," says Judt, "the worse the social problems: a statement which appears to be true for rich and poor countries alike. What matters is not how affluent a country is but how unequal it is. Thus Sweden, or Finland, two of the world's wealthiest countries by per capita income or GDP, have a very narrow gap separating their richest from their poorest citizens— and they consistently lead the world in indices of measurable wellbeing."[290]

The Power Elite knew they could not compete in the arena of ideas and political persuasion. They knew what they wanted was not what the majority of the American population wanted, so they decided to advance their interests by stealth and by gaming the system.

MacLean found documents stored at the University of Virginia exposing the need for secrecy. "These papers revealed something else as well: how and why stealth became so intrinsic to this movement. Buchanan had realized the value of stealth long ago, while still trying to influence Virginia politicians. But it was Koch who institutionalized this policy. In his first big gift to Buchanan's program, Charles Koch signaled his desire for the work he funded to be conducted behind the backs of the majority. "Since we are greatly outnumbered," Koch conceded to the assembled team, the movement could not win simply by persuasion. Instead, the cause's insiders had to use their knowledge of "the rules of the game"— that game being how modern democratic governance works— "to create winning strategies."[291]

Forces of domination created a landscape of fertile ground giving birth to Trumpism. Although Trumpism embraces white supremacy, it is driven by greed, not racism, which is but a tool for the greedy. Distinction must be made, however, between Trumpism and Trump. Trump is a psychopath, according to an array of psychologists, with a profound predilection for breaking things. His business failures are many and self-destructive actions too numerous for listing. When faced with a choice of working within a system or smashing the system, Trump invariable selected destruction.

This penchant for breaking things coincides with political forces advancing a strategic agenda for breaking the American government, the so-called Movement Conservatives. These forces existed at the beginning of the country, strenuously resisting the very formation of the country before the outbreak of war with England. The Articles of Confederation, a notoriously weak basis for governing, highlights the fissures between the colonies and the palpable desire for independence from each other, in addition to England. The Civil War is a product of these sentiments and mocks the very idea of a United States.

Power elites focused on their power, control and wealth enhancing enterprises. At the turn of the 20th century countervailing forces advocating for Common Good threatened the power elite. World War II represented a clear danger to them and the economic systems favoring them. Forces for change were a direct threat, prompting the power elite to fight back. And fight back they did, but they did so covertly, away from public scrutiny, because the patriotic America of the mid-20th century would never support them. Instead, they hid their agenda, their goals and objectives. Using the latest and most sophisticated techniques for Public Relations (propaganda), they reframed issues so their self-interested initiatives were defined as efforts for Freedom and Liberty strategically disguising their real agenda.

Creating a foundation for the required social and political landscape would not be easy. It demanded a long-term strategy shaping public opinion, utilizing sophisticated mass communication techniques based upon social psychological manipulation, and seizing control of one of the political parties serving as the vanguard of America's dismantlement.

"The Koch team's most important stealth move," says MacLean, "and the one that proved most critical to success, was to wrest control over the machinery of the Republican Party, beginning in the late 1990s and with sharply escalating determination after 2008. From there it was just a short step to lay claim to being the true representatives of the party, declaring all others RINOS— Republicans in name only. But while these radicals of the right operate within the Republican Party and use that party as a delivery vehicle, make no mistake about it: the cadre's loyalty is not to the Grand Old Party or its traditions or standard-bearers. Their loyalty is to their revolutionary cause."[292]

What was to gain by dismantling America? Enormous wealth and power.

The power elite desired every greater expansion of their empires unfettered by government rules and regulations, just as the slave masters did in Barbados under the banner of Protestant Supremacy. They wanted freedom from human rights and rules for worker management. They wanted few taxes and a government that existed solely for military defense purposes and for military aggressive purposes when foreign governments posed an obstacle. They despised FDR's New Deal and Social Security.

Government did not exist, the power elite believed, for serving the Common Good; government existed for facilitating individual gain; their wealth eventually trickling down to the masses.

"We no longer ask," says Judt, "of a judicial ruling or a legislative act: is it good? Is it fair? Is it just? Is it right? Will it help bring about a better society or a better world? Those used to be the political questions, even if they invited no easy answers. We must learn once again to pose them."[293]

The slave masters and their corporate compatriots work strategically and tirelessly to bring America back to the Articles of Confederation. The courts have been a key target. Since the 1970s, the Supreme Court has been transformed and set itself on a track for dismantlement of the American government.

What have the slave masters achieved?

The Constitution is an organizational document. The Legislature is responsible for confronting problems before the country. The legislature passes laws and provides funding for resolving problems. The Executive implements and administers laws. Judiciary adjudicates disputes involving the unconstitutionally passed laws or the executive performing tasks outside the laws that were passed by the legislature.

Over the past 100 years, problems confronting the nation have included:

- Elderly eating dog food for survival;
- Black people segregated from jobs, housing, health care, education, and participation in the political process;
- Poisoned air and water due to industrial polluters;
- Workers killed at work due to unsafe conditions;
- Women killed obtaining an abortion;
- Unions met with brute force by employers who demanded supremacy;
- Weapons readily accessible by killers—even slaughtering children in their classrooms;
- Workers surviving on their wages suddenly without a job with no source of income for survival;
- Business enterprises, averse to free market principals, buying out competitors, so they do not face any competition;
- Corrupted political leader who sold their soul to people who wanted influence, consider Nixon slush fund.

These problems were addressed by Social Security Act; Civil Rights Act, 1964 and Voting Rights Act of 1965; Clean Air and Water Act; Reorganization Plan 3 that created the EPA; OSHA; Supreme Court decision in Roe v Wade; Fair Labor Standards Act; State gun laws and Brady Act; Sherman Antitrust Act; McCain-Feingold Campaign Finance Act.

Since 1970, Republicans and the Republican Court have reversed answers to these problems. The problems are now not resolved.

At the close of World War II, Americans loved their country and their government. Today America is facing insurrection, led by their elected representatives. Something happened. The slave masters and their corporate compatriots, deploying a long-term strategy, drove wedges between Americans. The goal is to end American Democracy so the slave masters can return to power and operate their criminal enterprise unhampered by law.

Politico's Heidi Przybyla recalled that in his 2021 memoir, former Republican speaker John Boehner said of this faction: "What they're really interested in is chaos.... They want to throw sand in the gears of the hated federal government until it fails and they've finally proved that it's beyond saving." And they are tied tightly to right-wing media: "Every time they vote down a bill, they get another invitation to go on Fox News or talk radio," he said. "Its a narcissistic—and dangerous—feedback loop."

Brute force unrestrained by law or morality represents the heart of America. Invasion, occupation and exploitation of lands, natural resources and peoples enslaved on the land; all in service of personal wealth and power for the rich and powerful; represent the actually history of the United States. This is a history of crimes against humanity: genocide; hideous crimes of enslavement, rape, murder and torture; and massive corruption of government including bribery, conspiracy and sabotage of foreign powers in service of the on-going crime.

The evidence presented establishes probable cause of criminal acts, supporting return of a True Bill of Indictment accusing the United States of Crimes Against Humanity to include:

- Illegally invading the lands of North America
- Illegally occupying those lands
- Illegally extracting resources from those lands
- Illegally holding and exploiting enslaved peoples
- Perpetration of Genocide
- Enslavement of Native peoples
- Rape of enslaved peoples
- Rape of Native peoples

- Torture of enslaved people
- Murder of enslaved people
- Murder of Native people
- Conspiracy to bribe government
- Bribery of government officials
- Conspiracy to sabotage foreign governments

PART THREE

Closing

Closing Argument

THE STATE PROSECUTOR IS ASKING you to return an indictment, a formal charge or set of charges, against the United States of America. In doing so, the prosecutor is asking you to confront and contradict the propaganda apparatus of the United States; a force that has propagated a tale, an untrue story, designed to promote the country as noble and honorable, while hiding its use of brute force in achieving its status as a leading world power. The tale is deeply imbedded in the hearts, minds and souls of Americans.

It is difficult, if not near impossible, for people to confront the darkness of the past. Often, they respond defensively with anger and violence directed at the people now providing a true history. The task before you comes with considerable risk that cannot be minimized or trivialized.

The truth, however, is the only mechanism for redressing the insults and injuries inflicted upon the victims of Americanism. Their anguished cries demand no less. Not all, but a sizeable portion of those with wealth and power, have enjoyed luxurious lives, at the expense of their victims. It is past time for them to be held accountable. That choice is yours. This is my case.

Notes

[1] Stephen Howe, *Empire: A Very Short Introduction*

[2] Harari, Y.N. (2018) **21 Lessons for the 21st Century** (p. 73). Random House Publishing Group. Kindle Edition.

[3] Aslan, R. (2017) **God: A Human History** (p. 58). Random House Publishing Group. Kindle Edition. https://www.c-span.org/video/?443471-15/god

[4] Wells, Spencer (2010-06-03). **Pandora's Seed: The Unforeseen Cost of Civilization** (pp. 52-53). Random House, Inc. Kindle Edition. Also, See Wells, (p. 13-15). Random House, Inc. Kindle Edition. https://www.c-span.org/video/?179633-1/the-journey-man Wells, Spencer (2007-11-20). **Deep Ancestry: The Landmark DNA Quest to Decipher Our Distant Past** (Kindle Locations 1901-1902). Random House Inc Clients. Kindle Edition.

[5] Meredith, Martin (2014-10-14). **The Fortunes of Africa: A 5000-Year History of Wealth, Greed, and Endeavor** (Kindle Locations 1707-1708). PublicAffairs. Kindle Edition.

[6] Armstrong, Karen (2014-10-28). **Fields of Blood: Religion and the History of Violence** (p. 12). Knopf Doubleday Publishing Group. Kindle Edition.

[7] See: "Slavery Routes," A short history of human trafficking (2021) Deutsche Welle. Also see UNESCO 1992. https://www.c-span.org/video/?296230-1/slave-trade https://vimeo.com/441910944 Slavery Routes, Also see UNESCO **General History of Africa, Vol. III, Abridged Edition: Africa from the Seventh to the Eleventh Century (Volume 3)** (1992) University of California Press

[8] Taylor, Alan (2002) **American Colonies: The Settling of North America** (The Penguin History of the United States, Volume1) (p. 5). Penguin Group US. Kindle Edition. See also "Native American Mitochondrial DNA Analysis Indicates That the Amerind and the Nadene Populations Were Founded by Two

Independent Migrations" Antonio Torroni,* Theodore G . Schurr, Chi-Chuan Yang, Emoke J . E. Szathmary, Robert C. Williams, Moses S. Schanfield, Gary A. Troup, William C. Knowler, Dale N. Lawrence, Kenneth M. Weiss and Douglas C. Wallace **Genetics Society of America, 1992.** Bailyn, Bernard. (2012) **The Barbarous Years: The Peopling of British North America: The Conflict of Civilizations, 1600-1675** (Kindle Locations 313-314). Knopf Doubleday Publishing Group. Kindle Edition.

[9] Stannard, David E. (1992) **American Holocaust: Columbus and the Conquest of the New World** (Ideologies of Desire) (pp. 8-9). Oxford University Press. Kindle Edition.

[10] Taylor, Alan (2001) **American Colonies:** (p. 15). Taylor, Alan. (2001) **American Colonies:** (p. 21)..

[11] Bailyn, Bernard. (2012) **The Barbarous Years** (Kindle Locations 365-368). Bailyn, Bernard (2012) (Kindle Locations 690-693)

[12] Reséndez, Andrés (2017) **The Other Slavery: The Uncovered Story of Indian Enslavement in America** (p. 13-14). Houghton Mifflin Harcourt. Kindle Edition. https://benfranklinsworld.com/episode-387-jean-pfaelzer-california-and-slavery/

[13] Naimark, Norman M. (2017) **Genocide: A World History** (New Oxford World History) (p. 7). Oxford University Press. Kindle Edition.

[14] Naimark, Norman M (p. 8)

[15] Naimark, Norman M (p. 8-13).

[16] Dunbar-Ortiz, R. (2014 **An Indigenous Peoples' History of the United States** (ReVisioning American History) (pp. 198-199). Beacon Press. Kindle Edition.

[17] **For as much of you,** *Christopher Columbus***, are going by our command, with some of our vessels and men, to discover and subdue some Islands and Continent in the ocean, and it is hoped that by God's assistance, some of the said Islands and Continent in the ocean will be discovered and conquered by your means and conduct, therefore it is but just and reasonable, that since you expose yourself to such danger to serve us, you should be rewarded for it.** *Privileges and Prerogatives Granted by Their Catholic Majesties to Christopher Columbus : 1492* www.avalon.law.yale.edu

[18] Meredith, Martin (2014-10-14). **The Fortunes of Africa: A 5000-Year History of Wealth, Greed, and Endeavor** (Kindle Locations 2043-2045). PublicAffairs. Kindle Edition.

[19] Beckert, Sven (2014-12-02). **Empire of Cotton: A Global History** (Kindle Locations 778-786). Knopf Doubleday Publishing Group. Kindle Edition.

[20] Beckert, Sven (Kindle Locations 905-909).

[21] Taylor, Alan (2002-07-30). **American Colonies:** (p. x) **Additional Notes:**
https://www.c-span.org/video/?321631-1/an-indigenous-peoples-history-united-states
https://www.c-span.org/video/?413277-1/qa-nancy-isenberg
https://www.c-span.org/video/?113124-1/the-story-american-freedom
https://www.c-span.org/video/?321423-1/the-half-told&buy=
https://www.c-span.org/video/?419681-4/washington-journal-carol-anderson-discusses-white-rage&event=419681

[22] Gerbner, K. (2018) **Christian Slavery: Conversion and Race in the Protestant Atlantic World (Early American Studies)** (Kindle Locations 43-54). University of Pennsylvania Press. Kindle Edition.

[23] Gerbner, K. (2018), (Kindle Locations 74-76).
See also, (Kindle Locations 91-92). https://benfranklinsworld.com/episode-206-katharine-gerbner-christian-slavery/

[24] Sirmans, M. Eugene. (2012) **Colonial South Carolina** (Published by the Omohundro Institute of Early American History and Culture and the University of North Carolina Press) (p. 27). Omohundro Institute and University of North Carolina Press. Kindle Edition.

[25] Gerbner, K. (Kindle Locations 292-294).

[26] MacLean, Nancy (2017) **Democracy in Chains: The Deep History of the Radical Right's Stealth Plan for America** (pp. 144-145). Penguin Publishing Group. Kindle Edition. https://www.theguardian.com/news/audio/2021/nov/30/barbados-becomes-a-republic-and-britain-faces-a-reckoning

[27] Jordan, D. (2017), **White Cargo: The Forgotten History of Britain's White Slaves in America** (p. 205-207). Kindle Edition.

[28] Calloway, Colin G. (2018) **The Indian World of George Washington** (pp. 27-28). Oxford University Press. Kindle Edition.

[29] Gordon-Reed, Annette (2011). **Andrew Johnson: The American Presidents Series: The 17th President, 1865-1869**. Henry Holt and Co.. Kindle Edition.

[30] Wiencek, Henry (2003) An **Imperfect God** (p. 43). Farrar, Straus and Giroux. Kindle Edition.

[31] Vaver, Anthony (2011-06-30). **Bound with an Iron Chain: The Untold Story of How the British Transported 50,000 Convicts to Colonial America** (p. 91). Pickpocket Publishing. Kindle Edition.

[32] Jordan (Kindle Locations 179-182)

[33] Linebaugh, Peter (2014) **Stop, Thief!: The Commons, Enclosures, and Resistance** (Spectre) . PM Press. Kindle Edition, loc 233

[34] Taylor, Alan. **American Colonies** (p. 120).

INDICTING AMERICA

[35] Taylor, Alan (2002) **American Colonies** (p. 120-122).

[36] Dunbar-Ortiz, R. (2014), **An Indigenous Peoples'** (p. 35).

[37] Dunbar-Ortiz, R. (2014), (p. 40)

[38] Bailyn, Bernard (2012-11-06). **The Barbarous Years:** (Kindle Locations 1563-1598).

[39] Linebaugh, Peter (2014) Kindle Edition, loc 233

[40] Wiencek, Henry (2003) **An Imperfect God** (pp. 51-52). Farrar, Straus and Giroux. Kindle Edition.

[41] Vaver, Anthony (2011-06-30). Loc. 134

[42] Vaver, Anthony (p. 56).https://www.bbc.co.uk/programmes/b00b1m9b

[43] Vaver, Anthony (2011-06-30). (pp. 7-8).

[44] McGhee, Heather. **The Sum of Us: What Racism Costs Everyone and How We Can Prosper Together** (p. 125). Random House Publishing Group. Kindle Edition.

[45] The Civil War: Why They Fought: Year In Review 2011." *Britannica Book of the Year, 2012. Encyclopædia Britannica Online.* Encyclopædia Britannica Inc., 2012. Web. 12 Dec. 2012. <http://www.britannica.com/EBchecked/topic/1793303/Civil-War-Why-They-Fought-The

[46] Dunbar-Ortiz, Roxanne. **Loaded: A Disarming History of the Second Amendment (City Lights Open Media)** (p. 29). City Lights Publishers. Kindle Edition.

[47] Taylor, Alan (2002-07-30). **American Colonies:** (p. 428).

[48] Middlekauff, Robert (2005-01-05). **The Glorious Cause: The American Revolution, 1763-1789** (Oxford History of the United States) (p. 7). Oxford University Press. Kindle Edition.

[49] Rakove, Jack (2010-05-06). **Revolutionaries: A New History of the Invention of America** (Kindle Locations 236-239). Houghton Mifflin Harcourt. Kindle Edition.

[50] Calloway, Colin G. (2018) (pp. 12-13)https://lehrmaninstitute.org/history/founders-land.html

[51] Wiencek, Henry. (2003) **An Imperfect God** (p. 19). Kindle Edition.

[52] Calloway, Colin G. (2018) (p. 4).

[53] Calloway, Colin G. (2018) (p. 181)

[54] Calloway, Colin G. (2018) (p. 180)

[55] Middlekauff, Robert (2005-01-05). (p. 27).

[56] Rakove, Jack (2010-05-06). **Revolutionaries:** (Kindle Locations 1375-1380).

NOTES

[57] Rakove, Jack (2010-05-06). (Kindle Locations 796-798). Edition.

[58] Applebaum, Y. (2015) "America's Fragile Constitution," **The Atlantic** October, 2015, **Settler Colonialism**

[59] Dunbar-Ortiz, R. (2014), **An Indigenous Peoples' History of the United States** (ReVisioning American History) (p. 6). Beacon Press. Kindle Edition. https://www.c-span.org/video/?417790-1/all-real-indians-died-off

[60] Griffin, P. (2007) **American Leviathan: Empire, Nation, and Revolutionary Frontier** (p. 97). Farrar, Straus and Giroux. Kindle Edition.

[61] Calloway, Colin G. (p. 182).

[62] Taylor, Alan. **American Revolutions: A Continental History, 1750-1804** (p. 75). W. W. Norton & Company. Kindle Edition.

[63] Calloway, Colin G. (2018) (p. 184).

[64] Calloway, Colin G. (2018) (p. 184).

[65] Griffin, P. (2007) **American Leviathan: Empire, Nation, and Revolutionary Frontier** (p. 154). Farrar, Straus and Giroux. Kindle Edition.

[66] Griffin, P. (2007) (p. 154).

[67] Taylor, Alan. **American Colonies:** (p. 201).

[68] Taylor, Alan. **American Colonies:** (p. 390).

[69] Isenburg, N. (2016) **White Trash: The 400-year untold history of class in America.** New York: Penguin Random House. Pp 106-107

[70] Taylor, Alan. **American Revolutions:** (p. 57).

[71] Steven M. Wise (2005) **Though the Heavens May Fall: The Landmark Trial That Led to the End of Human Slavery** (p. xiii). Kindle Edition.

[72] Blumrosen, A.W.; Blumrosen, R. G. (2006-11-01) **Slave Nation: How Slavery United the Colonies and Sparked the American Revolution** (Kindle Locations 1529-1533). Sourcebooks, Inc. Kindle Edition.

[73] Blumrosen, A.W.; Blumrosen, R. G. (Kindle Locations 1529-1533).

[74] Waldstreicher, David (2009) **Slavery's Constitution: From Revolution to Ratification** (pp. 38-40). Farrar, Straus and Giroux. Kindle Edition.

[75] Poser, Norman S. (2013-09-01). **Lord Mansfield: Justice in the Age of Reason** (p. 300). MQUP. Kindle Edition.

[76] Calloway, Colin G. (2018) (p. 201)..

[77] "Dirty little secret," by Simon Schama, **Smithsonian**, May, 2006.

[78] Wiencek, Henry. (2013) Master of the Mountain (p. 45). Farrar, Straus and Giroux. Kindle Edition.

[79] Parkinson, Robert G.. **Thirteen Clocks: How Race United the Colonies and Made the Declaration of Independence** (Published by the Omohundro Institute of Early American History ... and the University of North Carolina Press) (p. 2). Omohundro Institute and UNC Press. Kindle Edition.

[80] Parkinson, Robert G. (2021) (p. 2).

[81] Parkinson, Robert G. (2021) (p. 2)

[82] Blumrosen, Alfred W.; Blumrosen, Ruth G. (2006-11-01). (Kindle Locations 1208-1220).

[83] Blumrosen, Alfred W.; Blumrosen, Ruth G. (2006-11-01). (Kindle Locations 1208-1220).

[84] Foner, E. (2010) **The Fiery Trial: Abraham Lincoln and American Slavery** (p. 44). W. W. Norton & Company. Kindle Edition.

[85] Foner, E. (2010) **The Fiery Trial:** (p. 45).

[86] Roosevelt III, K. (2022) **The Nation That Never Was: Reconstructing America's Story Kindle Edition**

[87] Brown, Vincent. **Tacky's Revolt: The Story of an Atlantic Slave War** (p. 8). Harvard University Press. Kindle Edition.

[88] O'Shaughnessy, Andrew Jackson. **An Empire Divided: The American Revolution and the British Caribbean (Early American Studies)**. University of Pennsylvania Press, Inc.. Kindle Edition.

[89] Native America, PBS

[90] Ellis, Joseph J. (2015) **The Quartet: Orchestrating the Second American Revolution, 1783-1789** (Kindle Locations 91-93). Knopf Doubleday Publishing Group. Kindle Edition.

[91] Bilder, Mary Sarah. (2015) **Madison's Hand: Revising the Constitutional Convention** (Kindle Locations 322-328). Harvard University Press. Kindle Edition.
https://www.c-span.org/video/?523455-1/reconstruction-americas-story
https://www.c-span.org/video/?c4782124/user-clip-george-washington-native-americanspart-2
https://lehrmaninstitute.org/history/founders-land.html
https://www.globalsecurity.org/military/world/usa/government/jefferson-1784.htm
https://www.nytimes.com/interactive/2019/08/14/magazine/1619-america-slavery.html
https://www.nytimes.com/2020/01/23/podcasts/1619-podcast.html
https://www.c-span.org/video/?430379-2/democracy-chains
https://www.c-span.org/video/?404805-1/jane-mayer-discusses-dark-money

[92] Bilder, Mary Sarah (2015) (Kindle Locations 223-225).

NOTES

[93] Griffin, Patrick. Kindle Edition, loc 3865

[94] Baptist, Edward E. (2014) **The Half Has Never Been Told: Slavery and the Making of American Capitalism** (Kindle Locations 4617-4624). Basic Books. Kindle Edition.

[95] Wiencek, Henry (2014) **Master of the Mountain** (p. 252).

[96] Wiencek, Henry. (2014) (p. 257).

[97] McPherson, James M. (1988-02-25). **Battle Cry of Freedom: The Civil War Era (Oxford History of the United States)** (p. 8-9). Oxford University Press. Kindle Edition.

[98] David Brion Davis. (2006) **Inhuman Bondage: The Rise and Fall of Slavery in the New World** (Kindle Locations 4186-4221. Kindle Edition.

[99] Foner, Eric (2010) **The Fiery Trial:** (pp. 16-17).

[100] McGhee, Heather (2021) (p. 103).

[101] An Illustrated Business History of the United States Hardcover – Download: Adobe Reader, May 21, 2021 by Richard Vague (2021) University of Pennsylvania Press

[102] Baptist, Edward E (2014) (Kindle Locations 4943-4949).

[103] Baptist, Edward E (2014) (Kindle Locations 5312-5313). https://www.c-span.org/video/?298322-2/watch-online-annette-gordon-reed&event=298322&playEvent

[104] Howe, Daniel Walker (2007-10-29). **What Hath God Wrought (p. 277).** Oxford University Press. Kindle Edition.

[105] Madley, B. (2016) **An American Genocide: The United States and the California Indian Catastrophe, 1846-1873 (The Lamar Series in Western History)** (Kindle Locations 3480-3484). Yale University Press. Kindle Edition.

[106] Wood, Gordon S. (2009-10-10). **Empire of Liberty: A History of the Early Republic, 1789-1815 (Oxford History of the United States)** (Kindle Locations 2446-2450). Oxford University Press. Kindle Edition.

[107] Howe, Daniel Walker (2007-10-29). (pp. 255-256).

[108] Wood, Gordon S. (Kindle Locations 2518-2526).

[109] Taylor, Alan (2002-07-30). **American Colonies:** (p. 391).

[110] Wortman, Marc (2009-07-30). **The Bonfire: The Siege and Burning of Atlanta** (pp. 28-29). Perseus Books Group. Kindle Edition.

[111] Wortman, Marc (2009-07-30). (pp. 33-34).

[112] Foner, Eric (2010) **The Fiery Trial:** (pp. 261-262).

[113] https://www.senate.gov/about/powers-procedures/investigations/joint-committee-conduct-of-war.htm

[114] Dunbar-ortiz, Roxanne . **Not "A Nation of Immigrants": Settler Colonialism, White Supremacy, and a History of Erasure and Exclusion** (p. 22). Beacon Press. Kindle Edition.

[115] Madley, B. (2016). Kindle Edition, P 31.

[116] Madley, B. (2016) (Kindle Locations 3493-3495)

[117] Madley, B. (2016) (Kindle Locations 3497-3501)

[118] Madley, B. (2016) , Benjamin (2016) (Kindle Locations 3619-3623).

[119] Madley, B. (2016) , Benjamin (2016) (Kindle Location 3746)

[120] Madley, B. (2016) , Benjamin (Kindle Locations 4148-4150).

[121] Madley, B. (2016) , Benjamin. (Kindle Locations 4180-4182).

[122] Madley, B. (2016) , Benjamin (2016 (Kindle Locations 4186-4191

[123] Madley, B. (2016) , Benjamin. (2016) (Kindle Locations 4229-4234

[124] Madley, B. (2016) , Benjamin (2016) (Kindle Locations 4247-4427). https://www.c-span.org/video/?427014-5/an-american-genocide

[125] McPherson, James M. (1988-02-25). **Battle Cry of Freedom: The Civil War Era (Oxford History of the United States)** (p. 13). Oxford University Press. Kindle Edition.

[126] Howe,Daniel Walker (2007-10-29). (pp. 251-252).

[127] McPherson, James M. (1988-02-25). (pp. 14-15).

[128] McPherson, James M. (1988-02-25). (p. 22).

[129] McPherson, James M. (1988-02-25). (pp. 12-13).

[130] Howe,Daniel Walker (2007-10-29). (pp. 1-2).

[131] McPherson, James M. (1988-02-25). (p. 39)

[132] Foner, Eric.(2010) **The Fiery Trial:** (p. 9).r

[133] Queen Victora's Empire https://www.pbs.org/empires/victoria/

[134] Racism: A History, the Color of Money https://www.imdb.com/title/tt1916252/
Motherland, best documentary 2010 https://www.imdb.com/title/tt1220221/
Slavery: A history BBC https://www.imdb.com/title/tt1916252/
500 Years Later https://www.amazon.com/500-Years-Later-Paul-Robeson/dp/B000YGE18C

[135] The First World War https://www.amazon.com/First-World-War-Complete/dp/B0009S2K9C

[136] Congo: White King, Red Rubber, Black Death https://www.imdb.com/title/tt0404551/
Taylor, A.J.P. (1954) **The struggle for mastery in Europe 1848-1918** Oxford University Press

[137] Osterhammel, Jürgen.(2009) **The Transformation of the World: A Global History of the Nineteenth Century (America in the World)** (pp. 401-402). Princeton University Press. Kindle Edition.

[138] Beckert, Sven (2014-12-02). (Kindle Locations 166-173).

[139] Osterhammel, J. (2014) (p. xv).

[140] Armstrong, Karen (2014) (p. 284).

[141] Beckert, Sven. (Kindle Locations 87-90).

[142] Armstrong, Karen (2014) (p. 285)..

[143] Herman, Arthur (2008) **Gandhi & Churchill: The Epic Rivalry that Destroyed an Empire and Forged Our Age**. Random House Publishing Group. Kindle Edition. Loc 446

[144] Armstrong, Karen (2014) (p. 285).

[145] **Art of war: Sun Tzu's legendary victory manual comes to life** (DVD) History Channel, 2009

[146] Foner, Eric (2010) **The Fiery Trial:** (pp. 15-16).

[147] https://avalon.law.yale.edu/19th_century/lincoln1.asp
https://www.nps.gov/linc/learn/historyculture/lincoln-second-inaugural.htm

[148] https://www.ourdocuments.gov/doc.php?flash=false&doc=38&page=transcript

[149] Foner, Eric.(1990) **A Short History of Reconstruction** (p. 1). HarperCollins. Kindle Edition

[150] Beckert, S. (2014) (Kindle Locations 899-902)..

[151] Madley, B. (2016) loc 193,.

[152] Whitman, James Q. (2017) **Hitler's American Model: The United States and the Making of Nazi Race Law** (pp. 1-2). Princeton University Press. Kindle Edition.

[153] Kendi, Ibram X. (2016) **Stamped from the Beginning: The Definitive History of Racist Ideas in America** (p. 340). PublicAffairs. Kindle Edition.

[154] Whitman, James Q. (2017) (p. 8).

[155] Whitman, James Q.(2017) (p. 9)..

[156] Whitman, James Q. (2017) (pp. 9-10).
https://www.ourdocuments.gov/doc.php?flash=false&doc=34&page=transcript

https://www.ourdocuments.gov/doc.php?flash=false&doc=38&page=transcript
http://www.civil-war.net/pages/ordinances_secession.asp

[157] Kendi, Ibram X.(p. 230-231)..

[158] Foner, E (1990). **A Short History of Reconstruction** (p. 33).

[159] http://www.abrahamlincolnonline.org/lincoln/speeches/last.htm

[160] Foner, E (1990). **A Short History of Reconstruction** (p. 33). HarperCollins. Kindle Edition.

[161] Gordon-Reed, Annette. **Andrew Johnson: The American Presidents Series: The 17th President, 1865-1869** (Kindle Locations 60-62). Henry Holt and Co. Kindle Edition.

[162] Gordon-Reed, Annette. (Kindle Locations 187-188)..

[163] Lane, C. (2009) **The Day Freedom Died: The Colfax Massacre, the Supreme Court, and the Betrayal of Reconstruction** (p. 2). Henry Holt and Co.. Kindle Edition.

[164] Foner, Eric (2010-10-19). **A Short History of Reconstruction** (p 109). HarperCollins. Kindle Edition.

[165] Foner, Eric (2010-10-19). **A Short History of Reconstruction** (p 127). HarperCollins. Kindle Edition.

[166] "There's One Heresy That Sets Bernie Apart From All Other Dem Contenders to Unseat Trump: And it's not simply that he calls himself a socialist," Grandin, G. **The Nation**, July 29, 2019

[167] Stevenson, Bryan (2014-10-21). **Just Mercy: A Story of Justice and Redemption** (Kindle Locations 4646-4651). Random House Publishing Group. Kindle Edition.

[168] Stevenson, Bryan (2014-10-21). (Kindle Locations 4655-4659)..

[169] Shay, J. (2010) **Achilles in Vietnam: Combat Trauma and the Undoing of Character**, p xx New York: Simon & Schuster

[170] Wilson, C.R. (1980) **Baptized in blood: The religion of the lost cause, 1865-1920** Athens, Georgia: Georgia University Press, p. 4.

[171] Wilson, C.R. (1980) p. 5.

[172] Cone, J.H. (2011) **The Cross and the Lynching Tree**, loc 201 Orbis Books. Kindle Edition.

[173] Foner, Eric (2010-10-19). **A Short History of Reconstruction** (p. 53). HarperCollins. Kindle Edition.

[174] Lane, Charles. (p. 18)..

[175] Foner, Eric. **A Short History of Reconstruction** (pp. 117-118). HarperCollins. Kindle Edition.

[176] Lane, Charles. (p. 47).

[177] Lane, Charles. (pp. 56-86).

[178] Lane, Charles. (p. 220).

[179] Lemann, Nicholas. **Redemption: The Last Battle of the Civil War** (p. 21). Farrar, Straus and Giroux. Kindle Edition.

[180] Wiencek, Henry. (2013) **Master of the Mountain** (p. 250). Farrar, Straus and Giroux. Kindle Edition. Wiencek, Henry. (2013) (p. 258).

[181] https://www.nbcnews.com/news/nbcblk/animated-frederick-douglass-calls-slavery-compromise-prageru-video-rcna99246

[182] Taylor, Alan. **American Republics:** (p. 152).
Taylor, Alan. (p. 154).
Taylor, Alan. (pp. 151-152).

[183] Beckert, Sven. (Kindle Locations 2331-2333)

[184] Buruma, Ian (2003-02-04). **Inventing Japan: 1853-1964** (Modern Library Chronicles Series Book 11) (p. 11). Random House Publishing Group. Kindle Edition.

[185] Dower, J.W. (1999) **Embracing defeat: Japan in the wake of World War II**, p 19 New York: W.W. Norton & Co.

[186] Feifer, G. (2006) **Breaking open Japan: Commodore Perry, Lord Abe, and American Imperialism in 1853**, p 62. New York: Smithsonian Books

[187] Whitman, James Q. (2017) **Hitler's American Model: The United States and the Making of Nazi Race Law** (p. 9). Princeton University Press. Kindle Edition. See The Convention of Kanagawa: The Treaty between the United States and the Empire of Japan. Commodore Matthew The United States Government The Tokugawa Shogunate of Japan. Kindle Edition
For an extensive examination of the Scramble for Africa see Parkenham, T. (1991) **The scramble for Africa: white man's conquest of the dark continent from 1876-1912.** New York: Random House.

[188] Kinzer, Stephen (2006) Overthrow: **America's Century of Regime Change from Hawaii to Iraq** (pp. 87-88). Henry Holt and Co.. Kindle Edition.

[189] Kinzer, Stephen (2013): **John Foster Dulles, Allen Dulles, and Their Secret World War** (Kindle Locations 158-162). Henry Holt and Co.. Kindle Edition.

[190] Immerwahr, Daniel (2019) **How to Hide an Empire** (p. 212). Farrar, Straus and Giroux. Kindle Edition.

[191] Kinzer, Stephen (2006) **Overthrow:** (p. 80-88).

[192] Immerwahr, Daniel (p. 113).

[193] Immerwahr, Daniel (p. 113).

[194] Kinzer, Stephen (2006) **Overthrow:** (p. 89).

[195] Kinzer, Stephen (2013): **John Foster Dulles,** (Kindle Locations 5083-5085). Kindle Edition.

[196] Talbot, David. (2015) **The Devil's Chessboard: Allen Dulles, the CIA, and the Rise of America's Secret Government** (p. 259). HarperCollins. Kindle Edition.

[197] Weiner, T. (2008) **Legacy of ashes: the history of the CIA**. P. 107 New York: Anchor Books.

[198] Immerwahr, Daniel (2019) (p. 347).

[199] Talbot, David. (2015) (pp. 251-252)..

[200] Kinzer, Stephen (2006) **Overthrow:** (pp. 129-130).

[201] https://www.youtube.com/watch?v=eJ3RzGoQC4s Century of Self, BBC Kinzer, Stephen (2006) **Overthrow:** (p. 134)..

[202] Immerwahr, Daniel (2019) (p. 114)..

[203] Kinzer, Stephen (2006) **Overthrow:** (p. 3).

[204] Kinzer, Stephen (2006) **Overthrow:** (p. 57).

[205] Kinzer, Stephen (2006) **Overthrow:** (p. 65).

[206] Immerwahr, Daniel (2019) (p. 348).

[207] Hotta, Eri (2013-10-29). **Japan 1941: Countdown to Infamy** (Kindle Locations 913-921). Knopf Doubleday Publishing Group. Kindle Edition. https://www.c-span.org/video/?316712-1/japan-1941-countdown-infamy&playEvent

[208] Mitter, Rana (2014) **Forgotten Ally: China's World War II, 1937–1945**. Houghton Mifflin Harcourt. Kindle Edition. Loc 487

[209] Mitter, Rana (2014) Kindle Edition. Loc 942

[210] CHAPTER I Memory and Self-Observation The Perpetuation of the Nineteenth Century, Osterhammel, Jürgen (2009) (p. 3).

[211] https://www.bbc.co.uk/programmes/b098bt3h

[212] Osterhammel, Jürgen.(2009) (pp. 401-402) Also see, Beckert, Sven (2014-12-02). (Kindle Locations 177-182). https://www.bbc.co.uk/programmes/b03ffkfd

[213] "20th-century international relations". *Encyclopædia Britannica. Encyclopædia Britannica Online.* Encyclopædia Britannica Inc., 2014. Web. 07 Jan. 2014 Retrieved from <http://www.britannica.com/EBchecked/topic/291225/20th-century-international-relations>.

NOTES

[214] Mitter, Rana (2014) Kindle Edition. Loc 180

[215] Mitter, Rana. (p. 346).

[216] Mitter, Rana (2014) Kindle Edition. Loc 187

[217] Mitter, Rana. (2014) (p. 17)

[218] Mitter, Rana (2014) Kindle Edition. Loc 178

[219] Logevall, Fredrik. **Embers of War: The Fall of an Empire and the Making of America's Vietnam** (pp. 75-76). Random House Publishing Group. Kindle Edition.

[220] Immerwahr, Daniel (2020) (pp. 265-266).

[221] Immerwahr, Daniel (2020) (p. 269).

[222] Wilson, Mark R. **Destructive Creation: American Business and the Winning of World War II** (American Business, Politics, and Society) (pp. 97-98). University of Pennsylvania Press. Kindle Edition.

[223] Wilson, Mark R. (p. 3).

[224] Wilson, Mark R. (p. 112).

[225] Wilson, Mark R. (pp. 248-249).

[226] Oreskes, Naomi; Conway, Erik M. (2023) **The Big Myth: How American Business Taught Us to Loathe Government and Love the Free Market** (pp. 16-17). Bloomsbury Publishing. Kindle Edition.

[227] Oreskes, Naomi; Conway, Erik M (2023). (p. 18).

[228] Oreskes, Naomi; Conway, Erik M. (2023) (p. 82).

[229] Oreskes, Naomi; Conway, Erik M. (2023) (p. 85).

[230] Oreskes, Naomi; Conway, Erik M. (p. 128)

[231] Oreskes, Naomi; Conway, Erik M. (p. 138)

[232] Oreskes, Naomi; Conway, Erik M. (p. 138).

[233] https://www.britannica.com/event/New-Economic-Policy-Soviet-history

[234] Pool, J. (1997) **Who financed Hitler: The secret funding of Hitler's rise to power, 1919-1933** New York: Pocket Books

[235] Storrs, Landon R.Y (2013). **The Second Red Scare and the Unmaking of the New Deal Left (Politics and Society in Modern America)** (p. 1). Princeton University Press. Kindle Edition.

[236] Storrs, Landon R.Y. (p. 1).

[237] Storrs, Landon R.Y. (p. 2).

[238] MacLean, Nancy. (pp. 50-51).

[239] MacLean, Nancy. (p. xv).

[240] MacLean, Nancy. (p. xv).

[241] Gergel, Richard (2019) **Unexampled Courage** p. 4 Farrar, Straus and Giroux. Kindle Edition.

[242] Gergel, Richard (2019) (p. 113)

[243] Gergel, Richard (2019) (p. 217).

[244] Gergel, Richard (2019) (p. 218).

[245] Gergel, Richard (2019) (p. 219).

[246] Perlstein, Rick (2015) **The Invisible Bridge: The Fall of Nixon and the Rise of Reagan** (p. 91). Simon & Schuster. Kindle Edition.

[247] Stevens, Stuart (2020) **It Was All a Lie** (p. 19). Knopf Doubleday Publishing Group. Kindle Edition.

[248] https://www.archives.gov/legislative/features/voting-rights-1965/johnson.html

[249] History Channel **LBJ And Vietnam: In the eye of the storm**

[250] Sony Pictures (2004) **The fog of war: an Errol Morris Film.**

[251] **Heroes under fire: shadow warriors** (DVD) The History Channel, 2005

[252] **Showdown with Iran** (DVD) Frontline, PBS, 2007

[253] https://www.imdb.com/title/tt0432232/ The Century of Self, BBC documentary

[254] Letters from an American, Heather Cox Richardson, June 9, 2024

[255] MacLean, Nancy (2017) (p. 177-179).

[256] https://www.c-span.org/podcasts/subpage/?series=lecturesHistory History of Abortion University of California, Davis, law professor Mary Ziegler discussed the history of abortion and contraception laws in the United States. June, 22, 2024

[257] Judt, Tony (2010) **Ill Fares the Land** (p. 2). Penguin Publishing Group. Kindle Edition.

[258] "Milton Friedman and the Chicago School of Economics" **Foundation for Economic Education**, R.M. Ebeling.

[259] https://www.nytimes.com/2018/03/05/books/review/adam-winkler-we-the-corporations.html "How Businesses Became People" **By ZEPHYR TEACHOUT** MARCH 5, 2018 https://www.thenation.com/article/america-has-a-monopoly-problem-and-its-huge/

[260] Stiglitz, Joseph E. (2010) **Freefall: America, Free Markets, and the Sinking of the World Economy** (p. 148). W. W. Norton & Company. Kindle Edition.

NOTES

[261] The Warning (2009) PBS Frontline **The Flaw: What happens when the rich get richer** (2010) Studio Lambert

[262] America's Monopoly Problem: How big business jammed the wheels of innovation DEREK THOMPSON **OCTOBER 2016 ISSUE**
https://www.theatlantic.com/magazine/archive/2016/10/americas-monopoly-problem/497549/
Also see:
https://www.theatlantic.com/magazine/archive/1881/03/the-story-of-a-great-monopoly/306019/
https://hbr.org/2009/07/the-end-of-rational-economics
https://www.nytimes.com/2018/06/04/upshot/reagan-deregulation-and-americas-exceptional-rise-in-health-care-costs.html?hp&action=click&pgtype=Homepage&clickSource=story-heading&module=second-column-region&region=top-news&WT.nav=top-news

[263] Packer, George. (2013) **The Unwinding: An Inner History of the New America** (p. 115-116). Farrar, Straus and Giroux. Kindle Edition.

[264] Harari, Y. N. (2018) (p. 8).

[265] Judt, Tony (2010) (pp. 19-20).

[266] Tooze, Adam (2018) **Crashed** (p. 36). Penguin Publishing Group. Kindle Edition.

[267] Tooze, Adam (2018) (p. 54).

[268] Tooze, Adam (2018) (p. 64).

[269] Tooze, Adam (2018) (p. 63). Edition. Tooze, Adam (2018) (p. 70).

[270] Tooze, Adam (2018) (p. 162).

[271] Tooze, Adam (2018) (p. 166).

[272] Judt, Tony (2010) (p. 112). Penguin

[273] **The Untouchables: Money, power and Wall Street** (2013) PBS Frontline

[274] Tooze, Adam (2018) (pp. 18-19).

[275] Tooze, Adam (2018) (p. 203).

[276] Tooze, Adam (2018) (p. 463).

[277] Tooze, Adam (2018) (p. 21).

[278] Tooze, Adam (2018) (p. 465).

[279] Tooze, Adam (2018) (p. 468).

[280] Judt, Tony (2010) (p. 217).

[281] **The Flaw: What happens when the rich get richer** (2010)

[282] https://www.c-span.org/video/?523455-1/reconstruction-americas-story

[283] MacLean, Nancy. (p. 5).

[284] MacLean, Nancy (pp. 75-76).

[285] MacLean, Nancy. (p. 151).

[286] Heather Cox Richardson newsletter Nov. 11, 2022. https://www.rightwingwatch.org/post/nick-fuentes-says-the-results-of-the-2022-elections-prove-why-we-need-a-dictatorship/utm_source=substack&utm_medium=email

[287] Phillips-Fein, Kim. **Invisible Hands: The Businessmen's Crusade Against the New Deal** . W. W. Norton & Company. Kindle Edition.

[288] MacLean, Nancy. (p. xx). See also: **Koch Brothers Exposed** (2012) Brave New Foundation

[289] MacLean, Nancy. (p. 134).

[290] Judt, Tony (2010)(pp. 19-20).

[291] MacLean, Nancy. (p. xx).

[292] MacLean, Nancy. (p. xxvii). See: https://www.youtube.com/watch?v=eJ3RzGoQC4s **Century of self** O'Shaughnessy, N. (2016) **Selling Hitler: Propaganda and the Nazi Brand** Kindle Edition Hurst Babiak, P. & Hare, R.D. (2009) **Snakes in Suits** HarperCollins e-books. Kindle Edition.

[293] Judt, Tony (2010) (pp. 1-2).

Bibliography and Video References

Allison, D.K. & Ferreiro, L.D. (2018) **The American Revolution: A world war** Smithsonian Books.

Amar. A.R. (2005) **America's Constitution: A biography**, New York: Random House

Anderson, C. (2016) **White Rage: The unspoken truth of our racial divide.** United Kingdom: Bloomsbury. See also C-Span https://www.c-span.org/video/?417268-10/carol-anderson-discusses-race-relations

"Andrew Johnson". En*cyclopædia Britannica. Encyclopædia Britannica Online.*
Encyclopædia Britannica Inc., 2014. Web. 22 Oct. 2014 <http://www.britannica.com/EBchecked/topic/305256/Andrew-Johnson>.

Applebaum, Y. (2015) "America's Fragile Constitution," **The Atlantic** October, 2015,

Armstrong, Karen (2011). **History of God** (Kindle Locations 688-699). New York: Random House Publishing Group. Kindle Edition.

Armstrong, Karen (2014). **Fields of blood: Religion and the history of violence** (2014) New York: Alfred A. Knopf. Kindle Edition. See also C-Span Lectures in History https://www.c-span.org/video/?322547-1/after-words-karen-armstrong

Aslan, R. (2014) **Zealot: the life and times of Jesus of Nazareth** New York: Random House

Aslan, R. (2017) God: **A Human History** Random House Publishing Group. Kindle Edition.

astrolabe. (2014). In Encyclopædia Britannica. Retrieved from http://www.britannica.com/EBchecked/topic/39959/astrolabe

Babiak, P. & Hare, R.D. (2009) **Snakes in Suits** HarperCollins e-books. Kindle Edition

Bailyn, B. (1992) **The ideological origins of the American Revolution:** New York: Harvard University Press. See also C-Span https://www.c-span.org/video/?174896-1/to-begin-world-anew

Bailyn, B. (1986) **The peopling of British North America: An introduction** New York: Alfred A Knopf

Bailyn, B. (2011) **Voyagers to the west: A Passage in the Peopling of America on the Eve of the Revolution** New York: Random House

Bailyn, B. (2012) **The barbarous years: the peopling of British North America : the conflict of civilizations, 1600– 1675** New York: Alfred Knopf

Baptist, E.E. (2014) **The half has never been told: slavery and the making of American capitalism** New York: Basic Books

Beard, C. A. (1913) **An economic interpretation of the Constitution of the United States** New York: The Free Press.

Beckert, Sven (2014) **Empire of Cotton: A Global History** New York: Knopf Doubleday Publishing Group. Kindle Edition. See also C-Span Lectures in History https://www.c-span.org/video/?324267-1/empire-cotton

Sven Beckert and Seth Rockman. (2016) **Slavery's Capitalism: A New History of American Economic Development (Early American Studies)** University of Pennsylvania Press. Kindle Edition.

Belew, K. and Gutiérrez, R.A. (2022) **A Field Guide to White Supremacy** University of California Press. Kindle Edition.

Bilder, Mary Sarah. (2015) **Madison's Hand: Revising the Constitutional Convention** Harvard University Press. Kindle Edition.

BIBLIOGRAPHY AND VIDEO REFERENCES

"black code". *Encyclopædia Britannica. Encyclopædia Britannica Online.* Encyclopædia Britannica Inc., 2014. Web. 22 Oct. 2014 <http://www.britannica.com/EBchecked/topic/67722/black-code>.

Blackmon, D.A. (2009) Slavery by another name: the Re-Enslavement of Black Americans from the Civil War to World War II New York: Anchor Books

Blight, D.W. (2007) **A Slave No More: Two Men who Escaped to Freedom Including Their Own Narratives of Emancipation.** New York: Harcourt Books

Blumrosen, A.W. & Blumrosen, R.G. (2006) **Slave Nation: how slavery united the colonies & sparked the American revolution.** Illinois: Source Books. See also C-Span https://www.c-span.org/video/?c4780602/aw-blumrosen-thomas-hearing

Bogus, C.T. (ed) (2000) **The second amendment in law and history: historians and constitutional scholars on the right to bear arms** New York: The New Press

Bordewich, F.M. **America's great debate: Henry Clay, Stephen A. Douglas, and the compromise that preserved the union** (2012) New York: Simon & Schuster

Bown, S.R. (2010) **Merchant Kings: When Companies Ruled the World, 1600-1900** New York: St. Martin's Press

Brookhiser, R. (2003) **Gentleman revolutionary: Gouverneur Morris, the rake who wrote the Constitution** New York: Free Press

Brown, V. (2020) **Tacky's Revolt: The Story of an Atlantic Slave War Kindle Edition**

Buruma, I. (2003) **Inventing Japan 1853-1964** New York: Random House

Buruma, Ian (2013) **Year Zero: A History of 1945** Penguin Publishing Group. Kindle Edition.

Calloway, C.G. (2018) **The Indian World of George Washington: The first President, the first Americans, and the birth of a nation.** Oxford University Press. Kindle Edition.

Christian, D. (2018) **Origin Story: A Big History of Everything** New York: Little, Brown & Co.

The Civil War: Why They Fought: Year In Review 2011." *Britannica Book of the Year, 2012. Encyclopædia Britannica Online.* Encyclopædia

Britannica Inc., 2012. Web. 12 Dec. 2012. <http://www.britannica.com/EBchecked/topic/1793303/Civil-War-Why-They-Fought-The

Cone, J.H. (2011) **The cross and the lynching tree** New York: Orbis Books

Cotter, W.R. (1994) "The Somerset Case and the Abolition of Slavery in England," pp. 31-56 **History 79 (1994):31**

Davis, D.B. (2006) **Inhuman bondage: the rise and fall of slavery in the new world.** New York: Oxford University Press

Davis, D.B. (2014) **The problem of slavery in the age of emancipation** New York: Alfred A. Knopf

de Waal, Frans (2013) **The Bonobo and the Atheist: In Search of Humanism Among the Primates** W. W. Norton & Company. Kindle Edition.

Diamond, J. (1999) **Guns, germs and steel: The fates of human societies.** New York: WW Norton

Dower, J.W. (1999) **Embracing defeat: Japan in the wake of World War II**, p 19New York: W.W. Norton & Co.

Dower, John W. (2017) **The Violent American Century: War and Terror Since World War II** Haymarket Books. Kindle Edition.

Downey, K. (2014) **Isabella: The warrior queen** New York: Anchor Books

Dunbar-Ortiz, R. (2014) **An indigenous people's history of the United States (Revisioning American History)** Massachusetts: Beacon Press. See also C-Span Lectures in History https://www.c-span.org/video/?321631-1/an-indigenous-peoples-history-united-states and https://www.c-span.org/video/?442127-1/nation-immigrants-mythology

Dunbar-Ortiz, R. (2021) **Not "A Nation of Immigrants": Settler Colonialism, White Supremacy, and a History of Erasure and Exclusion** Kindle Edition

Dunbar-Ortiz, R. (2018) **Loaded: A Disarming History of the Second Amendment (City Lights Open Media)** Kindle Edition

Ehrenreich, B. (1997) **Blood rites: origins and history of the passions of war** New York: Henry Holt and Company

Ellis, J.J. (2007) **American Creation 1st Edition, Kindle Edition** New York: Vintage

BIBLIOGRAPHY AND VIDEO REFERENCES

Ellis, Joseph J. (2015-05-12). **The Quartet: Orchestrating the Second American Revolution, 1783-1789** New York: Alfred A. Knopf

Eltis, D. (2000) **The rise of African Slavery in the Americas** New York: Cambridge University Press

Engerman, S., Drescher, S. & Paquette, R. (editors) (2001) **Slavery, Oxford Readers** Oxford University Press

English Civil Wars. (2013). In *Encyclopædia Britannica*. Retrieved from http://www.britannica.com/EBchecked/topic/187936/English-Civil-Wars

Exploration of North America. (2013) *The History Channel website.* Retrieved 4:45, May 23, 2013 from http://history.com/topics/exploration-of-north-america

Feifer, G. (2006) **Breaking open Japan: Commodore Perry, Lord Abe, and American Imperialism in 1853** New York: Smithsonian Books

Finkelman, P. (2003) **Defending slavery: proslavery thought in the old south, a brief history with documents.** Massachusetts: The Bedford series in history and culture.

Finkelman, P. (2018) **Supreme injustice: slavery in the nation's highest court** Massachusetts: Harvard University Press

Fynn-Paul, J. (2009) "Empire, monotheism and slavery in the greater Mediterranean region from antiquity to the early modern era." **Past and Present, no 205 (Nov. 2009)**

Foner, E. (1990) **A short history of reconstruction 1863-1877** New York: Harper, See also C-Span Lectures in History https://www.c-span.org/video/?428340-1/reconstruction-civil-rights

Foner, E. (2010) **The fiery trial: Abraham Lincoln and American slavery** (2010) New York: W.W. Norton and Co.

Foner, E. (2019) **The second founding: How the Civil War and Reconstruction remade the Constitution** New York: W.W. Norton and Co.

"French and Indian War". *Encyclopædia Britannica. Encyclopædia Britannica Online.*
Encyclopædia Britannica Inc., 2017. Web. 29 Sep. 2017
<https://www.britannica.com/event/French-and-Indian-War>.

Gates, H.L. "Ending the slavery blame-game" April 23, 2010, **New York Times.**

Gerbner, K, (2018) Christian Slavery: Conversion and Race in the Protestant Atlantic World (Early American Studies) Pennsylvania: University of Pennsylvania Press. Also see Ben Franklin's World Podcast, Episode 206 https://www.benfranklinsworld.com/episode-206-katharine-gerbner-christian-slavery/

Gergel, Richard (2019) **Unexampled Courage** Farrar, Straus and Giroux. Kindle Edition.

Goodall, J. C-Span Lectures in History https://www.c-span.org/video/?458280-1/abraham-lincoln-andrew-johnson-constitution

Gordon-Read, (2011) **Andrew Johnson: The American Presidents** New York: Henry Holt & Company.

Griffin, P. (2007) **American leviathan: empire, nation, and revolutionary frontier** New York: Hill and Wang

Harari, Y.N. (2018) **21 Lessons for the 21st Century** New York: Spiegel & Grau

Hart, Bradley W. (2018) **Hitler's American Friends: The Third Reich's Supporters in the United States** (p. 223). St. Martin's Press. Kindle Edition.

Herman, Arthur (2008) **Gandhi & Churchill: The Epic Rivalry that Destroyed an Empire and Forged Our Age** . Random House Publishing Group. Kindle Edition.

History of Europe. (2014). In *Encyclopædia Britannica*. Retrieved from http://www.britannica.com/EBchecked/topic/195896/history-of-Europe/58403/Revolution-and-the-growth-of-industrial-society-1789-1914

Hochschild, Arlie Russell (2018) **Strangers in Their Own Land: Anger and Mourning on the American Right** The New Press. Kindle Edition.

Hofstadter, R. (2012) "White servitude," retrieved from http://www.montgomerycollege.edu/Departments/hpolscrv/whiteser.html

Hofstadter, R. (1955) **The age of reform: from Bryan to FDR.** New York: Vintage Books

BIBLIOGRAPHY AND VIDEO REFERENCES

Holton, W. (1999) **Forced founders: Indians, debtors, slaves, and the making of the American Revolution in Virginia** North Carolina: University of North Carolina Press

Horne, G. (2014) **The counter revolution of 1776: Slave resistance and the origins of the United States of America** New York: New York University Press

Horwitz, T. (2014) "PTSD: The Civil War's hidden legacy," **Smithsonian** January, 2015

Hotta, E. (2013) **Japan 1941: Countdown to infamy** New York: Alfred A. Knopf

Howe, Stephen (2002) **Empire: A Very Short Introduction** (Very Short Introductions Book 76). OUP Oxford. Kindle Edition.

Howe, D.W. (2007) **What hath God wrought: the transformation of America, 1815-1848** New York: Oxford University Press, The Oxford History of the United States.

Hyman, L. & Baptist, E. E. (2016) **American Capitalism: A reader** New York: Simon & Schuster

Immerwahr, D. (2019) **How to hide an empire: a history of the greater United States** New York: Macmillan USA

Industrial Revolution. (2014). In *Encyclopædia Britannica*. Retrieved from http://www.britannica.com/EBchecked/topic/287086/Industrial-Revolution

Isenburg, N. (2016) **White Trash: The 400-year untold history of class in America.** New York: Penguin Random House.

"Jim Crow laws," http://en.wikipedia.org/wiki/Jim_Crow_laws

Johnston, D.C. (2016) **The making of Donald Trump** New York: Melville House

Jordan, D. & Walsh, M. (2017) **White Cargo: The Forgotten History of Britain's White Slaves in America** Amazon Digital Services

Jordan, W.D. (1974) **White man's burden: historical origins of racism in the United States** New York: Oxford University Books.

Jordan, W.D. (1968) **White over black: American attitudes toward the Negro 1550-1812** University of North Carolina press.

Judt, T. (2005) **Postwar: A History of Europe Since 1945** New York: Penguin

Judt, T. (2010) **Ill fares the land** New York: Penguin

Kendi, X.O. (2016) **Stamped from the beginning: the definitive history of racist ideas in America** New York: Nation Books

Kinzer, S. (2013) **The brothers: John Foster Dulles, Allen Dulles, and their secret world war** New York: Times Publishing

Kinzer, S. (2006) **Overthrow: America's century of regime change from Hawaii to Iraq.** New York: Henry Holt and Co.

Lane, C. (2009) **The Day Freedom Died: The Colfax Massacre, the Supreme Court, and the Betrayal of Reconstruction** New York: Henry Holt and Co.. Kindle Edition.

Lee, Bandy X. **The Dangerous Case of Donald Trump** (p. 477). St. Martin's Publishing Group. Kindle Edition.

Lemann, N. (2006) **Redemption: The last battle of the Civil War** New York: Farras, Straus & Giroux

Linebaugh, P. (2014) **Stop, Thief!: The Commons, Enclosures, and Resistance** (Spectre) Kindle Edition New York: PM Press

Logevall, Fredrik. **Embers of War: The Fall of an Empire and the Making of America's Vietnam** Random House Publishing Group. Kindle Edition.

Lovejoy, P.E. (2011) **Transformations in Slavery: A History of Slavery in Africa (African Studies Book 117) 3rd Edition, Kindle Edition** Cambridge University Press

Lowe, K. (2013) **Savage Continent: Europe in the aftermath of World War II** New York: St. Martin's Press

MacLean, N. (2017) **Democracy in chains: the deep history of the radical right's stealth plan for America** New York: Penguin Books

Madley, B. (2016) **An American genocide: The United States and the California Indian Catastrophe, 1846-1873** Yale University Press. See also C-Span Lectures in History https://www.c-span.org/video/?427014-5/an-american-genocide and https://www.c-span.org/video/?414117-1/killing-native-americans-california

Maier, P. (2010) **Ratification: the people debate the Constitution, 1787-1788** New York: Simon and Schuster.

May, G. **Bending toward justice: The voting rights act and the transformation of American democracy** (2013) New York: Basic Books

May, G. **The informant: The FBI, the Ku Klux Klan, and the murder of Viola Liuzzo** (2005) Connecticut: Yale University Press

Mayer, J. (2016) **Dark money: the hidden history of the billionaires behind the rise of the radical right** New York: Anchor Books

Mayer, J. (2009) **Dark Side: The inside story of how the war on terror turned into a war on American ideals** New York: Anchor Press

McGhee, H. (2021) **The Sum of Us: What Racism Costs Everyone and How We Can Prosper Together** Kindle Edition, One World Publishing

McKitrick, E.L. (ed) **Slavery defended: the views of the old south.** New York: Columbia University Press.

McPherson, J.M. (1988) **Battle cry of freedom: the Civil War era** New York: Oxford University Press. The Oxford History of the United States.

Meredith, M. (2014) **The fortunes of Africa: a 5000 year history of wealth, greed and endeavor** New York: Public Affairs

Meredith, M (2005) **Fate of Africa: a history of fifty years of independence** New York: Public Affairs

Middlekauff, R. (2005) **The glorious cause: The American revolution 1763-1789** New York: Oxford University Press.

Mitter, R. (2014) **Forgotten Ally: China's World War II, 1937–1945** New York: Houghton Mifflin Harcourt. Kindle Edition.

Myers, Barton. "Sherman's Field Order No. 15." New Georgia Encyclopedia. 17 September 2014. Web. 22 October 2014.

Naimark, Norman M. (2017) **Genocide: A World History** (New Oxford World History) Oxford University Press. Kindle Edition.

Newby-Alexander, C. Interview Ben Franklin's World podcast Episode 250 https://www.benfranklinsworld.com/episode-250-virginia-1619/

Oreskes, Naomi; Conway, Erik M. (2023) **The Big Myth: How American Business Taught Us to Loathe Government and Love the Free Market** Bloomsbury Publishing. Kindle Edition.

O'Shaughnessy, A.J. (2015) **An Empire Divided: The American Revolution and the British Caribbean (Early American Studies) Kindle Edition**

O'Shaughnessy, N. (2016) **Selling Hitler: Propaganda and the Nazi Brand** Kindle Edition Hurst

Osterhammel, J. (2014) **The Transformation of the World: A Global History of the Nineteenth Century (America in the World)** New Jersey: Princeton University Press. Kindle Edition.

Packer, George. (2013) **The Unwinding: An Inner History of the New America** Farrar, Straus and Giroux. Kindle Edition.

Pappas, G. D. (2017) **The literary and legal genealogy of native American dispossession: The Marshall trilogy cases** New York: Routledge

Parkenham, T. (1991) **The scramble for Africa: white man's conquest of the dark continent from 1876-1912.** New York: Random House.

Parkinson, Robert G. (2021) **Thirteen Clocks** (Published by the Omohundro Institute of Early American History and Culture and the University of North Carolina Press) Kindle Edition.

Peniel, J. C-Span Lectures in History https://www.c-span.org/video/?458781-2/civil-rights-ronald-walters-career

Perlstein, R. (2009) **Before the storm: Barry Goldwater and the unmaking of the American Consensus.** Nation Books.

Perlstein, Rick. (2015) **The Invisible Bridge: The Fall of Nixon and the Rise of Reagan.** Simon & Schuster. Kindle Edition.

Perlstein, Rick. (2010) **Nixonland: The rise of a President and the fracturing of America** New York: Scriber Kindle Edition.

Perlstein, Rick. (2020) **Reaganland: America's Right Turn 1976-1980 Kindle Edition** Simon& Schuster

Perry, Matthew. **The Convention of Kanagawa: The Treaty between the United States and the Empire of Japan.** The United States Government. The Tokugawa Shogunate of Japan, Kindle Edition

Phillips-Fein, Kim. **Invisible Hands: The Businessmen's Crusade Against the New Deal**. W. W. Norton & Company. Kindle Edition.

Pool, J. (1997) **Who financed Hitler: The secret funding of Hitler's rise to power, 1919-1933** New York: Pocket Books

Poser, N.S. (2013) **Lord Mansfield: Justice in an age of reason** London: McGill-Queens University Press.

Privileges and Prerogatives Granted by Their Catholic Majesties to Christopher Columbus : 1492, retrieved from http://avalon.law.yale.edu/15th_century/colum.asp

Rabin, D. (2011) 'In a Country of Liberty?': Slavery, Villeinage and the Making of Whiteness in the Somerset Case (1772) Hist Workshop J (2011) 72 (1): 5-29. doi: 10.1093/hwj/dbq050 First published online: August 23, 2011

"Radical Republican". *Encyclopædia Britannica. Encyclopædia Britannica Online.* Encyclopædia Britannica Inc., 2014. Web. 22 Oct. 2014 <http://www.britannica.com/EBchecked/topic/488729/Radical-Republican>.

Rakove, J.N. (2010) **Revolutionaries: A New History of the Invention of America Kindle Edition** New York: Vintage E-Books.

Rakove, J.N. (1990) **Original Meanings: Politics and Ideas in the Making of the Constitution Kindle Edition** New York: Random House

"Reconstruction". *Encyclopædia Britannica. Encyclopædia Britannica Online.*
Encyclopædia Britannica Inc., 2014. Web. 22 Oct. 2014 <http://www.britannica.com/EBchecked/topic/493722/Reconstruction/295416/The-end-of-Reconstruction>

Reconstruction Acts. (2014, October 22). In *Wikipedia, The Free Encyclopedia.* Retrieved 12:06, October 22, 2014, from http://en.wikipedia.org/w/index.php?title=Reconstruction_Acts&oldid=630600976

Resendez, A. (2016) **The other slavery: the uncovered story of Indian enslavement in America** New York: Houghton Mifflin

Reynolds, E. (1985) **Stand the storm: A history of the Atlantic Slave Trade.** Illinois: Elephant Paperbacks.

Rhiannon Koehler. (2018). "Hostile Nations: Quantifying the Destruction of the Sullivan-Clinton Genocide of 1779." **American Indian Quarterly, 42(4), 427–453.** https://doi.org/10.5250/amerindiquar.42.4.0427

Richardson, Heather Cox, (2020) **How the South won the Civil War: oligarchy, democracy, and the continuing fight for the soul of America** Oxford University Press,

Rodney, W. "African slavery and other forms of social oppression on the Upper Guinea Coast in the context of the Atlantic slave-trade," **The Journal of African History, Vol 7, No. 3 (1966) pp. 431-443.**

Roosevelt III, K. (2022) **The Nation That Never Was: Reconstructing America's Story Kindle Edition**

Ryback, T.W. **(2008) Hitler's private library: The books that shaped his life New York: Alfred A. Knopf**

Scaife, W. R. (1993) **The campaign for Atlanta** (1993)

"Dirty little secret," by Simon Schama, **Smithsonian**, May, 2006.

"sextant". *Encyclopædia Britannica. Encyclopædia Britannica Online.* Encyclopædia Britannica Inc., 2014. Web. 25 Sep. 2014 <http://www.britannica.com/EBchecked/topic/537066/sextant>.

Shay, J. (2010) **Achilles in Vietnam: Combat Trauma and the Undoing of Character** New York: Simon & Schuster

Sirmans, M.E. (2012) **Colonial South Carolina: A Political History, 1663-1763 (Published by the Omohundro Institute of Early American History and Culture and the University of North Carolina Press) Kindle Edition**

"Slaughterhouse Cases". *Encyclopædia Britannica. Encyclopædia Britannica Online.*
Encyclopædia Britannica Inc., 2014. Web. 22 Oct. 2014 <http://www.britannica.com/EBchecked/topic/548140/Slaughterhouse-Cases>.

Slack, P. (2012) **Plague: a very short introduction** New York: Oxford University Press

Slap, A. C-span Lectures in History https://www.c-span.org/video/?458280-1/abraham-lincoln-andrew-johnson-constitution

Sloan, C. and McKean, D. (2009) **The great decision: Jefferson, Adams, Marshall, and the battle for the Supreme Court** New York: Public Affairs.

The Case of JAMES SOMMERSETT, a Negro, on a Habeas Corpus,* King's-Bench: 12 GEORGE III. A.D. 1771-72. The Somerset Case *Howell's State Trials*, vol. 20, cols 1-6, 79-82 retrieved from http://www.nationalarchives.gov.uk/pathways/blackhistory/rights/transcripts/somerset_case.htm

Stannard, D.E. (1992) **American Holocaust: Columbus and the Conquest of the New World** New York: Oxford University Press. Kindle Edition.

Stevens, Stuart (2020) **It Was All a Lie** Knopf Doubleday Publishing Group. Kindle Edition.

Stevenson, Bryan (2014) **Just mercy: a story of justice and redemption** New York: Spiegel and Grau

Stiglitz, Joseph E. (2010) **Freefall: America, Free Markets, and the Sinking of the World Economy** W. W. Norton & Company. Kindle Edition.

Stilwell, S. (2014) **Slavery and Slaving in African History (New Approaches to African History Book 8) Kindle Edition** Cambridge University Press

Storrs, Landon R.Y (2013). **The Second Red Scare and the Unmaking of the New Deal Left (Politics and Society in Modern America)** Princeton University Press. Kindle Edition.

Stringer, C. (2012) **Lone survivors: how we came to be the only humans on earth** New York: Henry Holt & Co.

Talbot, David. (2015)**The Devil's Chessboard: Allen Dulles, the CIA, and the Rise of America's Secret Government** HarperCollins. Kindle Edition.

Taylor, A. (2002) **American colonies: the settling of North America.** New York: Penguin Books, Penguin History of the United States.

Taylor, A. (2013) **The internal enemy: slavery and war in Virginia, 1772-1832** New York: W.W. Norton.

Taylor, A. (2016) **American Revolutions: A continental history, 1750-1804** New York: W.W. Norton.

Taylor, A. (2021) **American Republics: A Continental History of the United States, 1783-1850** New York: W.W. Norton

Taylor, A.J.P. (1954) **The struggle for mastery in Europe 1848-1918** Oxford University Press

Teachout, Zephyr (2014) **Corruption in America: From Benjamin Franklin's Snuff Box to Citizens United** Massachusetts: Harvard University Press. Kindle Edition.

"There's One Heresy That Sets Bernie Apart From All Other Dem Contenders to Unseat Trump: And it's not simply that he calls himself a socialist," Grandin, G. **The Nation**, July 29, 2019

Thomas, H. (1997) **The slave trade: the story of the Atlantic slave trade: 1440-1870.** New York: Simon and Schuster

Thornton, J. (1992) **Africa and Africans in the making of the Atlantic World, 1400-1800, second edition** by John Thornton (1998) New York: Cambridge University Press

Thyssen family. (2014). In *Encyclopædia Britannica*. Retrieved from http://www.britannica.com/EBchecked/topic/594746/Thyssen-family

Tick, E. (2005) **War and the soul: healing our nation's veterans from post traumatic stress disorder** Illinois: Quest Books

Toland, J. (1970) **The rising sun: The decline and fall of the Japanese empire 1936-1945** Volume 1. New York: Random House

Tooze, Adam (2018) **Crashed** Penguin Publishing Group. Kindle Edition.

Traub, J. (2016) **John Quincy Adams: militant spirit**. New York: Basic Books.

Trump, M. (2020) **Too Much and Never Enough: How My Family Created the World's Most Dangerous Man** Kindle Edition New York: Simon & Schuster

"20th-century international relations". *Encyclopædia Britannica. Encyclopædia Britannica Online.*
Encyclopædia Britannica Inc., 2014. Web. 07 Jan. 2014 Retrieved from <http://www.britannica.com/EBchecked/topic/291225/20th-century-international-relations>.

UNESCO **General History of Africa, Vol. III, Abridged Edition: Africa from the Seventh to the Eleventh Century (Volume 3)** (1992) University of California Press

Vague, R. (2021) **An illustrated Business history of the United States** University of Pennsylvania Press

Van Der Zee, J. (1985) **Bound over: indentured servitude & American conscience** New York: Simon & Schuster

Vance, J. D. (2018) **Hillbilly Elegy: A Memoir of a Family and Culture in Crisis** (p. 3). HarperCollins. Kindle Edition

BIBLIOGRAPHY AND VIDEO REFERENCES

Vaver, A. (2011) **Bound with an iron chain: the untold story of how the British transported 50,000 convicts to colonial America.** Massachusetts: Pickpocket Publishing.

Victor, G. (1998) **Hitler: the pathology of evil** Washington: Brassey's

Waldron, L & Hartmann T. (2005) **Ultimate sacrifice: John and Robert kennedy, the plan for a coup in Cuba, and the murder of JFK** New York: Carroll & Graf

Waldron, L. (2013) **The hidden history of the JFK assassination: the definitive account of the most controversial crime of the Twentieth Century** California: Berkeley

Waldstreicher, D. (2009) **Slavery's constitution: From revolution to ratification.** New York: Hill and Wang.

Walter, B. F. (2022) **How Civil Wars Start** New York: Crown. Kindle Edition.

Waugh, J. C. (1997) **Reelecting Lincoln: the battle for the 1864 Presidency** New York: Crown Publishing

Weatherford, Jack. (2004) **Genghis Khan and the Making of the Modern World** . Crown/Archetype. Kindle Edition

Weiner, R. C-Span Lectures in History https://www.c-span.org/video/?458124-2/origins-world-war-ii-europe

Weiner, T. (2007) **Legacy of ashes: The history of the CIA** New York: Anchor Books

Weld, T.D. (2011) **American slavery as it is: testimony of a thousand witnesses** University of North Carolina

Wells, S. (2007) **Deep ancestry: the landmark DNA quest to decipher our distant past** Washington, D.C.: National Geographic.

Wells, S. (2010) **Pandora's seed: the unforeseen cost of civilization** New York: Random House.

Whitman, J. Q. (2017) **Hitler's American model: the United States and the making of Nazi race law** New Jersey: Princeton University Press

Wiecek, W. M. (1977) **The sources of antislavery Constitutionalism in America, 1760-1848** London: Cornell University Press.

Wiecek, W.M. (1974) **Somerset: Lord Mansfield and the Legitimacy of Slavery in the Anglo-American World** The University of Chicago Law Review, Vol. 42, No. 1 (Autumn, 1974) pp. 86-146 (61 pages)

Wiencek, H. (2003) **An imperfect God: George Washington, his slaves and the creation of America.** New York: Farrar, Straus and Giroux

Wiencek, H. (2013) **Master of the mountain: Thomas Jefferson and his slaves.** New York: Farrar, Straus & Giroux

Wilson, C.R. (1980) **Baptized in blood: The religion of the lost cause, 1865-1920** Athens, Georgia: Georgia University Press

Wilson, Mark R. (2016) **Destructive Creation: American Business and the Winning of World War II (American Business, Politics, and Society)** University of Pennsylvania Press. Kindle Edition.

Winik, J. (2001) **April 1865: The month that saved America.** New York: Harper Collins

Winik, J. (2007) **Great Upheaval: America and the Birth of the Modern World, 1788-1800** New York: Harper Collins

Wise, S. M. (2005) **Though the heavens may fall: the landmark trial that led to the end of human slavery.** Massachusetts: Da Capo Press.

Woodard, C. (2011) **American nations: A history of the eleven rival regional cultures of North America** New York: Penguin Books

Woodward, C. (2016) **American character: a history of the epic struggle between individual liberty and the common good** New York: Penguin Random House

Wood, G.S. (2009) **Empire of liberty: a history of the early Republic, 1789-1815.** New York: Oxford University Press. The Oxford History of the United States.

World War I. (2013). In *Encyclopædia Britannica*. Retrieved from http://www.britannica.com/EBchecked/topic/648646/World-War-I

Wortman, M. (2009) **The Bonfire: The siege and burning of Atlanta** New York: Public Affairs

Wright, R. (2010) **The evolution of God** Massachusetts: Back Bay Books

Yergin, D. and Stanislaw, J. (1993) **The prize: the epic quest for oil, money, and power** New York: Simon & Schuster

Zinn, H. (2005) **A people's history of the United States, 1492-Present** New York: Harper.

Videos:

500 Nations (1994) Warner Home Video

500 Years Later (2007) Halaqua Productions

BIBLIOGRAPHY AND VIDEO REFERENCES

Aftershock: Beyond the Civil War (2006) The history channel.
The African Americans: many rivers to cross (2013) PBS
Amazing Grace (2010) Bristol Bay Productions
America: The Story of US: Rebels (2010) A&E Networks
America Before Columbus (2009) National Geographic
Art of war: Sun Tzu's legendary victory manual comes to life (DVD) History Channel, 2009
Boogie Man: The Lee Atwater Story (2009) Interpositive Media
The Century of Self (2002) BBC
The Civil War (2007) A&E Networks
Congo: White King, Red Rubber, Black Death (2003) ArtMattan Productions
Conquest of America History Channel (2012)
The Doctrine of Discovery: Unmasking the Domination Code (2015) 38Plus2Productions
Documenting Hate: Charlottesville & New American Nazis (2018) PBS
Egalite for All: Toussaint Louverture and the Haitian Revolution (2009)
The first world war (DVD) Lew Strachan, 2004
The Flaw: What happens when the rich get richer (2010) Beek Street Films
The Fog of War (2004) Sony Pictures
Founding Fathers (2000) A&E Networks
The Genographic Project (2005) National Geographic
Great Human Odyssey (2015) Nova
The Gulf War (1996) PBS
Guns, germs and steel National Geographic (2005)
Harvest of Empire (2012)
Heroes Under Fire: Shadow Warriors (2005) A&E Networks
How the earth was made (2009) A&E Networks
How the earth was made (2007) Smithsonian
The Industrial Revolution (2001) Cerebellum
Iran: The Hundred Years War (2008) Arte France

Journey of man (2005) National Geographic
The Ku Klux Klan
Kock Brothers Exposed (2012) Brave New Foundation
The last white knight: Is reconciliation possible? (2013) Virgil films and entertainment.
LBJ and Vietnam: In the eye of the storm (2008) A&E Network
The LBJ Tapes (2021) LBJ Library
Legacy: The Origins of Civilization (2009) Acorns Productions
Looking for answers (2001) Frontline, PBS
The Louisiana Purchase (2003) History Channel
Making of North America Nova (2015)
Mankind: the story of all of us History Channel (2012)
The Mexican American War (2006) History Channel
Motherland (2010)
Native America (2018) PBS
Paris 1919: Inside the peace talks that changed the world (2008) National Film Board of Canada
The Power of Big Oil (2022) PBS
Queen Victoria's Empire (2001) PBS
Racism: A History, the Color of Money https://www.imdb.com/title/tt1916252/
Reconstruction: The second civil War (2004) American Experience
Sherman's March (2007) History Channel
Showdown with Iran (DVD) Frontline, PBS, 2007
Slavery: A history BBC https://www.imdb.com/title/tt1916252/
Slavery and the Making of America (2004) PBS
Slavery Routes: A short history of human trafficking (2021) Deutsche Welle
Slavery by Another Name (2012) TPT National Productions
Thomas Jefferson: a film by Ken Burns (1996) PBS
Trail of Tears (2009) Rich Heape Films
The Untouchables: Money, Power and Wall Street (2013) PBS
Vietnam: A television history (1970) PBS

The Vietnam War (2017) PBS
The War that made America (2005) PBS
The Warning (2009) PBS

Appendix

James Somerset Clauses

Articles of Confederation: Article IV.

The better to secure and perpetuate mutual friendship and intercourse among the people of the different States in this Union, the free inhabitants of each of these States, paupers, vagabonds, and fugitives from justice excepted, shall be entitled to all privileges and immunities of free citizens in the several States; and the people of each State shall free ingress and regress to and from any other State, and shall enjoy therein all the privileges of trade and commerce, subject to the same duties, impositions, and restrictions as the inhabitants thereof respectively, **provided that such restrictions shall not extend so far as to prevent the removal of property imported into any State, to any other State, of which the owner is an inhabitant; provided also that no imposition, duties or restriction shall be laid by any State, on the property of the United States, or either of them**. (Bold text aimed directly at Somerset and Lord Mansfield)

If any person guilty of, or charged with, treason, felony, or other high misdemeanor in any State, shall flee from justice, and be found in any of the United States, he shall, upon demand of the Governor or executive power of the State from which he fled, be delivered up and removed to the State having jurisdiction of his offense.

Full faith and credit shall be given in each of these States to the records, acts, and judicial proceedings of the courts and magistrates of every other State.

Constitution: Article. IV, Section. 2.

The Citizens of each State shall be entitled to all Privileges and Immunities of Citizens in the several States.

A Person charged in any State with Treason, Felony, or other Crime, who shall flee from Justice, and be found in another State, shall on Demand of the executive Authority of the State from which he fled, be delivered up, to be removed to the State having Jurisdiction of the Crime.

No Person held to Service or Labour in one State, under the Laws thereof, escaping into another, shall, in Consequence of any Law or Regulation therein, be discharged from such Service or Labour, but shall be delivered up on Claim of the Party to whom such Service or Labour may be due. (Bold highlights Somerset.)

Fugitive Slave Act of 1793

An Act respecting fugitives from justice, and persons escaping from the service of their masters.

Be it enacted, &c., That, whenever the Executive authority of any State in the Union, or of either of the Territories Northwest or South of the river Ohio, shall demand any person as a fugitive from justice, of the Executive authority of any such State or Territory to which such person shall have fled, and shall moreover produce the copy of an indictment found, or an affidavit made before a magistrate of any State or Territory as aforesaid, charging the person so demanded with having committed treason, felony, or other crime, certified as authentic by the Governor or Chief Magistrate of the State or Territory from whence the person so charged fled, it shall be the duty of the executive authority of the State or Territory to which such person shall have fled, to cause him or her arrest to be given to the Executive authority making such demand, or to the agent when he shall appear; but, if no such agent shall appear within six months from the time of the arrest, the prisoner may be discharged: and all costs or expenses incurred in the apprehending, securing, and transmitting such fugitive to the State or Territory making such demand, shall be paid by such State or Territory.

SEC. 2. *And be it further enacted*, That any agent appointed as aforesaid, who shall receive the fugitive into his custody, shall be empowered to transport him or her to the State or Territory from which he or she shall have fled. And if any person or persons shall, by force, set at liberty, or rescue the fugitive from such agent while transporting, as aforesaid, the person or persons so offending shall, on conviction, be fined not exceeding five hundred dollars, and be imprisoned not exceeding one year.

SEC. 3. *And be it also enacted,* That when a person held to labor in any of the United States, or in either of the Territories on the Northwest or South of the river Ohio, under the laws thereof, shall escape into any other part of the said States or Territory, the person to whom such labor or service may be due, his agent or attorney, is hereby empowered to seize or arrest such fugitive from labor, and to take him or her before any Judge of the Circuit or District Courts of the United States, residing or being within the State, or before any magistrate of a county, city, or town corporate, wherein such seizure or arrest shall be made, and upon proof to the satisfaction of such Judge or magistrate, either by oral testimony or affidavit taken before and certified by a magistrate of any such State or Territory, that the person so seized or arrested, doth, under the laws of the State or Territory from which he or she fled, owe service or labor to the person claiming him or her, it shall be the duty of such Judge or magistrate to give a certificate thereof to such claimant, his agent, or attorney, which shall be sufficient warrant for removing the said fugitive from labor to the State or Territory from which he or she fled.

SEC. 4. *And be it further enacted,* That any person who shall knowingly and willingly obstruct or hinder such claimant, his agent, or attorney, in so seizing or arresting such fugitive from labor, or shall rescue such fugitive from such claimant, his agent or attorney, when so arrested pursuant to the authority herein given and declared; or shall harbor or conceal such person after notice that he or she was a fugitive from labor, as aforesaid, shall, for either of the said offences, forfeit and pay the sum of five hundred dollars. Which penalty may be recovered by and for the benefit of such claimant, by action of debt, in any Court proper to try the same, saving moreover to the person claiming such labor or service his right of action for or on account of the said injuries, or either of them.

Approved [signed into law by President George Washington], February 12, 1793.

Fugitive Slave Act of 1850

Section 1

Be it enacted by the Senate and House of Representatives of the United States of America in Congress assembled, That the persons who have been, or may hereafter be, appointed commissioners, in virtue of any act of Congress, by the Circuit Courts of the United States, and Who, in consequence of such appointment, are authorized to exercise the powers that any justice of the peace, or other magistrate of any of the United States, may exercise in respect to offenders for any crime or offense against the United States, by arresting, imprisoning, or bailing the same under and by the virtue of the thirty-third section of the act of the twenty-fourth of September seventeen hundred and eighty-nine, entitled "An Act to establish the judicial courts of the United States" shall be, and are hereby, authorized and required to exercise and discharge all the powers and duties conferred by this act.

Section 2

And be it further enacted, That the Superior Court of each organized Territory of the United States shall have the same power to appoint commissioners to take acknowledgments of bail and affidavits, and to take depositions of witnesses in civil causes, which is now possessed by the Circuit Court of the United States; and all commissioners who shall hereafter be appointed for such purposes by the Superior Court of any organized Territory of the United States, shall possess all the powers, and exercise all the duties, conferred by law upon the commissioners appointed by the Circuit Courts of the United States for similar purposes, and shall moreover exercise and discharge all the powers and duties conferred by this act.

Section 3

And be it further enacted, That the Circuit Courts of the United States shall from time to time enlarge the number of the commissioners, with a view to afford reasonable facilities to reclaim fugitives from labor, and to the prompt discharge of the duties imposed by this act.

Section 4

And be it further enacted, That the commissioners above named shall have concurrent jurisdiction with the judges of the Circuit and District Courts of the United States, in their respective circuits and districts within the several States, and the judges of the Superior Courts of the Territories, severally and collectively, in term-time and vacation; shall grant certificates to such claimants, upon satisfactory proof being made, with authority to take and remove such fugitives from service or labor, under the restrictions herein contained, to the State or Territory from which such persons may have escaped or fled.

Section 5

And be it further enacted, That it shall be the duty of all marshals and deputy marshals to obey and execute all warrants and precepts issued under the provisions of this act, when to them directed; and should any marshal or deputy marshal refuse to receive such warrant, or other process, when tendered, or to use all proper means diligently to execute the same, he shall, on conviction thereof, be fined in the sum of one thousand dollars, to the use of such claimant, on the motion of such claimant, by the Circuit or District Court for the district of such marshal; and after arrest of such fugitive, by such marshal or his deputy, or whilst at any time in his custody under the provisions of this act, should such fugitive escape, whether with or without the assent of such marshal or his deputy, such marshal shall be liable, on his official bond, to be prosecuted for the benefit of such claimant, for the full value of the service or labor of said fugitive in the State, Territory, or District whence he escaped: and the better to enable the said commissioners, when thus appointed, to execute their duties faithfully and efficiently, in conformity with the requirements of the Constitution of the United States and of this act, they are hereby authorized and empowered, within their counties respectively, to appoint, in writing under their hands, any one or more suitable persons, from time to time, to execute all such warrants and other process as may be issued by them in the lawful performance of their respective duties; with authority to such commissioners, or the persons to be appointed by them, to execute process as aforesaid, to summon and call to their aid the bystanders, or posse comitatus of the proper county, when necessary to ensure a faithful observance of the clause of the Constitution referred to, in conformity with the provisions of this act; and all good citizens are hereby commanded to aid and assist in the prompt and efficient execution of this law, whenever their services may be required, as aforesaid, for that purpose; and said warrants shall run, and be executed by said officers, any where in the State within which they are issued.

Section 6

And be it further enacted, That when a person held to service or labor in any State or Territory of the United States, has heretofore or shall hereafter escape into another State or Territory of the United States, the person or persons to whom such service or labor may be due, or his, her, or their agent or attorney, duly authorized, by power of attorney, in writing, acknowledged and certified under the seal of some legal officer or court of the State or Territory in which the same may be executed, may pursue and reclaim such fugitive person, either by procuring a warrant from some one of the courts, judges, or commissioners aforesaid, of the proper circuit, district, or county, for the apprehension of such fugitive from service or labor, or by seizing and arresting such fugitive, where the same can be done without process, and by taking, or causing such person to be taken, forthwith before such court, judge, or commissioner, whose duty it shall be to hear and determine the case of such claimant in a summary manner; and upon satisfactory proof being made, by deposition or affidavit, in writing, to be taken and certified by such court, judge, or commissioner, or by other satisfactory testimony, duly taken and certified by some court, magistrate, justice of the peace, or other legal officer authorized to administer an oath and take depositions under the laws of the State or Territory from which such person owing service or labor may have escaped, with a certificate of such magistracy or other authority, as aforesaid, with the seal of the proper court or officer thereto attached, which seal shall be sufficient to establish the competency of the proof, and with proof, also by affidavit, of the identity of the person whose service or labor is claimed to be due as aforesaid, that the person so arrested does in fact owe service or labor to the person or persons claiming him or her, in the State or Territory from which such fugitive may have escaped as aforesaid, and that said person escaped, to make out and deliver to such claimant, his or her agent or attorney, a certificate setting forth the substantial facts as to the service or labor due from such fugitive to the claimant, and of his or her escape from the State or Territory in which he or she was arrested, with authority to such claimant, or his or her agent or attorney, to use such reasonable force and restraint as may be necessary, under the circumstances of the case, to take and remove such fugitive person back to the State or Territory whence he or she may have escaped as aforesaid. In no trial or hearing under this act shall the testimony of such alleged fugitive be admitted in evidence; and the certificates in this and the first [fourth] section mentioned, shall be conclusive of the right of the person or persons in whose favor granted, to remove such fugitive to the State or Territory from which he escaped, and shall prevent all molestation of such person or persons by any process issued by any court, judge, magistrate, or other person whomsoever.

Section 7

And be it further enacted, That any person who shall knowingly and willingly obstruct, hinder, or prevent such claimant, his agent or attorney, or any person or persons lawfully assisting him, her, or them, from arresting such a fugitive from service or labor, either with or without process as aforesaid, or shall rescue, or attempt to rescue, such fugitive from service or labor, from the custody of such claimant, his or her agent or attorney, or other person or persons lawfully assisting as aforesaid, when so arrested, pursuant to the authority herein given and declared; or shall aid, abet, or assist such person so owing service or labor as aforesaid, directly or indirectly, to escape from such claimant, his agent or attorney, or other person or persons legally authorized as aforesaid; or shall harbor or conceal such fugitive, so as to prevent the discovery and arrest of such person, after notice or knowledge of the fact that such person was a fugitive from service or labor as aforesaid, shall, for either of said offences, be subject to a fine not exceeding one thousand dollars, and imprisonment not exceeding six months, by indictment and conviction before the District Court of the United States for the district in which such offence may have been committed, or before the proper court of criminal jurisdiction, if committed within any one of the organized Territories of the United States; and shall moreover forfeit and pay, by way of civil damages to the party injured by such illegal conduct, the sum of one thousand dollars for each fugitive so lost as aforesaid, to be recovered by action of debt, in any of the District or Territorial Courts aforesaid, within whose jurisdiction the said offence may have been committed.

Section 8

And be it further enacted, That the marshals, their deputies, and the clerks of the said District and Territorial Courts, shall be paid, for their services, the like fees as may be allowed for similar services in other cases; and where such services are rendered exclusively in the arrest, custody, and delivery of the fugitive to the claimant, his or her agent or attorney, or where such supposed fugitive may be discharged out of custody for the want of sufficient proof as aforesaid, then such fees are to be paid in whole by such claimant, his or her agent or attorney; and in all cases where the proceedings are before a commissioner, he shall be entitled to a fee of ten dollars in full for his services in each case, upon the delivery of the said certificate to the claimant, his agent or attorney; or a fee of five dollars in cases where the proof shall not, in the opinion of such commissioner, warrant such certificate and delivery, inclusive of all services incident to such arrest and examination, to be paid, in either case, by the claimant, his or her agent or attorney. The person or persons authorized to execute the process to be issued by such commissioner for the arrest and detention of fugitives from service or labor as aforesaid, shall also be entitled to a fee of five dollars each for each person he or they may arrest, and take before any commissioner as aforesaid, at the instance and request of such claimant, with such other fees as may be deemed reasonable by such commissioner for such other additional services as may be necessarily performed by him or them; such as attending at the examination, keeping the fugitive in custody, and providing him with food and lodging during his detention, and until the final determination of such commissioners; and, in general,

APPENDIX

for performing such other duties as may be required by such claimant, his or her attorney or agent, or commissioner in the premises, such fees to be made up in conformity with the fees usually charged by the officers of the courts of justice within the proper district or county, as near as may be practicable, and paid by such claimants, their agents or attorneys, whether such supposed fugitives from service or labor be ordered to be delivered to such claimant by the final determination of such commissioner or not.

Section 9

And be it further enacted, That, upon affidavit made by the claimant of such fugitive, his agent or attorney, after such certificate has been issued, that he has reason to apprehend that such fugitive will he rescued by force from his or their possession before he can be taken beyond the limits of the State in which the arrest is made, it shall be the duty of the officer making the arrest to retain such fugitive in his custody, and to remove him to the State whence he fled, and there to deliver him to said claimant, his agent, or attorney. And to this end, the officer aforesaid is hereby authorized and required to employ so many persons as he may deem necessary to overcome such force, and to retain them in his service so long as circumstances may require. The said officer and his assistants, while so employed, to receive the same compensation, and to be allowed the same expenses, as are now allowed by law for transportation of criminals, to be certified by the judge of the district within which the arrest is made, and paid out of the treasury of the United States.

Section 10

And be it further enacted, That when any person held to service or labor in any State or Territory, or in the District of Columbia, shall escape therefrom, the party to whom such service or labor shall be due, his, her, or their agent or attorney, may apply to any court of record therein, or judge thereof in vacation, and make satisfactory proof to such court, or judge in vacation, of the escape aforesaid, and that the person escaping owed service or labor to such party. Whereupon the court shall cause a record to be made of the matters so proved, and also a general description of the person so escaping, with such convenient certainty as may be; and a transcript of such record, authenticated by the attestation of the clerk and of the seal of the said court, being produced in any other State, Territory, or district in which the person so escaping may be found, and being exhibited to any judge, commissioner, or other office, authorized by the law of the United States to cause persons escaping from service or labor to be delivered up, shall be held and taken to be full and conclusive evidence of the fact of escape, and that the service or labor of the person escaping is due to the party in such record mentioned. And upon the production by the said party of other and further evidence if necessary, either oral or by affidavit, in addition to what is contained in the said record of the identity of the person escaping, he or she shall be delivered up to the claimant, And the said court, commissioner, judge, or other person authorized by this act to grant certificates to claimants or fugitives, shall, upon the production of the record and other evidences aforesaid, grant to such claimant a certificate of his right to take any such person identified and proved to be owing service or labor as aforesaid, which certificate shall authorize such claimant to seize or arrest and transport such person to the State or Territory from which he escaped: Provided, That nothing herein contained shall be construed as requiring the production of a transcript of such record as evidence as aforesaid. But in its absence the claim shall be heard and determined upon other satisfactory proofs, competent in law.

Approved, September 18, 1850.

Made in the USA
Columbia, SC
16 January 2025

a8824196-a6af-4890-b92c-107a5e547dd4R01